ADVANCES IN RESEARCH AND SERVICES FOR
CHILDREN WITH SPECIAL NEEDS

LES RECENTS DEVELOPPEMENTS DANS LE SECTEUR DES
SERVICES AUX ENFANTS AYANT DES BESOINS SPECIAUX

ADVANCES IN RESEARCH & SERVICES FOR CHILDREN WITH SPECIAL NEEDS

LES RECENTS DEVELOPPEMENTS DANS LE SECTEUR DES SERVICES AUX ENFANTS AYANT DES BESOINS SPECIAUX

Edited by

Geraldine Schwartz

Traductions par

David Bélanger

UNIVERSITY OF BRITISH COLUMBIA PRESS
VANCOUVER

ADVANCES IN RESEARCH AND SERVICES
FOR CHILDREN WITH SPECIAL NEEDS

LES RECENTS DEVELOPPEMENTS DANS LE SECTEUR DES
SERVICES AUX ENFANTS AYANT DES BESOINS SPECIAUX

© The University of British Columbia 1983

This book has been published with the help of a grant from the Canada Council and from the Woodward Foundation, Vancouver. A grant for translation was fully funded by The Secretary of State of Canada.

Canadian Cataloguing in Publication Data

Main entry under title:
    Advances in research and services for children
    with special needs

Essays adapted from a conference held in 1979
at the University of British Columbia.
    ISBN 0-7748-0164-6

    1. Handicapped children—Congresses. 2. Handicapped children—Can-
ada—Congresses. 3. Handicapped children—Services for—Congresses. I.
Schwartz, Geraldine J.
    HV888.A39   362.7'95   C82-091382-0

ISBN 0-7748-0-0164-6

Printed and bound in Canada by John Deyell Company

Dedication

DR. SYDNEY ISRAELS   DR. JACK McCREARY

This volume is dedicated to the memory of *Dr. Sydney Israels* and *Dr. Jack McCreary*. Those who knew, worked with, and loved these men will know that it is a particularly fitting tribute to them and their work. Both of them worked tirelessly during their lifetimes to foster the spirit of multi-disciplinary co-operation and friendship. They both looked beyond the borders of our country and were responsible for bringing to Vancouver as permanent residents and as visiting scholars, scientists of stature from all over the world. They each broke down long standing interdisciplinary barriers. The Institutions* they founded, fostered and built remain as monuments pulsating with life and hope, dedicated to the idea of serving the whole child. This volume, which will have an international distribution, will provide their ideas with spiritual wings to fly to five continents—to small and large centres—to bear fruit in new grounds. It is an enterprise of which they would both be proud. It is a most fitting tribute since their energy and vision did so much to bring this conference about.

* The Jack McCreary Health Sciences Centre at U.B.C.
* The Sydney Israels Memorial Fund Children's Hospital Research Facilities.

Dédicace

Ce volume se veut un hommage à la mémoire du *docteur Sydney Israels*, et du *docteur Jack McCreary*. Ceux qui ont connu ces hommes, qui ont travaillé avec eux et les ont aimés reconnaîtront que c'est là un hommage particulièrement approprié à leur personne et à leur oeuvre. Ils se sont employés tous deux inlassablement, leur vie durant, à promouvoir l'esprit d'amitié et de collaboration interdisciplinaire. Tous les deux ont franchi les frontières de leur pays et on leur doit d'avoir attiré à Vancouver, en permanence ou à titre de visiteurs distingués, des hommes de sciences éminents venus de toutes les parties du monde. Ils ont l'un et l'autre, renversé des barrières interdisciplinaires de longue durée. Les institutions* qu'ils ont fondées, construites et au développement desquelles ils se sont consacrés sont aujourd'hui des monuments, pétillants de vie et d'espoir, dédiés à l'idée qu'il faut se mettre au service de l'enfant considéré comme un tout. Ce volume qui sera distribué à travers le monde donnera à leurs idées des ailes qui les conduiront sur les cinq continents—vers les grands et les petits centres—pour porter semence dans des terrains neufs. Il s'agit d'une entreprise dont ils seraient fiers tous les deux. Cet hommage ne pourrait mieux leur convenir puisque leur énergie et leur vision des choses a tellement contribué à la réalisation de cette conférence.

* Le Centre des Services de Santé Jack McCreary à l'Université de British Columbia.
* Les laboratoires de recherche du Sydney Israels Memorial Fund Children's Hospital.

Contents

Acknowledgements

Editing a book in which the authors write in one of two languages and come from seven countries, six provinces and the Northwest Territories of Canada, and six U.S. States is an ambitious enterprise. Such a feat could not have been accomplished without the help of many people.

I would like to thank my co-editors, Drs. Geof Robinson, Bob Wilson, John Crichton, Jean-Marie Honerez, Pat Woodward and Mr. Don McEachern for taking the conference presentations in whatever form they were and preparing a workable manuscript.

The art of translation requires a special talent. Several years ago when I read David Belanger's beautiful translation of noted psychologist Donald Hebb's work, I said, "If I ever need anything translated, I must ask Dr. Belanger. He's the best." David graciously consented to do this book. Those of you who read the French translation will recognize the quality of his work.

I must also thank Nadine Serrouya, who is my French eyes and who consented to read the French manuscript in friendship well beyond the call of duty.

Dr. Georgia Adams, Secretary General of the International Council of Psychologists, used her experience and wise editorial talent to provide a smooth copy of the final manuscript, in spite of a schedule which appears busier in retirement than when she was supposed to be working full time. I must also thank Dr. Jane C. Fredeman, Senior Editor at U.B.C. Press whose expertise and guidance made it possible to put a book with so many pieces together.

The members of the Conference Steering Committee—Dr. Bob Wilson, representing the Canadian Psychological Association; John Crichton, the Canadian Paediatric Association; Sue Penfold, the Canadian Psychiatric Association; and Anne Crichton, who prepared the plenary association—put together an extraordinary conference, to celebrate IYC. They are responsible for the content and quality of this book, since it was this committee that invited the speakers from such far flung places and from so many disciplines.

The Vancouver Children's Hospital both sponsored and hosted the IYC Conference. A special vote of thanks is offered to their Board, their administration and staff, both professional and volunteer, who gave many hours in 1979 to preparing the conference and to making it the truly memorable event it was. Many delegates remind me, when we meet at other events, of the wonderful hospitality they received in Vancouver. Special recognition is due to my three conference secretaries, Audrey Withers, who started it, and Sue Erb and Doreen Gaddes who finished the job. Dr. G.R.F. Elliot, who took over at the Woodward Foundation after Jack McCreary died, was responsible for helping us get a grant to publish this work. His efforts and wise counsel were most appreciated. I would also like to thank the directors of the Woodward Foundation for their important support.

The Secretary of State of Canada provided a grant so that simultaneous translation was available at the conference and so that the French language part of this book was possible. This grant allowed the participation of French colleagues from Quebec and France; it also made the message of the conference accessible to an international audience in both languages. It is a wonderful contribution for both IYC and I.Y.D.P. It promotes the message proudly of what Canada is all about.

This book is the result of many contributions of effort and talent. Each of the authors listed below has made a special statement from their own country and discipline to an international disciplinary audience. Since many are working at the leading edge of their science, the freshness of their statements reaches into the future. In addition to the long list above, many others remain unnamed. It is my hope that all its contributors will be rewarded, as I am, by the depth, quality, and scope of its message.

Geraldine Schwartz, Ph.D.
Editor

Introduction

A book is a very different experience from a conference. When the book is the child of a landmark event, a conference that brought together leading scientists from three continents, ten disciplines and two language groups to speak to an audience of their fellows from an even wider range of eighteen disciplines, it is more than a book. It becomes a hybrid product which must reflect both the uniqueness and excitement of the conference and the scholarly and thoughtful work of its contributors. It becomes an event of a third kind. It is to such an experience that the reader is now invited.

The conference was a celebration of the International Year of the Child, sponsored by the Canadian Associations of Psychology, Paediatrics and Psychiatry, the British Columbia Association of Psychology and the International Council of Psychologists. The atmosphere of celebration pervaded the summer campus at the University of British Columbia in Vancouver. Feelings were high. We knew we were participating in a first time event, one that crossed the defended lines of discipline, language and country to share our scientific findings about advances in research and services for children with special needs; to develop liaisons that would lead to future joint research and communication; to address ourselves to our common concern for the well-being of children everywhere.

We were working towards the ideal, one that others have glimpsed—we were about to look at the whole child as a unity of mind, body and spirit—from each of our different perspectives with the purpose of documenting, and then disseminating, advances in research and services to children with special needs throughout the world.

We considered the special needs of the child above all as a child, as an indivisible whole that can not be dissected into parts belonging to the paediatrician, the psychologist or the educator. It was a multi-disciplinary meeting in the true sense of the word. The concern underpinning the conference—the theme permeating every meeting—was that while for the purposes of study we may need to begin with the parts, we cannot treat, nurture or educate even the smallest part of a child without considering the whole that is larger and infinitely more complex than the sum of its parts.

We came together as friends who accept and respect each other's views—not to convince each other that any one of our perspectives was the right one about children, but to add each of our perspectives to a new, expansive multi-faceted way of looking at children.

Nor would we strive for simplicity, because we were studying the most complex organism in the universe, about which there are more unknowns than any other. In attempting to be unitary and simplistic, we may overlook the subtleties and the complexities. Instead, we were prepared to cope with the complexity by accepting the co-existence of many perspectives and views and we were ready to do so in friendship rather than in competition.

In 1960, C.S. Lewis, in his book *The Four Loves*, wrote of the kingliness of friendship, where people meet like sovereign princes of independent states, abroad, on neutral ground—freed from their contexts—to be together, not out of any duty but with joyous free will, each thinking himself indeed fortunate to be among such company. It was with such a spirit that we began the dialogue, in an attempt to learn to communicate not only in the two languages of Canada, English and French, but in the language of each other's discipline, philosophy and culture. It is the goal—the dream of this volume—that by sharing this meeting with others through this book, we can continue the dialogue with a wider number of our colleagues around the world.

You will note that the current addresses of all the participants are printed at the back of this volume. This list has a special purpose. It is meant to allow, indeed encourage, direct communication between the reader and the participating scientists.

Is there an idea that intrigues you, a research project that has special applications to your work, and you would like to know more? Write to the author, continue the dialogue. The barriers of language, discipline and nation have been lowered so that you can do this. This was the purpose of the international multi-disciplinary conference and it remains the expressed purpose and special invitation of this volume, its editors and authors.

The opportunity of editing this book and reading in depth the twenty—three contributions of the participants was very different from hearing these reports at the conference where due to simultaneous sessions one could see only half the picture. After careful and thoughtful reading, new understandings emerged, immediately applicable to my own discipline and research. Again and again I found pieces of the puzzle slipping into place. I had many personal "aha" experiences when I understood for the first time, "So that's why the neurologist says that!" or "That's the genetic basis of this factor" or "That's why the psychiatrists have this problem." I felt that the reading gave new breadth, depth and scope to my understanding of the child who was disabled, of his caretakers and of the problems of many of the professionals who undertook to care for him. I was excited by some of the ways in which the writers addressed the problems.

This volume is especially addressed to our colleagues from developing countries and those who work in areas remote from centres of expertise. They will see the current state of the art and will glean some new ideas. They will also recognize many of the problems. They will see that all over the world, their colleagues are working with dedicated effort toward solutions, but that the problems they perceive in their own areas are also present to some degree in the most developed countries. Our hope is that it will encourage them to design new solutions from their own experience, and to engage themselves in the sharing of this information at subsequent meetings and in future publications.

Finally, we must ask ourselves, why devote such enormous energy to finding better ways of helping handicapped children? Should we not just let them grow in a natural way and face whatever disease or disaster life has to offer? Surely they will survive, and in fact, perhaps in this way the fittest will survive as they always have, and we will have fewer children with special needs in the generations to come. That question reminds me of the story of the giant who, when strolling through the fields one day, picked up a handful of earth rich with seeds and flung it into the wind. Some of the seeds fell into a garden tended by a small boy, who viewed them with wonder. He planted them carefully, watered and nourished them until they grew into magnificent blossoms. After several years, the giant happened to pass through the fields and saw many acres of beautiful wildflowers blowing in the breeze, but in one corner of the field there was a magnificent patch which attracted his attention. Each blossom was extraordinary in beauty, fragrance, colour and form. It is not that the wildflowers were not beautiful, he thought, but blossom for blossom they looked stunted and pale beside the nurtured blooms.

This analogy is also true for children. True, left in their natural context, they will grow and some will flourish, but it is extraordinary how special nurturing will allow hitherto undiscovered potential to emerge. Thus, every ounce of energy we expend jointly to nurture the children in our corner of the field will produce untold dividends and this will be especially so if we share our discoveries with our friends in other parts, so that they too can tend their own gardens and share what they learn with their neighbours.

THE CONFERENCE

The delegates were welcomed to the conference by Dr. Doug Kenny, President of the University of British Columbia. He noted that the Province of British Columbia and the University combined the dynamism of a frontier society and the cordial hospitality of warm people whose vision had been centered around the sea, the mountains and the forests. He invited the delegates to take away golden memories and new friendships.

Mr. Tom Tucker spoke for the Honourable Mr. Robert McLelland, the Minister of Health, who was unexpectedly detained. He brought greetings from Mr. Bill Bennett, Premier of British Columbia and from the Government.

Mr. Tucker pointed to the problem of the economics of providing a broad and comprehensive range of health care to all people. He said the Government of British Columbia was particularly interested in prevention and he would be listening most closely to our session which addressed itself to that topic so that British Columbia could consider the advice of international experts.

Dr. Pat McGeer, Minister of Education, introduced the plenary session. Dr. McGeer spoke of the pressure in British Columbia to provide more services. This pressure has resulted, he said, in our devoting our attention to disseminating current knowledge. Compared to other developed countries, Canada was not yet delivering its rightful share of contributions to research and to the development of new ideas. He was looking forward to the wise counsel of the speakers and hoped to hear some suggestions as to what activities could be undertaken in the future.

The conference was divided into seven sessions, three sets of two simultaneous sessions and a plenary session.

THE BOOK

This volume is divided into seven chapters. Each section was edited to communicate the speakers' main thrust in a version that could be read in a short period. While the topics are integrated by their common theme, each topic can also be considered a separate unit.

The first section, DELIVERY OF SERVICES TO EXCEPTIONAL CHILDREN IN REMOTE AREAS, was organized, chaired and edited by Dr. Geoffrey Robinson, Professor and Head of the Division of Population Paediatrics at U.B.C. Dr. Robinson said, "The word remote usually implies "at a distance from, far away or out of the way," but it can have other implications too, including climatic, cultural and linguistic differences. The delivery of services to remote areas, therefore, may involve dealing with the special problems of access imposed by geography and climate; or of lifestyle, beliefs and priorities of cultural groups; or of communication when professional and patient speak different languages. To these may be added logistical problems arising from the sparsely populated nature of many remote areas, such as unemployment, poor housing, etc. Finally, there are the crucial issues of staff selection, staff training, and turnover.

The five writers have all had personal involvement in delivery of services to children in remote areas in Canada and the follow-up presentations illustrate their approaches to various problems. These include an innovative experiment to evaluate a teaching programme for parents of deaf children in rural Newfoundland

and Labrador; a multidisciplinary assessment and management team for exceptional children in northern Saskatchewan; a general discussion of policy development for service delivery programmes and a specific programme for the care of the retarded Inuit, both in the Northwest Territories.

The second session, A CROSS–CULTURAL STUDY OF COGNITIVE DEVELOPMENT AND CHILD REARING PRACTICES was organized and edited by Dr. Robert Wilson, who represented the Canadian Psychological Association on the Conference Steering Committee. The session was chaired by Dr. Walter Lonner, noted cross–cultural researcher, of the University of Western Washington.

In this unit, the authors attempt to deal with the significant goal of cross–cultural psychology, which is the development of a nearly universal set of principles that apply to all human populations while recognizing the new trend of understanding the cultural uniqueness of different populations. In the third article in this section, Dr. Walter Lambert looks at the universal problem of child-rearing in the unique context of nine countries. As well, he examines the immigrant groups from these countries to North America. While there are certainly many differences, some of the common factors in child–rearing practices may surprise you. This presentation was selected for translation and is also available in French.

The third session was organized, chaired and edited by Dr. John Crichton, Chairman of the Dept. of Neurology at the Vancouver Children's Hospital. The authors describe studies which demonstrate the persistence of learning disabilities identified in kindergarten regardless of the school's attempt at remedial intervention. In fact, not only do the children who are identified early continue to have learning problems in school, but the degree of impairment also appears to remain constant over time, and to affect school performance throughout the person's academic career. The call for new methods of intervention is clearly stated. In the last paper the author describes a multi-disciplinary intervention programme which has apparently achieved satisfactory results.

The fourth topic on the PREVENTION OF DEVELOPMENTAL DISABILITIES was organized, edited and chaired by Dr. Bluma Tischler, Medical Director of Woodlands, a large residential school for the mentally retarded in British Columbia.

In this unit the incidence of disabilities after a rubella epidemic is described, and a screening procedure used in B.C. for identifying known abnormalities in newborns is outlined. In this section, the article on neurological aspects of learning disorders, by Dr. J.K. Brown, was chosen for translation.

The fifth topic on the TREATMENT OF THE MULTIPLY HANDICAPPED CHILD was organized and chaired by Dr. Roger Freeman, noted child psychiatrist and Professor of Psychiatry at the University of British Columbia.

This unit was edited by Don McEachern, psychologist, educator and administrator at Douglas College in Vancouver. The chapter describes some of the problems of working with the multi-handicapped child. The importance of early diagnosis and long term planning by trained and compassionate caretakers is underlined. In this section, the paper by Dana Brynelsen uses letters and the case study method to describe the problems experienced by staff in getting adequate services to plan long term care for multiply handicapped children. This paper was selected for translation and is available in French.

The sixth session on CHILD ABUSE was presented in French by scientists from France and French Canada. Simultaneous translation was provided at the conference and English translations are available in this volume. The session was organized and chaired by Dr. Francois Desrosiers, Chairman of the Psychology Dept. of Laval University in Quebec City. It was edited by Dr. Jean-Marie Honorez of Ste. Justine's Hospital for Children in Montreal. Dr. Honorez suggests that abuse is not a unique phenomenon related only to children, but that it is part of the overall pattern of social violence current in our society. He feels that the most fruitful way to approach the problem is by treating the fragile family structure. The authors who follow, point to the diverse forms of child abuse throughout the whole class structure of our society and the studies describe the continuing effect of early abuse in the later lives of these children.

The plenary session, organized by Dr. Anne Crichton, sociologist and member of the Department of Health Care Planning at U.B.C. was chaired by Dr. Graham Clarkson, noted speaker, consultant to governments and institutions in health care. This section was edited for this volume by Dr. Patricia Woodward, Director of Educational Services at Woodlands, a residential institution for the mentally retarded in B.C., and Chairperson of the Scientific Programme for this conference.

The six conference sessions were organized to highlight the advances in research, to outline the problems, and to report on some of the solutions in the delivery of health care to exceptional children. The purpose of the plenary session was to provide the conference with some thoughtful directions by experienced health care planners in how to go about getting some of these services in place.

Dr. George Silver, Professor, School of Public Health, Yale University, calls for the formation of special advocacy groups and separate services to clearly delineate policy and programmes for children. He points to some impressive European models as examples of what could be done in North America. He feels that once there are services for children in general, the exceptional child would be well cared for within that context.

Dr. Robert Haggerty, Programme Director of the Robert Wood Johnson Foundation, points to the effect of family stress in social, economic and behavioural areas, which increase the likelihood of illness and the use of health services. He calls for the integration of medical, educational and social programmes where in addition to dealing with the whole child in the context of the family, great economies could be effected through the use of parents and non−medical personnel. He feels that such an integrated service would be in the best interest of the exceptional child whose disability places great strains on the family unit.

Introduction

Un volume et une conférence sont deux expériences bien différentes. Quand le volume est le résultat concret d'un évènement marquant, soit un conférence qui a réuni d'éminents personnages scientifiques provenant de trois continents, représentant dix disciplines et appartenant à deux groupes linguistiques différents, pour qu'ils s'adressent à un auditoire constitué de collègues représentant une gamme plus vaste encore de dix-huit disciplines, c'est plus qu'un livre. L'oeuvre devient hybride, car elle doit être le reflet tant du caractère unique et sensationnel de la conférence que de l'érudition et de la sagesse de ses participants. Elle devient un évènement d'un troisième niveau. C'est à une expérience de ce genre que le lecteur est présentement convié.

La conférence a été convoquée pour célébrer l'Année Internationale de l'Enfant, sous le patronnage des Sociétés canadiennes de Psychologie, de Pédiatrie et de Psychiatrie, de l'Association de Psychologie de Colombie Britannique et du Conseil International des Psychologues. L'atmosphère de fête se retrouvait sur tout le campus estival de l'Université de British Columbia à Vancouver. Il y avait de l'électricité dans l'air. L'enthousiasme était grand. Nous savions que nous participions à une première, à un évènement qui violait les remparts des disciplines, des langues et des nationalismes pour mettre en commun nos données scientifiques sur les progrès récents de la recherche et des services offerts aux enfants ayant des besoins spéciaux, pour créer des liens en vue de futures recherches conjointes et d'une communication accrue, et pour réfléchir ensemble sur nos préoccupations communes pour le bien–être de tous les enfants du monde.

Nous allions réaliser l'idéal, ce que les autres disaient qu'il fallait faire—nous étions sur le point de considérer l'enfant pris globalement dans son unité d'intelligence, de corps et d'esprit—à partir de chacune nos différentes perspectives dans le but de déterminer et de diffuser ensuite le progrès accompli dans la recherche et les services offerts à travers le monde aux enfants présentant des besoins spéciaux.

Nous avons considéré cet enfant défavorisé comme un enfant avant tout, comme un tout indivisible qui ne pouvait être disséqué en sections appartenant au pédiatre, au psychologue ou à l'éducateur. Ce fut une réunion pluridisciplinaire dans le vrai sens du terme. On ne pourra jamais assez faire ressortir que le thème central de la conférence, celui qui était au coeur de chacune des réunions, c'était que, bien qu'il soit peut-être nécessaire pour fins didactiques de commencer par les parties, on ne saurait jamais traiter, soigner ou éduquer, fût-ce la plus petite partie d'un enfant, sans tenir compte du tout qui est plus grand et infiniment plus complexe que la somme des parties.

Nous nous sommes accueillis comme des amis capables d'accepter et de respecter les points de vue des uns des autres, des amis dont le but n'était pas de convaincre les autres du bien-fondé de leurs opinions ou de leurs façons de comprendre les enfants, mais de présenter chacune de leurs perspectives pour constituer une image nouvelle, plus complète et à multiples facettes de ces enfants.

Nous ne nous proposions pas non plus de chercher à simplifier, car nous nous trouvions en face de l'organisme le plus complexe de l'univers, qui présente plus d'inconnues que tout autre organisme. En visant l'unité et la simplicité, nous aurions risqué de laisser échapper les aspects subtils et complexes. Nous étions, au contraire, préparés à affronter la complexité, en acceptant la coexistence de plusieurs perspectives et façons de voir, et nous étions décidé à le faire dans l'amitié plutôt que dans la rivalité.

En 1960, dans son livre *The Four Loves*, C.S. Lewis parlait de la royauté de l'amitié où les gens se rencontrent à l'étranger, en terrain neutre, comme des princes souverains d'états indépendants—libérés de leur entourage—pour se retrouver ensemble, non par devoir mais librement, joyeusement, de plein gré, chacun se considérant privilégié de se trouver en telle compagnie. C'est dans un esprit semblable que nous avons engagé le dialogue, dans un effort pour apprendre à échanger non seulement dans les deux langues du Canada, l'anglais et le français, mais dans celle de chacune de nos disciplines, de nos philosophies et de nos cultures. C'est l'objectif—l'ambition de ce volume—d'arriver, en partageant les fruits de cette conférence avec d'autres par le truchement de cette publication, à poursuivre le dialogue avec un nombre plus grand de collègues à travers le monde.

Vous pourrez constater que les coordonnées actuelles de chacun des participants apparaissent à l'endos de ce volume. Cette liste a un but bien précis. Celui de permettre, voire d'encourager, la communication directe entre le lecteur et les participants.

S'il y a une idée qui vous intrigue, un projet de recherche qui se rapporte plus particulièrement à votre travail et si vous vouliez en savoir plus long, écrivez à l'auteur, continuez ce dialogue. Les barrières entre langues, disciplines et nationalités ont été ouvertes de façon à vous le permettre. C'était le but initial de cette conférence pluridisciplinaire internationale et cela reste le but exprès et l'invitation spéciale transmise par ce volume, ses éditeurs et ses auteurs.

L'expérience découlant de la préparation de l'édition de ce livre et le privilège s'y rattachant de lire en profondeur les vingt-trois présentations des participants ont été bien différents de l'audition de ces compte-rendus lors de la conférence où, à cause des séances simultanées, personne n'était en mesure d'apercevoir plus qu'une moitié de tableau. La lecture lente et attentive a suscité chez moi de nouvelles façons de comprendre qui s'appliquaient directement à ma propre discipline et à ma recherche. A maintes reprises je voyais des éléments du puzzle tomber en place. J'ai fait plusieurs découvertes personnelles qui m'amenaient par exemple à me dire: "voilà donc pourqoui les neurologues disent ceci!" ou "c'est là la base génétique de ce facteur" ou "voilà pourqoui les psychiatres ont ce problème". Cette lecture donnait plus d'ampleur, de profondeur et de portée à ma compréhension de l'enfant handicapé, de ceux qui en prennent soin, et des problèmes rencontrés par plusieurs des professionnels qui ont entrepris de l'aider. J'ai été très intéressée par la façon dont certains des auteurs abordaient les problèmes.

Ce volume s'adresse tout particulièrement à nos collègues des pays en voie de développement et à ceux qui travaillent dans des régions éloignées des centres d'expertise. Ils constateront où nous en sommes présentement et ils recueilleront de nouvelles idées. Ils reconnaîtront également plusieurs des problèmes. Ils verront que partout dans le monde leurs collègues s'emploient à rechercher des solutions, mais que les problèmes qui sont les leurs se rencontrent aussi à des degrés divers dans les pays les plus industrialisés. On doit espérer que ces constatations les amèneront à trouver des solutions à partir de leur propre expérience et à participer eux-mêmes à des échanges d'information, à des rencontres subséquentes et dans des publications à venir.

Nous pouvons nous demander enfin s'il vaut la peine de consacrer tant d'énergie à la recherche de meilleurs moyens d'aider les enfants handicapés. Ne devrions-nous pas tout simplement les laisser grandir de façon naturelle et affronter les maladies ou les catastrophes que la vie leur réserve? Ils survivraient sûrement et, en fait, peut-être qu'ainsi ce serait, comme toujours, les mieux constitués qui tiendraient le coup, de sorte que dans les générations futures il y aurait moins d'enfants ayant des besoins spéciaux. Ces considérations me rappellent l'histoire du géant qui, un jour, en se promenant à travers les champs, ramassa une poignée de terre remplie de grains et la lança dans le vent. Certains de ces grains tombèrent dans un jardin cultivé par un petit garçon qui s'émerveilla de leur apparition. Il les planta soigneusement, les arrosa et les engraissa jusqu'à ce qu'ils croissent et donnent des fleurs magnifiques. Après plusieurs années, le géant se trouva à passer à travers les champs et vit plusieurs acres de belles fleurs sauvages qui étaient bercées par le vent, mais dans un coin du champ il y avait une parcelle de terrain magnifique qui attira son attention. Chaque fleur y était d'une beauté, d'un parfum, d'une couleur et d'une forme extraordinaires. Les fleurs sauvages sont pourtant belles, pensait-il, mais, fleur pour fleur elles avaient l'air pâles et rabougries à côté des plantes cultivées.

Cette analogie s'applique également aux enfants. Bien sûr, ils grandiront et certains s'épanouiront, si on les laisse dans leur environnement naturel, mais il est extraordinaire de constater jusqu'à quel point des soins spéciaux permettent à un potentiel caché jusque là de se manifester. Ainsi, chaque gramme d'énergie que nous mettons en commun pour pourvoir aux besoins des enfants dans notre parcelle du terrain rapportera des dividendes incalculables et ceci se réalisera d'autant plus que nous aurons partagé nos connaissances et nos découvertes avec nos amis d'ailleurs, de façon à ce qu'ils puissent, eux aussi, cultiver leurs propres jardins et partager avec leurs voisins ce qu'ils auront appris.

La Conference

Le docteur Doug Kenny, président de l'Université de British Columbia, souhaita la bienvenue aux délégués. Il fit remarquer que la Colombie Britannique et l'Université agissant ensemble présentaient le dynamisme d'une société de pionniers et l'hospitalité cordiale d'un peuple chaleureux dont la vision était orientée vers la mer, la montagne et la forêt. Il invita les délégués à rapporter dans leurs bagages des souvenirs merveilleux et des amitiés nouvelles.

Monsieur Tom Tucker parla au nom de l'honorable Robert McLelland, ministre de la santé, retenu ailleurs à la dernière minute. Il transmit aux délégués les salutations de l'honorable Bill Bennett, premier ministre de la Colombie Britannique, et celles des membres du Gouvernement.

Monsieur Tucker fit état des problèmes économiques associés au fait d'offrir à tous les citoyens une gamme complète de soins de santé. Il dit que le gouvernement de la Colombie Britannique s'intéressait tout particulièrement à la prévention et qu'il écouterait très attentivement ce qui se dirait durant la séance portant sur ce thème, de façon à ce que la province puisse étudier les conseils d'experts internationaux.

Le docteur Pat McGeer, ministre de l'éducation, ouvrit la séance plénière. Il parla des pressions exercées sur la Colombie Britannique pour l'amener à offrir plus de services. La conséquence de ces pressions a été, dit-il, d'attirer notre attention sur la nécessité de diffuser nos connaissances courantes. Par comparaison avec les autres pays industrialisés, le Canada ne contribue pas encore autant qu'il le devrait à la recherche et à l'élaboration d'idées nouvelles. Il dit qu'il attendait avec impatience les sages conseils des conférenciers et qu'il espérait recueillir des suggestions quant aux activités à entreprendre dans l'avenir.

La conférence était constituée de sept séances: trois séries de deux séances simultanées et une séance plénière.

Le Livre

Le volume comprend sept chapitres. Chaque section a été rédigée de façon à présenter l'argument principal des conférenciers sous une forme qui puisse se lire rapidement. Même si les sujets se trouvent intégrés en raison du thème qui leur est commum, chaque communication peut être considérée comme une unité distincte.

La première section, *Services offerts aux Enfants exceptionnels résidant dans des régions éloignées,* a été organisée, présidée et éditée par le docteur Geoffrey Robinson, professeur et directeur de la *Division de Pédiatrie de la Population* à l'Université de British Columbia. Le docteur Robinson faisait remarquer que le mot "éloigné" signifie d'habitude "à distance, loin, ou hors circuit". Mais le terme peut avoir d'autres connotations également, y compris les différences climatiques, culturelles et linguistiques. L'offre de services dans des régions éloignées peut donc entraîner la nécessité de s'attaquer aux problèmes d'accès spéciaux imposés par la géographie et le climat, ou aux problèmes de styles de vie, de croyances et de priorités des groupes culturels, ou aux problèmes de communication qui se présentent quand le professionnel et le patient parlent des langues différentes. Peuvent s'ajouter à ceux-ci les problèmes logistiques que pose le caractère raréfié de la population dans bien des régions éloignées, problèmes comme le chômage, la mauvaise qualité du logement, etc. Enfin, on doit faire face aux questions cruciales de la sélection, de la formation, et de l'instabilité du personnel.

Les cinq conférenciers ont tous été personnellement impliqués dans la diffusion de services aux enfants dans des régions éloignées du Canada et leurs descriptions de la situation illustrent leurs façons d'aborder les divers problèmes. Parmi ces comptes rendus on trouve une expérience innovatrice sur l'évaluation d'un programme d'enseignement pour parents d'enfants sourds dans les régions rurales de Terre-Neuve et du Labrador, un rapport sur le travail d'une équipe pluridisciplinaire d'évaluation et de prise en charge d'enfants exceptionnels dans le nord de la Saskatchewan, un débat général sur l'élaboration de politiques relatives à l'organisation de programmes de diffusion de services dans les territoires du Nord-Ouest s'adressant directement aux Inuits souffrant d'arriération mentale.

La seconde séance, *Etude transculturelle du développement cognitif et des façons d'élever les enfants,* a été organisée et éditée par le docteur Robert Wilson, représentant de la Société Canadienne de Psychologie et membre du Comité directeur de la conférence. Le docteur Walter Lonner, dont les travaux de recherches transculturelles sont bien connus et professeur de l'Université de Western Washington, a présidé la séance.

Les conférenciers de ce groupe se sont attaqués à l'objectif de la psychologie transculturelle qui est de définir un ensemble de principes quasi-universels qui s'appliqueraient à toutes les populations humaines, tout en se conformant à la nouvelle tendance vers une compréhension du caractère culturel propre à chaque population. Dans le troisième article de cette section le docteur Walter Lambert étudie les pratiques universelles d'éducation des enfants dans le contexte unique de neuf pays différents. Il examine également des groupes d'immigrants en

Amérique du Nord. Bien qu'il y ait évidemment de nombreuses différences, on pourra se surprendre de certains des facteurs communs dans la façon d'élever les enfants dans les divers pays. Cette conférence a été traduite et est présentée aussi en français.

La troisième séance a été organisée, présidée et éditée par le docteur John Crichton, directeur du Département de Neurologie de l'Hôpital de Vancouver pour les Enfants. Les conférenciers présentent des études qui démontrent la persistance, en dépit des efforts d'intervention corrective, des troubles d'apprentissage décelés à l'école maternelle. Effectivement, on observe non seulement que ces enfants, qui ont fait l'objet d'un dépistage précoce, continuent à avoir des problèmes d'apprentissage en classe, mais aussi que le degré de perturbation semble rester constant et affecter le travail et le rendement à l'école pendant toute la carrière académique de l'individu. Le besoin de méthodes d'intervention nouvelles est nettement affirmé. L'auteur du dernier article de cette série décrit un programme d'intervention pluridisciplinaire qui semble donner de bons résultats.

Le quatrième thème sur la *Prévention des défectuosités du développement* a fait l'objet d'une séance organisée, présidée et éditée par le docteur Bluma Tischler, directrice médicale de Woodlands, une grande école pensionnat pour arriérés mentaux en Colombie Britannique.

Sous ce thème on a présenté une description des cas de défectuosité constatés à la suite d'une épidémie de rubéole et on a fait l'esquisse d'une méthode utilisée en Colombie Britannique pour le dépistage d'anomalies précises chez les nouveaux-nés. Dans cette section, on a traduit l'article sur les aspects neurologiques des troubles d'apprentissage.

La séance sur les *Enfants à handicaps multiples* a été organisée et présidée par le docteur Roger Freeman, éminent spécialiste de la psychiatrie infantile et professeur de psychiatrie à l'Université de British Columbia.

L'édition des textes a été faite par Don McEachern, éducateur et administrateur au Collège Douglas à Vancouver. Le chapitre présente certains des problèmes que recontrent ceux qui travaillent auprès des enfants à handicaps multiples. On y fait ressortir l'importance de poser un diagnostic très tôt et d'une planification à long terme de la part de préposés aux soins bien entraînés et compatissants. Dans cette section, Dana Brynelsen a recours à des lettres de parents et à la méthode d'histoires de cas pour décrire les problèmes rencontrés par le personnel dans leur offre pour mobiliser des services permettant une planification à long terme des soins aux enfants à handicaps multiples. Cet article a été traduit et est présenté aussi en français.

La sixième séance sur l'*Enfant maltraité* a consisté dans une série de conférences en langue français de la part de scientifiques venant de France et du Canada français. Les auditeurs pouvaient bénéficier de services de traduction simultanée au moment des présentations et l'on trouvera dans ce volume une traduction de celles-ci en langue anglaise. La séance a été organisée et présidée par le docteur François Desrosiers, directeur de l'Ecole de psychologie de l'Université Laval à Québec. L'édition des textes est de monsieur Jean-Marie Honorez de l'Hôpital Sainte-Justine pour les Enfants à Montréal. L'un des conférenciers considére que le comportement abusif et violent n'est pas un phénomène isolé dirigé uniquement vers les enfants, mais plutôt un élément du tableau général de la violence sociale qui sévit présentement dans notre société. Il est d'avis que la façon la plus efficace d'aborder le problème est de s'attaquer à la fragilité de la structure familiale. Un autre conférencier décrit les diverses formes de sévices exercés sur les enfants dans toutes les classes sociales de notre société. Une autre étude porte sur l'effet continu des mauvais traitements subis durant la tendre enfance dans la vie ultérieure de ces victimes.

La séance plénière a été organisée par le docteur Anne Crichton, sociologue et membre du Département de Planification des Soins de Santé de l'Université de British Columbia. Le docteur Graham Clarkson, orateur de renom, conseiller sur les soins de santé auprès des gouvernements et des institutions, en a assumé la présidence. Le chapitre de ce volume a été édité par le docteur Patricia Woodward, directrice des services pédagogiques à Woodlands et présidente du comité du programme scientifique de cette conférence.

Les six séances de la conférence ont été conçues de façon à faire ressortir les progrès de la recherche, à circonscrire les problèmes et à présenter certaines des solutions qui s'appliquent à la diffusion des services de santé aux enfants exceptionnels. La séance plénière avait pour but de faire émaner au cours de cette conférence, de la bouche de planificateurs expérimentés en soins de la santé, de sages directives sur la façon de mettre en place certains de ces services.

Le docteur George Silver, professeur à L'Ecole de Santé Publique de l'Université Yale, a proposé la formation de groupes séparés de conseillers spéciaux et de préposés aux services, de façon à définir nettement les politiques et les programmes à appliquer aux enfants. Il a présenté des modèles européens impressionnants pour illustrer ce que l'on pourrait faire en Amérique du Nord. Il est d'avis que lorsqu'on aura institué des services pour les enfants en général, les enfants exceptionnels seront bien pourvus au sein d'un tel système.

Le docteur Robert Haggerty, directeur des programmes de la Fondation Robert Wood Johnson, a attiré l'attention sur l'influence exercée par le stress familial dans les sphères sociales, économiques et comportementales dans l'accroissement des risques de maladie et de l'utilisation des services de santé. Il propose l'intégration des programmes médicaux, éducationnels et sociaux afin que, en plus d'aborder l'enfant comme un tout dans le contexte de la famille, on puisse effectuer des économies importantes grâce à la participation des parents et d'un personnel non médical. A son avis, un tel service intégré répond au meilleur avantage de l'enfant exceptionnel dont l'invalidité impose des tensions considérables à la structure familiale.

I: DELIVERY OF SERVICES TO EXCEPTIONAL CHILDREN IN REMOTE AREAS

editor: Geoffrey Robinson

"Home Centred Video Taped Counselling Programmes: Description"

CLARE NEVILLE-SMITH, M.B. F.R.C.P. (C)

Abstract

In this project a method was developed for counselling parents of preschool children with severe or profound hearing impairments. The families included were from Newfoundland and Labrador. The project was evaluated in terms of its effects upon both parent competence in skills taught by the teacher, and children's language development, as well as in terms of its feasibility.

A one year trial period, using video tapes and telephone counselling by a qualified teacher of the hearing impaired, was successful in improving parent competence and children's language development. No problems were encountered with respect to feasibility. The preliminary findings were such that a similar programme was initiated by the Department of Education of Newfoundland through its School for the Deaf even before the completion of the final report.

Ce projet de recherche a consisté dans la création d'une méthode pour offrir des conseils aux parents d'enfants d'âge préscolaire, de Terre-Neuve et du Labrador, affectés de défectuosités graves ou profondes de l'audition. Le programme a été évalué en fonction de ses effets sur la compétence des parents dans les techniques enseignées, sur l'acquisition du langage chez les enfants et sur ses possibilités de réalisation.

On a pu, au cours d'une période d'essai d'une année, en utilisant des bandes de magnétoscope et le téléphone pour véhiculer les conseils d'un spécialiste de l'enseignement aux handicapés de l'ouïe, améliorer la compétence des parents et l'acquisition du langage des enfants. On n'a rencontré aucun problème dans la réalisation du projet. Les résultats préliminaires ont été assez encourageants pour amener le Ministère de l'Education de Terre-Neuve, par l'intermédiaire de son Ecole pour les Sourds, à mettre sur pied un programme semblable, avant même le compte rendu final.

Without doubt, to be born with, or to develop at an early age, a profound hearing impairment is to suffer one of the greatest handicaps. The affected child is prevented from acquiring that essential human attribute, his native language, by natural means, i.e., at his mother's knee.

For the prelingually deaf the ultimate level in social, emotional, and academic spheres appears to be higher when appropriate management is instituted in the preschool years, the period of optimal language learning. Early case finding and diagnosis is therefore a prerequisite; in Newfoundland, as in many other places, current practice leaves much to be desired. Even when a child has been diagnosed and hearing aids provided, the problem of continued parental counselling and language training remains. Various methods of meeting this need, which have been used in more populated areas, have proved to be impractical in our province with a total population of 560,000 scattered over 140,000 square miles. Our hearing impaired children (with an incidence rate of about 1/1000 live births) are scattered over a huge area. Only in St. John's is there a nursery school for the preschool deaf.

Memorial University of Newfoundland carries out "distance education" through a variety of media, such as the Hermes Satellite used by the Telemedicine Project of our Medical School and a number of community learning centres run by the Extension and Educational Television Departments. This programme has led to the idea of using direct videotape teaching of parents in their own homes. Consequently, a multi-disciplinary group has been formed to plan a project.

The objective was to develop a method of counselling parents of rural preschool children who had severe or profound hearing impairment but no other significant handicaps. Evaluation of the project was in terms of (1) its effects on parent competence in skills taught by the project, (2) its effects on the children's language development, and (3), evidence of the feasibility of this approach.

Children were eligible for the program if they (1) were less than six years of age, (2) had not been enrolled in a preschool nursery class for the hearing impaired, and (3) had severe or profound hearing impairment but no other significant handicap. Where it could be accurately measured, the third criterion was hearing loss of 70 db. or greater across the significant portion of the speech frequency range; in younger subjects the amount of hearing loss could not be accurately determined but was estimated to be at approximately this level. The etiology of deafness was Rubella in 9, familial in 6, and unknown in 12 cases.

There were 27 such children; their average age at diagnosis was 23 months (range 6–55 months). These 27 children belonged to 26 families distributed widely in the Island portion of the province. The only child known in Labrador was excluded on the basis of a significant handicap, namely cerebral palsy. Four of these families could be reached only by boat.

Twelve families had five or more children; six homes were considered to be grossly overcrowded. Other characteristics of the families included: 22 married mothers, three single mothers and one separated. Two mothers had less than Grade 8 education, seventeen of them had some high school education, the highest grade attended being between Grades 8 and 11; four had more than Grade 11; the educational level of three mothers was not known.

In the early months of 1977, the multidisciplinary committee met frequently. We realized that this would have to be a descriptive study, involving all the eligible children whose parents wished to participate, an unknown proportion at the outset. A teacher of the hearing impaired was recruited and the purchase of equipment arranged.

During this time, videotapes were prepared at the Inter-Provincial Hearing Handicap Resource in Amherst, Nova Scotia by three teachers of the preschool deaf. These teachers were sufficiently aware of the situation in Newfoundland to make these tapes relevant to our setting. Four series of twelve tapes each were made; these were appropriate to age groups between 0−60 months. Each 30 minute video tape consisted of five sections:

1) *General introduction*, which outlined topics to be covered.
2) *Lesson*, in which a teacher was seen giving a lesson to a child of the appropriate age using an auditory trainer with emphasis on good microphone techniques while stimulating language. On occasion she showed how to regain the interest of a child whose attention had wandered and how to cope with a child who became recalcitrant, even abandoning a lesson, if need be, to resume it later. Parents found the realism of these situations most helpful.
3) *More ideas*, which summarized the techniques shown in the lesson with suggestions for expanding them, for example, by using simple diaries or collections of pictures, e.g., "of granny's house," which could be produced each time the child planned to make such a visit.
4) *Things to remember*, which covered general information or technical comments, such as the care of the hearing aid, the importance of having colds treated because of the possibility of *serous otitis*, and a description of language development.
5) *Around the house*, which included suggestions to bring the activities of the lesson into everyday activities, e.g., having the child sit on the counter while mother peeled potatoes, as an opportunity for eye level contact while talking about the "here and now." In retrospect, we think that more fathers and other men should have been shown working and interacting with children. This oversight is a weakness; mothers were the main people involved.

The first workshop was held in St. John's in July 1977. All the children came with the 26 mothers and, in most cases, a second relative, (father, grandmother or older sibling). Much encouragement was given by a contact person nominated in each home area, usually the Public Health Nurse. Because of the numbers, the group was divided; the two workshops, each of four days, were held in consecutive weeks. These were made as informal as possible. Since Project staff, parents, and children stayed at the Newfoundland School for the

Deaf, they met in the evenings over meals. There were lectures and panel discussions on such topics as the ear and normal hearing, tests of hearing, audiograms, varieties of deafness, hearing aids, and on child development and management. Parents were given instruction regarding the equipment, videotape machines, T.V. monitors, and auditory trainers. These were not only demonstrated but also used individually under supervision. The competence of parents and the childrens' general development was assessed by a variety of methods.

All families agreed to take home the equipment. For a few families, the equipment had to be sent by bus, boat, and rail, taking up to three weeks. The teacher was the vital link and lifeline of the project during the ensuing 12 months. She mailed a videotape to each home every month and telephoned parents about three times a month. The calls were essential in assisting parents with any problems they might have, whether with the equipment, the content of video tapes, or in the management of the child. Every two months, the teacher mailed out some material on "new ideas," such as, ideas for homemade toys or the use of household materials. In the fall of 1977, she visited each home once, spending a full day at each. This gave her the opportunity to see how the families had managed to set up the equipment and use it. She also observed the mother teaching the child, helped her with techniques, and checked on how the parents were learning from the videotapes.

The next workshops were held in July 1978; the parents attended with the same group of professionals as in the previous year. Twenty-three of the original 26 families attended. Two of the three families who dropped out had severe socio-economic problems; contact was maintained with these families at home. In the third case, the mother had been placed under psychiatric care.

Several parents had asked to meet older deaf children and adults. They had also expressed interest in methods of communication other than oral. We noted that all but one child arrived at the second workshop wearing their hearing aids, all were obviously accustomed to them every waking hour. Several parents reported transferring aids to night clothes and removing them at "lights out." We saw children running to their parents when a battery was running low and replacing molds in their own ears. One 22-month-old was seen trying to get the prongs of the cord back into the body of the aid.

Parent competence was again informally assessed by the teachers to note changes from the 1977 base line. The children's progress was re-evaluated, with the same instruments being used by the same consultants.

From the outset we had considered one year too short a time in which to observe any marked change in language in a preschool deaf child. We hoped that on completion of the formal study, we would be able to continue the use of the video tapes and phone calls which appeared to be helping some parents. To this end, the Department of Education was kept informed of all activities and asked to send a representative to the second workshop. We were pleased when the Department made their first formal move into providing services to preschool deaf children in Newfoundland by an agreement to continue service for those 11 children still in the programme and not yet old enough to be admitted to school. The project teacher transferred to the employ of the Newfoundland School for the Deaf at the end of the program year.

It is interesting to note that the first year graduates who were admitted to the Newfoundland School for the Deaf were considered by the teacher to have much better listening skills and certainly a greater start on language as compared with children admitted in previous years. The Project's Educational Consultant considered the achievement of the children comparable to that of children in Nova Scotia and New Brunswick who had visited teachers weekly, and/or had attended preschool nursery classes.

The estimated cost of the service element, including pro-rated costs of the equipment for its expected life span, was nearly $2,500 per child per year.

2

"Home Centred Video Taped Counselling Programmes: Results"

MARIE O'NEILL, PH.D

Abstract

Twenty-three parents and 24 children who attended residential workshops were assessed at the beginning (1977) and the end (1978) of the programme. The Verbal Comprehension Scale of the Reynell Development Language Scales recorded an average improvement of 8.6 months, which was not significantly greater than the no-training predictions. On the Expressive Language Scale children averaged mean gains of 5.6 months, which was significantly greater than the no-treatment prediction ($p \leqslant .05$). Changes on the Hearing and Speech subscale and the Griffiths Mental Developmental Schedule were highly correlated ($r=0.83$) with changes in Reynell Expressive Language, but not with changes in Reynell Verbal Comprehension ($r=0.08$). Multiple regression analyses identified the best predictors of language development to be good parent competence in child management and in auditory training skills, good child development (excluding language), and frequent use of hearing aids.

Vingt-trois parents et vingt-quatre enfants ont participé à des ateliers en résidence et furent l'objet d'une évaluation au début (1977) et à la fin (1978) de l'application du programme. L'Echelle de Compréhension Verbale des Echelles de Développement du Langage de Reynell révéla une amélioration moyenne de 8,6 mois, qui n'était pas significativement plus grande que les prévisions pour la condition de contrôle (non-application du programme). L'Echelle de Langage Expressif donna des gains moyens de 5,6 mois, ce qui était significativement plus grand que les prévisions pour la condition de contrôle ($p \leqslant .05$). Les changements de l'Echelle de l'Audition et de la Parole et de l'Inventaire de Développement Mental de Griffiths entretiennent une corrélation très forte ($r=0,83$) avec les changements de l'Echelle de Langage Expressif de Reynell, mais non pas avec l'Echelle de Compréhension Verbale de Reynell, ($r=0,08$). Les analyses de régression multiple ont désigné comme meilleurs indices de prévision de l'acquisition du langage: la compétence des parents dans leurs relations avec les enfants et dans l'enseignement des aptitudes auditives, le développement (hors le langage) satisfaisant de l'enfant et l'usage fréquent des appareils acoustiques.

Evidence is accumulating to show that the language restrictions which are imposed on young deaf children by their handicap may be made less severe as their parents become able to provide those experiences that are basic to the acquisition of language. By the time the hearing loss is suspected (usually by twelve months) and certainly by the time the diagnosis is made (between eighteen months and three years) the parent has become a significant person in the child's life. Usually, the bonding necessary for cooperative work/play activities between parent and child has been established; time schedules in the home, as compared with those externally imposed by school, are fairly flexible. The situation is potentially favourable for home-based learning.

Luria has explained that in the normal child, true language begins at about eighteen months of age when symbolic processes develop. Between one and a half years and four to five years, the integration becomes more firmly established, with the eventual internalization of the process, so that language can be used as a vehicle for thought. These early years can be placed in a schedule in which progression is made from the time when the ability to hear at birth gives the child access to the development of verbal comprehension, and subsequently to concept formation, expressive language, and articulated speech. Reynell places this schedule in parallel with opportunities for verbal expression and communication being utilized by the developing child.

The deaf child, on the other hand, invariably needs several years "to reach even a three-year level of competence in the semantic, syntactic and morphologic aspects of language" (Ling, et.al). Ling and others have outlined the variety of educational options required to meet the needs of hearing-impaired children. There is abundant evidence to indicate that special help for deaf infants during the first three years of life is imperative. In order that parents may function effectively as home-based educators, they should be provided with appropriate information as rapidly as it can be absorbed, and they should receive the necessary psychological support for developing coping behaviour. Although not all parents learn to cope with the parent-oriented programmes, the effects of training are generally more enduring when parents, rather than teachers or therapists, are viewed as the primary agents of development.

The trial home based programme designed in St. John's, Newfoundland left open the question of whether to use a control group. This was not deemed feasible since, first, there was great uncertainty concerning what proportion of the target population might attend the first week-long workshop and then comply with the other components of the program; second, pre-school deaf populations in the most nearly comparable provinces—i.e. Prince Edward Island, Nova Scotia and New Brunswick—were already being served by programmes provided by the Amherst centre; and third, the exclusion of any children from the only available programme in this remote area might be regarded as ethically unsound.

MEASURES

1. Parent Assessments

Parent competence was evaluated by the *Parent Competence Evaluation Form*, which was completed independently by the three teachers/counsellors on the basis of observations of the same parents during each workshop and parent self report of behaviour at home. The project teacher completed this form after each of her home visits in the fall of 1977. Also, the *Monthly Teacher-Telephone Parent Competence Form* was completed by the project teacher at monthly intervals based on her telephone conversations that month with the parent.

During the 1978 Follow-up Workshop, each mother was administered the Family Concept Test (Van der Veen, 1974) by the research consultant. The test contains 80 items, each of which describes some social or emotional aspect of the whole family.

2. Assessment of Child Language Development

The standardized tests selected to assess child development were the *Reynell Developmental Language Scales* (Reynell, 1968) and the *Griffiths Mental Development Scales* (Griffiths, 1970). In addition, the Education Consultant made a global assessment of each child's language development level based on the criteria described by Dr. L. Owrid in his *Linguistic Schedules for Development of Speech*. Observers were used for both the Reynell and Griffith testing sessions; high inter-observer agreement in ratings was noted. As a further check, and since no control group was available, predictions of progress under no-training conditions were obtained from experts external to the study.

3. Case Studies

Case Studies have been included in the main report to give the reader a global view, as well as specific insights into the progress of 'typical' families over the year's program.

4. Acceptibility, Feasibility and Cost of the Programme

Parent participation was defined according to compliance with the study protocol. Parents also completed the *Parent Evaluation of the Workshop Questionnaire* and the *Mid-Year Parent Evaluation of the Programme Questionnaire*.

Throughout the period between workshops, an Equipment Repair Log was maintained. Costs which were covered by the three outside funding agencies were recorded for each phase of the programme.

ANALYSIS OF RESULTS

1. Parent Assessments

(a) Parent Competence. Four indices of parent competence were derived:

Index of Improvement in Parent Competence (i), Index of Parent Competence at the 1978 Follow-up workshop (ii), Index of Parent's Auditory Training Skills at the 1978 Follow-up workshop (iii), and Teacher's Global Assessment of Parent Competence(iv). Five parents consistently received a 'poor' classification and seven a 'good' classification on all four indices.

(b) Family Concept Test. Twelve global measures were based on the 80 items of this test. Family Effectiveness, (a measure of the adequacy of the functioning of the family), is based on 48 of these items. Most families in the present study received scores between 42 and 46 out of 48. Other subscales, including community sociability, family loyalty and closeness vs. estrangement, were markedly skewed towards positive scores. The parents received a wider distribution of scores on the other subscales: consideration vs. conflict, family actualization vs. inadequacy, open communication, family ambition, internal vs. external locus of control, togetherness vs. separation, family integration and adaptive coping.

For predicting the Index of Improvement in Parent Competence, open communication in the family, family loyalty, consideration in the family, separateness in the family, and family integration were the five best predictors (accounting for 39% of the variance). For predicting the Index of Parent Competence, the best predictors were: (i) open communication in the family, (ii) small number of children, (iii) husband employed and/or not on Social Assistance, (iv) mother not having completed secondary school, and (v) consideration within family. These variables accounted for 62% of the variance.

2. Child Language Development

In all comparisons, T-ratios were used to test group differences.

(a) *Reynell Developmental Language Scales*. On the Reynell test, the 24 children who attended the 1977 and the 1978 workshops showed a mean gain in developmental age of 8.6 months on Verbal Comprehension and 5.6 months on Expressive Language.

In addition, the 1978 mean Verbal Comprehension developmental age (18.6 months) was greater than the mean external predicted age (16.6 months) and significantly greater ($p<.05$) than the mean internal predicted age (15.4 months). The external ratings were made by outside specialists, the internal ratings by the project staff. Similarly, the 1978 mean Expressive Language developmental age (14.6 months) exceeded both the internal (12.3) and external (11.1 months) 'no training' predictions and was statistically significantly greater than both the mean predicted ages ($p<0.05$ and $p<0.005$ respectively).

(b) *Griffiths Mental Developmental Scales*. A comparison of the mean developmental ages of the children on the Locomotor, Eye/hand Coordination, Personal-Social Adjustment and Performance subscales and their developmental age on the Hearing and Speech subscale indicates that the children's development was severely delayed only in the hearing and speech developmental area.

The 1978 Hearing and Speech mean developmental age (17.4 months) was significantly greater (p<0.005) than both the Clinical Consultant's estimate (11.5 months) and the outside specialist's (12.8 months) "no training" predicted level. The mean developmental age at the 1978 workshop exceeded the 'no-training' predicted mean age by approximately five months.

A "good" parent competence rating at the 1978 workshop was the best predictor of change in verbal comprehension (Reynell) between workshops. A high score on the Griffiths Performance Scale, which can be interpreted as a crude measure of intellectual ability, was found best to predict changes in the expressive language scale of the Reynell. Use of the hearing aid was also a good predictor of language development; such use was correlated with both parent competence and intellectual ability of the child.

(c) *Education Consultant's Assessments.* The 1978 developmental ages indicated substantial gains in both comprehension of speech (14.0 months) and use of speech as communication (11.6 months). The 1978 global assessments of the Education Consultant exceeded her 'no-training' predictions and the differences were statistically significant (p>0.005).

3. Case Studies

Anne is the twelfth of thirteen children of first-cousin parents who have four deaf children and many deaf relatives. They live in a small overcrowded house with three deaf paternal aunts in an isolated outport. The family is well integrated. Although Anne was suspected of being deaf in infancy, this condition was accepted by the family whose attitude was that appropriate action would be taken at school age. However, after referral by the visiting nurse, the child was examined and severe deafness was confirmed at 42 months, some useful residual hearing being found in the lower frequencies.

The hearing tests were carried out during Anne's attendance (with her mother and deaf sister) at the first workshop. No hearing aid had been worn up to that time. The child was not generally cooperative during her language development sessions. She was able to score on gross and fine motor tests at reasonable levels. She had not learned to watch faces for cues and the mother resorted to gross manipulation of objects to help the child comprehend. She made very little sound at all (mostly crying or laughing noises) during the first workshop.

Despite severely crowded conditions in the home, the mother managed to work consistently with the child through the year, involving the whole family in the programme (one other sister was also a participant). She was always available for contact and grew in confidence during the year, improving in her ability to use the lessons and to hold Anne's attention. In her exceedingly busy life, she religiously adhered to a schedule of daily lessons, and improved her own aware-ness of the child's needs considerably.

At the time of retesting, Anne showed adequate progress. Her general deve-lopment was thought to be slow, but her response to procedures was greatly improved and her verbal measures increased above the expected gain.

4. Acceptance of the Programme

Four sociobiological variables were found to be good predictors of parent par-ticipation in the programme: (i) mother working less than five months of the year (30% of the variance), (ii) external locus of control and family actualization, (iii) a rating of 'good' on the global assessment of parent competence by the teacher, and (iv) a rating of 'good' on the 1978 Index of Parent Competence. The high rate of attendance at both workshops was also taken as evidence of the accep-tance of the programme by the parents.

Twenty-one of the parents returned the mid-year Parent Evaluation Question-naire. All indicated that the content of the videotapes had been useful and that they were satisfied with the educational components of the lessons. Twenty felt that they had been kept well informed of progress by the weekly telephone calls. Similar responses were received on the 1978 Workshop Evaluation Question-naire. The workshops and home visits were thought necessary and the parents appreciated the opportunity to meet other parents of hearing-impaired children. The auditory trainer was considered the most useful component of the pro-gramme.

The positive results with respect to improvement of parent competence and in rate of child language development are encouraging. However, the great range in results is not reflected in the averages presented. Some subjects did not seem to benefit from the programme. The range of results is nevertheless similar to that observed in children visited weekly by itinerant teachers from the Atlantic Provinces Resource Centre for the Hearing Handicapped.

In view of the excellent results achieved by some parents and children, the value of using such a videotaped programme, supported by regular telephone contacts, cannot be questioned. In Newfoundland, the severely and profoundly deaf children from rural areas had formerly arrived at the School for the Deaf with little or no language at five years of age.

The cost of this programme compares favourably with alternative methods of delivering language training to preschool hearing-impaired chilren. It would appear that correspondence courses, the least inexpensive alternative of all those reported in the literature, costs less than the programme described in this report.

References

Luria, A.R. *The Role of Speech in the Regulation of Normal and Abnormal Behaviour*. Pergamon, Oxford, 1961.

Reynell, J.K. Reynell Developmental Language Scales. Experimental Edition. N.F.E.R., Publishing Co. Ltd., Windsor, Berks, 1968.

Van der Veen, F. and Nevak, A.L. The Family Concept of the Disturbed Child: A Replication Study. *American Journal of Orthopsychiatry*. 44 (1974): 763-73.

Reynell, J.K. Reynell Developmental Language Scales Supplement to the Manual for Teachers of the Deaf. N.F.E.R. Publishing Company Ltd., Windsor, Berks, 1975.

Griffiths, R. *The Abilities of Young Children*. Child Development Research Centre, University of London, London, 1970.

3

Travelling Clinics in Saskatchewan—Diagnostic Assessment and Counselling

WITOLD ZALESKI, M.D., F.R.C.PSYCH., F.R.C.P. (C)

Abstract

The Alvin Buckwold Centre in Saskatoon provides outreach programmes for children in remote communities in Saskatchewan. Considerable problems are posed by geography, language, and culture, and in consequence the value of the service must be judged in frank and realistic terms. Emphasis must be placed upon involving community workers and families in the development of a feasible plan of management for each child. Several cases of successful projects are available. In an Indian Reserve inaccessible by road, a workshop, offering practical skills and evening classes for teenagers and parents, was added to a new school. Its success suggests that involving native people living in remote communities as co-partners in the delivery of services is a promising option.

Le Centre Alvin Buckwold de Saskatoon offre des programmes spéciaux pour atteindre les enfants des collectivités éloignées de la Saskatchewan. On décrit ici les problèmes considérables que posent la géographie, la langue et la culture et on évalue les services offerts en termes francs et réalistes. On insiste sur la nécessité d'intéresser les travailleurs communautaires et les familles à l'élaboration d'un plan réaliste de développement pour chaque enfant. Plusieurs exemples de projets réussis sont présentés. Dans une école neuve d'une réserve amérindienne située en dehors du réseau routier, on a ajouté un atelier pour offrir aux parents et aux adolescents des cours pratiques et des classes du soir. L'auteur propose de recruter des autochtones, vivant au sein même de groupes communautaires éloignés, pour les associer à la distribution des services.

The Alvin Buckwold Centre (A.B.C.) is a diagnostic, teaching and research centre for the prevention and treatment of mental retardation. It is a university-based and community-oriented facility, serving the entire province of Saskatchewan and operates as a section of the Department of Paediatrics of the University Hospital in Saskatoon. Of the various services of the A.B.C., I will mention only those which relate to the topic of this session—"Delivery of Services to Exceptional Children in Remote Areas".

How many kilometres are needed to make some place a "remote area"? In Saskatchewan, the population of under one million is concentrated in the southern belt of the province, within approximately 500 kilometers of the U.S. border. The province, however, extends for nearly 1200 kilometers to the north. It is easy to see that nearly two-thirds of the province is a remote area but it is less obvious that within the southern one-third of Saskatchewan too there are many remote areas.

There are many Indian reserves and the vast majority of these reserves could be characterized as remote areas. They are remote culturally and remote in language because many parents speak little or no English. The reserve is a remote area because there is no direct access, and permission must be obtained from the band's chief for a professional to enter the reserve to help a native family.

Saskatchewan's population is scattered in small towns, villages, hamlets and farms. Delivery of services in rural areas is difficult; some farm areas become very remote during winter or when the snow is melting.

TRAVELLING CLINICS

Recognizing the special needs for service delivery in Saskatchewan, the A.B.C., from its opening in 1967, has tried to reach as many areas of Saskatchewan as possible through travelling clinics. A clinical team from the Centre, composed of two to nine people, will visit on invitation any place in Saskatchewan. The objectives of the travelling clinics are not only to make diagnostic assessments and remedial suggestions and to counsel parents, teachers, and others, but also to include in this process the local resource people, both professional and volunteer, so that the greatest benefit can be derived by the child, his family, the school and the community as a whole.

Our visits to northern Saskatchewan are only a small part of the A.B.C. service program. We do not have any specific committment or any additional resources for service in remote areas. We consider it our obligation to respond to the needs of these communities in the same way that we respond to the needs of other areas of Saskatchewan.

The visits of travelling clinics are irregular. The frequency, as well as the locale, depends on someone's identifying a group of exceptional children who may need help and then contacting our centre. The clinics vary significantly from one place to another, depending on the local needs and the facilities available in each place. The basic process includes a comprehensive medical examination, psychological assessment, review of social history, and review of developmental, educational, emotional and behavioural functioning. Our staff meet with the local resource people to discuss the findings and make recommendations that would be feasible in that particular environment. They also counsel the parents and teachers. Biological specimens for further investigations are collected and processed at the University Hospital. A written report is eventually sent to all the people involved with the child; if the parents can read, a copy goes to them as well.

Interpersonal communication, especially counselling, is very difficult when parents can communicate only through an interpreter. Sometimes there are two Indian groups, within the same geographic area, who speak different languages, such as Cree and Chippewayan.

The validity of our assessments might be questioned, since some of the children referred may know little or no English. We have learned to make clinical evaluations of the children, relying more on non-verbal than verbal tests. True, we can diagnose a child as being mentally retarded only in the more obvious cases; we can proceed with more confidence in diagnosing children as being "exceptional", that is, as having special needs for education, training and management.

Although our primary interest is in delayed development, we see many children at the travelling clinics who are suffering from behaviour problems, emotional problems, physical, emotional and experiential deprivation, neglect and ill-treatment resulting from parental alcoholism, juvenile aggression, delinquency and juvenile drinking.

We often ask ourselves if our visits are an effective way of dealing with problems of exceptional children in northern Saskatchewan and on Indian reserves. The answer is obviously that we are very inefficient in the sense of cost-benefit ratio. We have to travel, sometimes by chartered aircraft; such a visit is also costly in terms of personnel time.

We recognize our inability to deal with the social ills and social needs in the area. We fail to deal with behaviour problems, aggression and violence, drinking problems, juvenile pregnancies or too many pregnancies. How can we help a well-meaning but inexperienced teacher who does not understand any Cree and who finds herself with children who do not speak any English? How can we help parents with whom we may be miscommunicating through an interpreter? How can we help even English-speaking parents who do not understand our meaning because of cultural differences? For instances, when I asked a native father in Buffalo Narrows what was the matter with his boy, he answered very logically, "Doctor, I brought him here and you are going to tell me what is the matter with him". The parents often do not see themselves as facing any special problem—it is the nurse's or the teacher's problem.

Why do we do it then? Why do we travel to communities which do not seem ready for medical and developmental counselling, intervention and remedial programmes? In my opinion, this service has to be continued because only through such persistent trials will these communities eventually recognize that the health, welfare and education of their children must be their greatest priority for the improvement and advancement of their communities.

At present, the welfare of the children is the concern of public health nurses and teachers; but many northern parents do not share our child-rearing concepts so as to be able to identify it as a high priority goal.

Among the native men who have become leaders of their people, the priorities seem to be political rights, self-determination, native land rights, etc. I hear little said about health and education. However, there are signs of gradual improvement. Some native women are taking leadership in these areas. I see increasing self-assertiveness of the native women, within the family and community, especially in the direction of improving the welfare of their children.

At present, we feel frustrated that we cannot offer more effective help to children within their own environment. If the child is significantly retarded, disturbed or neglected, the main resource seems to be foster homes, which are usually in the southern part of the province.

We must continue to identify the needs of children in remote communities, and we must be forceful and persistent in urging that these needs be met. Significant progress has been made in services to the provincial northern area, e.g., through the formation of the Department of Northern Saskatchewan. I am less certain of progress within the federally controlled services, except for advances in housing.

Another justification for continuance is that we are not altogether ineffective; some individual children and their families have benefited from assessment, diagnosis and treatment without the children having been removed from home. I meet many fine Indian families trying to do their best, often against overwhelming odds.

An important outcome of our visits is that the interest we show in the welfare of those communities acts as an encouragement for improved services and the initiation of new services. The devoted professional people who work in those areas, especially public health nurses, Indian Health Services nurses and the teachers, find our visits encouraging and motivating, as well as helpful in reducing their feelings of isolation.

As an example, I will relate one of my experiences while on a visit to Patuanak, at the invitation of the Indian band's council and their education committee. Patuanak is a reserve, inaccessible by road, which had a new school, new housing and various improvements. The visit was special in that the chief, several band counsellors and the education committee were actively involved in health and welfare work. They participated in the conference, together with the teachers and other resource people, discussed the children's needs and attempted to determine what could be done. The chief did not speak English and all discussions had to be carried on through an interpreter.

We were impressed that this remote community was a progressive one and could become a model for other reserves. During our visit, one of the local leaders asked us a very pertinent question: "What are you doing to help the parents learn how to manage a difficult child and to encourage kids to go to school?" In response, we recommended that an educational programme—

including films, talks, discussions and projects using practical skills—be set up for adults and teenagers in the community. The nurse, teachers, other occasional visitors and any local people with special skills could be involved. We also recommended that the school have a workshop in which older children could learn practical skills. Such a workshop could be of benefit to teenagers leaving school and also to children with lower academic abilities or interests. The workshop could also become a community centre for adults, offering evening classes for parents. Additional teachers would be needed. The school also needed a special education classroom and teacher, as well as native teachers' aides.

To achieve any of these gains, money would be needed from the Department of Indian Affairs. I sent written requests to both the federal and provincial authorities. Following up on my recommendations one year later, I found that the school had acquired a special education class and teacher, native aides, and an education programme for adults. However, at the same time, the future was very uncertain! Local politics were producing much friction in the community. The school principal had resigned because of friction, and the Indian band's leadership, including the chief, was changing. Since these changes, we have not had an opportunity for a return visit to this reserve.

OTHER PROGRAMMES

I shall briefly mention two other services which may be of some help to families with exceptional children, living far from specialized services.

1. University Hospital has a hostel unit where accomodation is available without charge for the child and parent (financed through the provincial health services programme). The child may attend a remedial preschool programme at the Alvin Buckwold Centre and a training programme may be prepared to take home. The child participates in a group programme with other children, as well as working in individual sessions with the parent and our developmental therapist.

2. The Early Childhood Development provided by the A.B.C. is home-based with optional weekly visits to the Centre. Parents are guided in stimulation and developmental therapy. The A.B.C. provides an outreach of 150 kilometres for this programme which includes regular home visits by our staff. In cooperation with the Saskatchewan Association for the Mentally Retarded and the Provincial Government mental retardation service, we are supporting, in an increasing number of communities, the formation of independent consumer groups which will run the programmes with our staff members helping as consultants.

This brief presentation of the travelling clinics will doubtless produce many questions without answering any. The broadest one that continually challenges us as we fly home from a northern clinic is, how can we do the job better? The obvious answer is that we must involve more native people living in those areas as our co-partners in the delivery of needed services.

4

"Delivery of Services to Exceptional Children in the Northwest Territories"

TRUDY USHER, MSW

Abstract

The Northwest Territories is a vast land, comprising one third of Canada's land mass, with only 42,000 inhabitants. There are 56 communities, almost all accessible only by aircraft. Yellowknife, the capital and largest city, has a population of 9,500 people. Forty-seven of these communities have populations of less than 1,000.

Of the 42,000 inhabitants, 30,000 belong to Inuit, Indian, and Métis groups. Cultural differences, minority lifestyles, and lack of the facilities available to urban areas, make the experiences described here relevant to similar communities all over the world.

This article embodies a commitment to use the strengths and resources found in the local population to plan for exceptional children so that they have the opportunity to grow and to reach their potential within the framework of family and community.

Les Territoires du Nord-Ouest forment une vaste superficie qui représente le tiers de la surface totale du Canada. Cet espace n'est occupé que par quarante-deux mille individus. Ils forment cinquante-six groupements communautaires. Yellowknife, la ville la plus importante et la capitale de cette région, a une population de neuf mille cinq cents (9,500) âmes. Quarante-sept de ces regroupements comptent moins de mille individus et, parmi ceux-ci, trente mille (30,000) appartiennent à des communautés d'Inuits, d'Amérindiens et de Métis. Les différences culturelles, les modes de vie et l'absence des installations et des moyens disponibles dans les régions centrales font que les expériences de ces populations entretiennent des rapports avec celles des groupements semblables à travers le monde.

L'auteur considère qu'il est de son devoir d'utiliser les énergies et les ressources de la population locale dans la planification de son action auprès des enfants exceptionnels, de façon à ce que ces derniers soient capables de se développer et de réaliser leurs potentialités au sein même de leur famille et de leur collectivité.

GEOGRAPHICAL AND CULTURAL ISSUES

The Northwest Territories (NWT) is bounded on the south by the 60th parallel, on the west by the Yukon Territory, on the north by the Arctic Ocean and on the east by the Atlantic Ocean. It comprises almost one-third of Canada's land mass.

The fact that this expanse stretches across three time zones adds to communication problems. It is divided into four regions: Inuvik, Fort Smith, Keewatin and Baffin.

The population of the NWT is approximately 42,000 people. There are approximately 16,000 Inuit, 7,000 status Indians, and 7,500 Métis and non-status Indians. The remainder are primarily people of Euro-Canadian descent. Fifty per cent of the population are under eighteen years of age. Sixty per cent of its communities have fewer than 500 people.

There is also a very marked difference between the Eastern and Western Arctic regions, which may be attributed to the differing length of contact with the southern lifestyle which has been greater in the West. Regional differences exist in the movement from nomadic hunting and fishing to organized settlement life, wage employment, transient lifestyle, breakdown of the extended family support system and alcohol and drug abuse.

For many years the Federal Government was responsible for delivering social services in the NWT. The major focus of the work was primarily crisis intervention, with few resources available to deal with prevention or development. In 1968, the Government of the NWT assumed responsibility for the delivery of social services. The Department of Social Services employs a network of 85 staff members who are resident in NWT communities. In addition, there are programme managers, support staff and clerical staff employed in field offices and in the headquarters in Yellowknife. More than half of the field staff positions are held by native northerners.

Historically, pre-settlement life has involved survival of the fittest. Extended family groups have supported themselves by hunting and fishing. They travelled across the land, as determined by the season and the availability of game. It was a hard rigorous life in which the less healthy died.

The extended family groups who travelled together did, however, offer some support in the raising of children. The present "southern" phenomena of the nuclear family and independent responsibility of parents for the children have only recently moved into the North. These imported customs have caused confusion and isolation of the person who has not previously experienced them.

Initially, people spent only a limited time in settlements, coming in mainly to replenish supplies. Currency was of little importance, while furs were exchanged for staples such as tea, flour and traps. However, when nursing stations and schools were introduced, people began to congregate in settlements and became introduced to the southern Canadian concepts of child-raising and child care.

Initially, the staff of nursing stations were the primary diagnostic and treatment providers. Many individuals were transported hundreds of miles to southern medical centres when the problem could not be treated locally. For instance once a child had been assessed and treated in the southern resource, it was all too easy to acknowledge the lack of resources in the north and thus simply to keep the child in the south. Communication was almost nil, transportation was expensive and limited, service personnel could not speak the native language, and the parent was unable to communicate by letter, hence they literally lost their children to southern institutions.

As staff in the service professions stabilized, they became more sensitive to the problems of dislocation and family breakdown. Lines of communication were developed, interpreters obtained, and compassionate visits arranged. At the same time, there came a recognition of, and desire to, develop appropriate services to diminish the need to refer children south for either assessment or ongoing care. The philosophy of home care, community involvement and the establishment of special education resources is now fully accepted in government policy.

THE PRESENT SITUATION

As we all know, philosophy and policy are fine words; but, when undertaking a major thrust in services, one must also deal with many realities, principally those of staffing and costs. The development of an inclusive network of support services is fraught with problems. Few highly skilled professionals (psychologists, paediatricians) choose to live in the north. Those who take up residence seldom stay long enough to have a thorough understanding of the people they serve or the tremendous differences between various geographic areas within the NWT.

The interested enthusiastic southern nurse, teacher or social worker finds that the word "challenge" which appealed to him so strongly in the ad in the Vancouver *Sun* or Toronto *Globe and Mail* also means isolation, becoming a member of a minority group, separation from family, friends and all the supportive community services which one had taken for granted. The end result is often disillusionment and a high staff turnover which in turn leads to a spasmodic service which lacks continuity and direction.

During the past ten years, the Department of Social Services has embarked upon a major program of staff recruitment and training of indigenous people. Although the Territorial Government is committed to such a policy, it is still difficult to recruit and retain good staff.

Furthermore, one must acknowledge that northern communities have massive problems in other areas, including unemployment or underemployment, inadequate housing, inadequate water and sanitation facilities, high cost of transportation, and a lack of recreational resources. These needs also compete for dollars and may command greater attention than the plight of exceptional children. We are, however, slowly expanding our capacity in the areas of medical, educational and social service resources. A far greater public awareness has led to a greater demand for service.

GUIDELINES FOR SERVICE DELIVERY PROGRAMS

In order to develop relevant and viable support services to a small diverse population, dispersed over a large territory, the following guidelines are suggested:

1. Since it is impossible to provide expertise in the majority of small communities, such expertise should be available for assessment, consultation and programme development in each major geographical region. Therefore, one must look to a core of professionals to provide consultation and guidance to teachers, nurses and social workers.
2. It is important to develop and maintain a registry of handicapped children so that early intervention and follow-up is possible.
3. Community-based services should be developed to deal with "at risk" children, i.e. infant stimulation programmes and developmental centres. Communities should be encouraged to provide their own solutions to the care and the future of young handicapped residents. Community people can be trained to administer these programmes. A valuable resource of non-professionals are the housewives who can work part-time.
4. There is a need for respite/training centres in which the caretakers can obtain support, guidance and physical/emotional relief when required.
5. Steps must be taken to develop the educational resources needed to meet special needs and establish special classrooms, with specially trained teachers and classroom assistants.

5

Proposal for the Handicapped Inuit in the Baffin Region, N.W.T.

RUTH GLENNIE, B.N.SC., D.S.P.A. Reg. OSHA

Abstract

"You people down south teach children in the wrong way. You start at the wrong end. When you are teaching a child, you don't start at the beginning, you start right at the end. So that he can see what he is working for. He does the last little bit, and your child never fails that way."

old Inuit man

The Baffin Region is one of the four areas in the Northwest Territories. It makes up the extreme northeast part of Canada. It extends north for more than one thousand miles. Much of the region lies within the Arctic Circle. The Inuit have inhabited this region for centuries.

Improved medical care has allowed for the survival of handicapped children. White men's laws and customs have prevented their destruction. As their number grew, many were placed in southern institutions. But it is being increasingly felt that children cared for in their own communities and subject to traditional ways would fit better into these communities as adults.

Accordingly, a programme, described here, has been proposed to support and supplement the care presently given to handicapped individuals in Arctic Settlements.

"Vous, les gens du sud, vous éduquez vos enfants de la mauvaise façon. Vous commencez du mauvais bout. Quand on enseigne à un enfant, on ne débute pas par le commencement, on part directement de la fin. De façon à ce qu'il puisse voir ce pour quoi il travaille. Il fait le dernier petit bout et, de cette manière, votre enfant n'échoue jamais."

Viel homme Inuit.

La région de Baffin est l'une de quatre régions des Territoires du Nord-Ouest. Elle constitue l'extrême portion nord-est du Canada. Elle s'étend sur plus de mille milles (quinze cent kilomètres) au nord. Une grande partie de cette région fait partie du cercle arctique. Les Inuits habitent cette région depuis des siècles.

L'amélioration des soins médicaux a permis la survie de plusieurs individus arriérés mentalement. Les lois et les coutumes de l'homme blanc ont empêché leur destruction. A mesure que leur nombre s'accroissait, plusieurs d'entre eux furent confiés à des institutions méridionales. On croit, cependant, qu'en prenant soin de ces enfants dans leurs propres communautés et en les soumettant aux façons de faire traditionnelles on assurerait chez eux une meilleure adaptation.

L'auteur décrit un programme visant à appuyer et à accroître les soins qui sont présentement prodigués aux arriérés mentaux des villages de l'arctique.

The Baffin Region, one of the four regions of the Northwest Territories (N.W.T.), makes up the extreme northeastern part of Canada. Beginning at about the 65th parallel, it extends north for more than 1000 miles, with much of the region lying within the Arctic Circle. During the past 25-50 years, small settlements have been established along the coast. The largest of these, Frobisher Bay, is the administrative centre for the Baffin Region. Although heavy supplies are brought by sea lift during the short summer, transportation between settlements is by air for the greater part of the year.

The Inuit have inhabited this Region for centuries. Their lifestyle ensured that only healthy, intelligent individuals survived to carry on the "tribal heritage." Individuals with birth defects or those who became seriously ill or injured did not survive. When the Inuit began to make contact with the white man, this way of life gradually changed. Whalers and priests brought the first glimpse of another way of life. Settlements grew as more and more people chose to leave the land for a more secure existence in the settlements.

The trade undertaken for a secure life, however, brought new dangers, including diseases which could leave crippling aftermaths. Improved medical attention ensured the survival of many who would have died previously. Tuberculosis, measles, meningitis and encephalitis left people with physical and intellectual disabilities. The handicapped individual was no longer a threat to group survival, and the white man's laws and customs were further safeguards. Slowly the number of handicapped Inuit grew. Their care remained largely with the families. From time to time children were sent south for assessment of their abilities; some returned home but many were placed in institutions in the south. Frequently, there was no contact between child and parents for years.

PRESENT STUDY

This project, undertaken by the Department of Social Services (Baffin Region), arose from a concern for the number of mentally retarded Inuit being cared for in southern Canada because of the lack of programmes and facilities in the Arctic region. The Department's mandate was to visit each person in his/her own environment, to assess his/her abilities, and to formulate an overall programme for the care of mentally retarded Inuit in the Baffin Region. A total of 42 were identified. Of these, 22 were children, 13 at home and 9 in institutions.

An attempt was made to determine each individual's level of functioning in self care, academic, social and work skills. In the Arctic settlements, it was possible to identify the individual's role within the community and to make a rough estimate of possible future needs.

An encouraging finding of the survey was the great degree of acceptance by Arctic settlements of people deviating from the norm in either intelligence or behaviour. The difference between the group of mentally retarded Inuit who had remained in the Arctic and those who were sent south was impressive. Except for very young children, all those in the north had learned a surprising number of self-care skills. Within the communities, mental retardation seemed to be accepted and there was a feeling of community responsibility for the handicapped person.

While it is generally agreed that children cared for in their own homes progress further than do institutionalized children, it is possible that other factors have also had an impact on the development of these people. The traditional Inuit methods of child-rearing may have been more effective in teaching skills than the methods used in the south.

The quality of physical care provided for the individual at the family and community level was generally excellent, but most families expressed a need for assistance in teaching the handicapped person skills beyond the basic living skills. The idea of instituting in the Arctic region programmes for mentally retarded individuals was enthusiastically endorsed by both the Inuit and whites.

PROPOSED PROGRAMME

The aim of the provincial programme should be to support and to supplement the care presently given to mentally retarded individuals in Arctic settlements. Assistance should be provided in a manner which permits local communities to maintain control of and responsibility for the care of their handicapped members. The proposed programme would utilize existing facilities and personnel, as well as methods familiar and acceptable to the Inuit. It would aim at clients being maintained in or returned to their home environments. Support systems would be coordinated and provided by personnel within the community, with itinerant workers acting in an advisory capacity for families, local helping personnel, and community groups.

PERSONNEL

1. *Existing Personnel*—It is recommended that the settlement social worker and nurse be involved in planning and supervising local programmes. Appropriate local committees should also be involved.

2. *Additional Personnel*—It is recommended that two workers trained in the development of programmes for mentally retarded children and adults be engaged. One would be an itinerant worker who would assist the settlements in setting up programmes. The other worker would be responsible for group home and community programmes in Frobisher Bay.

3. *Inuit Personnel*—It is recommended that Inuit people be used as much as possible in planning and carrying out programmes in the Arctic. Inuit social workers and local Inuit committees should be involved in the planning and carrying out of the programmes for handicapped individuals within their communities. Work programmes should involve Inuit as teachers and supervisors. Group home staff should be Inuit.

4. *Training Programme*—It is recommended that an apprentice training programme be set up in conjunction with the service programme for those Inuit employees who are interested in working with mentally retarded people.

Living Arrangements

1. It is recommended that, whenever possible, retarded individuals live in either their own homes or foster homes. Assistance within the home and parental respite programmes should be provided as necessary to keep the system working efficiently. Funds should be made available to the community so that this assistance can be administered locally.

2. *Group home*—It is recommended that a group home be established in Frobisher Bay. This home would serve as a residence for interim care, as a centre for the provision of short intensive training programmes and possibly as a permanent home for a few individuals.

DEVELOPMENTAL PROGRAMMES

It is recommended that programmes be initiated to help each individual to develop as far as possible in self care, socialization and work skills.

1. *Infant Stimulation Programme*—An infant stimulation programme should be started, so that care may be given to a child as soon as it is suspected that the child is retarded. The activities involved would aim to develop auditory and visual perception, motor development and pre-language skills. The programme

would be carried out by the family with the assistance and support of the community social worker and nurse. Another source of support would be the itinerant worker who would assist in planning individual programmes for each infant and would make suggestions as to how they could be implemented. Regular visits would be made so that parents and other people locally involved would be assured of regular ongoing support.

2. *Child Development Programme*—Similar home-based programmes should be implemented for young children. If there are two or more mentally retarded children in the community, meeting as a group for programmes would be beneficial. Parents and other interested people could take turns in working with the children with the support of the community social worker and itinerant worker. Such a programme would provide the children with regular contacts outside of their families, would tend to increase community involvement and would provide short periods of parent respite. Activities would be designed to improve gross and fine motor skills, language, and thinking strategies. Self help and social skills would also be emphasized.

3. *Skill Development Programme*—From time to time, it may be necessary for the child and one or both parents to be involved in an intensive programme for learning a certain skill, or a programme to help parents to learn how to teach their child. Such instruction could be carried out at the group home in Frobisher Bay, with each programme probably including several children and their parents.

4. *School Programme*—There are a number of children who would benefit from a modified school programme. Generally, the numbers would not justify special classes in each school. The child should be allowed to move with his age mates while working at his own level. With only one or two mentally retarded children in a school, the regular programme should not be adversely affected. The itinerant worker would also act as a resource person for the school.

5. *Work Programmes*—A number of teenage and adult mentally retarded Inuit are capable of learning simple tasks with supervision. There are a number of possible sources of work within the community in which they could be involved. These are:

   (i) Domestic work—Attempts should be made to place a mentally retarded person with people who clean public buildings, hotels, transient centres, laundries, etc.

   (ii) Greenhouse—A large greenhouse, to supply fresh vegetables for the Baffin Settlements, would not only be a useful undertaking for the community, but could employ some mentally retarded people for weeding, watering and harvesting.

   (iii) Garbage collection—A mentally retarded person could assist in regular garbage and honey bag collection. In addition, with supervision they could collect the trash littering each community.

(iv) Other work—Some higher functioning individuals could be trained as kitchen assistants or construction assistants.

CONCLUSION

Since the mentally retarded population is small, these programmes should not be difficult or expensive to implement. Once the system has been organized it can easily accommodate additional people. Although this study was initiated by the Department of Social Service, the cooperation of all Departments in the Baffin Region is essential to the success of the programme.

The adoption and implementation of these proposals is strongly urged. As Native Canadians, the Inuit have the right to expect that necessary care will be provided to the handicapped within their community. Action is imperative now while handicapped Inuit are still regarded as being the responsibility of the total community.

II. A CROSS-CULTURAL STUDY OF COGNITIVE DEVELOPMENT AND CHILD-REARING PRACTICES

editor: Robert Wilson

6

A Cross-cultural Study of Child-Rearing Practices: Trends, Issues and Problems

HARRY C. TRIANDIS

Abstract

Present-day cross-cultural investigation of child-rearing patterns suggests a trend away from applying to non-western population groups the ready-made theories conceived in Western cultures, such as the concept of intelligence. For a long time these concepts have been used under the assumption that they were universal. More recently, an increasing attempt to take culture-specific variables into account has been observed. In particular, great emphasis has been placed on the effects of cultural complexity, population density, and abundance versus scarcity of resources.

L'auteur examine les tendances, les questions et les problèmes liés à l'étude comparative des méthodes d'éducation des enfants adoptées dans les diverses sociétés. Son analyse semble indiquer qu'on est de plus plus porté à éviter d'appliquer des théories toutes faites et de conception occidentale, comme la notion d'intelligence, à des groupes de populations non-occidentales. Le recours à ces concepts était basé sur le postulat de leur universalité. Plus récemment, on a assisté à la manifestation d'un effort croissant pour tenir compte des variables propres à une culture. L'auteur traite, entre autres, de l'influence de la complexité culturelle, de la densité de la population et de l'abondance et de la pénurie relatives des ressources.

CHANGES IN THEORETICAL PERSPECTIVES

A major change in research in cross-cultural psychology has occurred during the last fifteen years. Rather than taking theories conceived in the West and attempting to find support for them in non-Western populations, there has been an increasing attempt to take into account culture-specific variables.

For example, measures of intelligence, a dimension defined in the West, have been widely used to assess intellectual abilities in different parts of the world. The assumption was that the meaning of the dimension is universally the same. Recent thinking, however, shows this view to be oversimplified and frequently wrong. Intelligence is defined differently in various cultures. For example, in

Africa it is not important to be *quick*, but it is important to be *right*, in order to be characterized as intelligent. Thus, when answering a Western intelligence test an African child is *not* likely to appreciate the importance of speed.

Any theoretical construct may be analyzed into *etic* (universal) and *emic* (culture-specific) variables. To the extent that we find similar relationships in different cultures, we can be confident that we are using etic variables. When analyzing role perceptions in two cultures, Triandis, Vassiliou and Nassiakou (1968) extracted, through factor analysis, both etic and emic factors. One can compare the two cultures on the etic factors, but there is additional information in the emic factors on which the cultures cannot be compared. Thus, in every case we can distinguish both universal factors and relationships, as well as culture-specific factors.

Culture-specific factors may be broken down into specific experiences, e.g., as cultural complexity, the definition of sex-role relationships in different cultures, the amount of schooling received by the individual and the exposure of the individual to rural or urban environments. At some point along this continuum are variables which are completely culture-specific, such as the concept of *philotimo* in Greece, or *amae* in Japan. This perspective concerning a continuum of etic through emic variables is emerging as a more and more powerful trend in the cross-cultural study of children.

There is no doubt that some theories developed in the West, such as Piaget's, may indeed have some aspects that are universally valid. Yet, their cross-cultural validity is probably greater for the very young child than for the older child and greater in certain domains than in others. Although the Piaget method of inquiry appears to be useful in every culture, the particular questions asked and the tasks used in testing should be made culture-specific. By thus ''starting from scratch'' in every individual culture studied, we may lay down a truly sound approach to cross-cultural research. The time has come to abandon the ethnocentric bias of Western psychologists, which has often led them to assume that people around the world are more or less the same, and that the researcher can therefore take any procedure developed in the West and use it everywhere.

Another trend in recent theorizing is toward greater recognition of the importance of ecological psychology. Barker and Wright's researches shows that different behaviour settings elicit different behaviours. This kind of theorizing has finally been taken seriously. Ecology is now linked with child-rearing practices and these are linked in turn with various levels of probability of different adult social behaviours. Related to this are theoretical attempts to link characteristics of the culture, such as cultural complexity, to characteristics of the individuals in the cultural setting, such as cognitive complexity. Although it is likely that *cultural* complexity be reflected in *cognitive* complexity, this remains an important unexplored area.

Still another trend is the increased emphasis on ethology and on biological determinants of behaviour. This trend is likely to emerge in new theorizing about child development in the near future.

But perhaps the most significant trend is the increased complexity in our thinking about psychological theory. Thirty years ago we thought of internal processes—libido, attitudes, values—as *the* important determinants of behaviour. Now we have a more complex interactionist viewpoint. Some variance in behaviour is attributed to the personality of the individual, an even greater amount to the ambient situation, and the greatest part to the interaction of personality and environment.

ISSUES AND PROBLEMS

The major issues concern *what* to study and *how* to study it. The major problems are concerned with determining which dimensions of ecology and culture, of history and language, influence child-rearing practices, and the probable consequences of various kinds of child-rearing practices.

Within this framework I see some major concerns. First, with respect to the antecedents of child-rearing, I see some dimensions emerging as more important than others. One such dimension is *cultural complexity*, which we have already discussed.

Cultural complexity is an important dimension in the analyses made by Sutton-Smith and Roberts (1980). They analyze games into those based on chance, those that require physical skill, and those that require strategy, such as chess. Some extremely simple societies have no games. Complex agricultural societies have all three kinds of games; but simple hunting, fishing and gathering societies tend to have only games of chance. Other relatively simple societies have only games of physical skill. In societies with authoritarian social structures there is a preference for arbitrary power games. The evident relationship between the complexity of a culture and the complexity of the games played in that culture is important. It suggests that the games of a society are microcosms representing that society. Since many attitudes and values that children assimilate from their culture are rehearsed in game situations, these findings suggest that the more complex attitudes and values develop in the more complex cultures.

A special aspect of complexity is family complexity. The simpler family structures are nuclear, while the extended family is more complex, requiring the person to take into account many interpersonal relationships.

A second major dimension may be described as *abundance* versus *scarcity* of resources per person. When resources are abundant, children tend to be raised in a warm social environment; when resources are scarce, they tend to be raised in a cold impersonal environment. The presence of many adult socializers means that there are more resources in the form of services and love for the child.

I am thinking of "resources" as economists do, that is, materials, qualities, skills or attitudes that are both usable in human development and scarce. The marginal value per unit of a resource is greatest when there is little of that resource available. As the resource becomes more and more abundantly available, its marginal value drops. So, if a child is constantly hugged and kissed, one more kiss means little, and under some circumstances it may even be aversive. These observations lead me to the hypothesis that a 3 by 3 table, such as Table 1, will reflect three rather different child-rearing patterns.

TABLE 1:

Hypothesized Relationship of Societal Complexity and Abundance of Resources, as Determinants of Child-Rearing Patterns

RESOURCES PER PERSON	CULTURAL COMPLEXITY		
	Low	*Intermediate*	*High*
Abundant	Warm Autonomous A	Somewhat Cold Controlling B	Warm Autonomous A
Intermediate	Cold Controlling B	Cold Very Controlling C	Cold Controlling B
Extremely Scarce	Abandonment D	Abandonment D	Abandonment D

Child-rearing pattern "A, warm-autonomous," has been described as "democratic" by some psychologists. It is a pattern found in societies with abundant resources and little complexity, where the tasks are simple and individual, such as hunting, fishing, or gathering fruit, undertaken singly or in small groups. Where resources are intermediate in abundance, as among the lower classes in industrial societies, parents tend to socialize their children severely, and harshly. Rejection of children is not uncommon. Emphasis on obedience, cleanliness, order, and conformity is high. This pattern has been described as "authoritarian" by some psychologists and is pattern B in Table 1. Pattern D is found in situations where resources are extremely scarce, such as conditions of extreme food deprivation, when children are abandoned, as happens in industrial societies in numerous cases of child-abuse, abandonment, and neglect. The mother who is too busy (lack of a time resource), who has to work in order to support her children, who even after work is too exhausted to hug and kiss, is likely to be cold and likely to let her children do as they please. This child-rearing pattern was called "laissez-faire" by some psychologists.

Ecologies with high population density, as pointed out by Berry (1979) require people to be sensitive to the needs of their neighbors. Parents then are likely to require their children to conform. Thus, we are likely to see more controlling child-rearing patterns in populations with high density. Such populations typically have relatively scarce resources per person. The combination of coldness due to limited resources, and control due to high density, leads to an extremely controlling and very cold pattern such as pattern C.

Following this brief review of some of the antecedents of child-rearing, let us consider probable consequences.

Warm child-rearing patterns tend to result in decreasing dependence, high self-evaluation, emotional responsiveness, a positive world view, emotional stability, low anxiety, generosity and nurturance. Cold parental relationships tend to result in personalities characterized by hostility, particularly towards peers, dependence, low self-evaluation, low emotional responsiveness, a negative world view, emotional instability, high anxiety, and little generosity and nurturance. Societies that withhold physical expressions of affection from children tend to have violent adults.

In other words, warm parents have warm children; cold parents have cold, anxious and unpredictable children. Warm parents are also more likely to have children high in cognitive complexity.

In my attempt to extract dimensions of social behaviour that will be important in every culture, I suggest that four dimensions are universal: association vs. dissociation, superordination vs. subordination, intimacy vs. formality and overt vs. covert. Any social behaviour can be conceived as a point in a multidimensional space, with a minimum of four dimensions. These four etic dimensions may be supplemented with several emic dimensions in each culture. Thus, the meaning of a behaviour may be represented by a point in 4-dimensional space. Although it is not sure that the four dimensions just mentioned are universal, the evidence to date seems consistent with this viewpoint. As the present discussion suggests, the first two dimensions can be found in the child-rearing patterns and also in the children's behaviours: warm corresponds to associative, cold to dissociative, conformity corresponds to subordination. Future investigations will study the behavioural correlates of intimacy and covert behaviour.

CONCLUSION

The major concern in the cross-cultural study of child-rearing are (1) what aspects or dimensions of culture influence child-rearing and (2) what are the effects of different child-rearing patterns. I suggested that cultural complexity, family structure, and the availability of resources may influence child-rearing patterns. The table I have presented here is offered as a basis for formulating hypotheses about the relationship between cultural complexity and the availability of resources on the one hand and child-rearing patterns on the other hand. The various child-rearing patterns so identified where hypothesized to result in particular behaviour patterns in adults socialized with these patterns.

We can study these problems by using the Human Relations Area Files. However, current trends in the methodology of cross-cultural research have shown increased emphasis on multimethod measurement and on the study of both etic and emic variables. Furthermore, what is being studied is influenced by what societies consider important; hence, because of the considerable interest in North America on human relations, justice equity, and related matters, the emphasis is more in the direction of studying specific problems of interest to that society than on studying the really important problem of what kind of culture is likely to have what kind of child-rearing patterns, and what are the probable consequences of each child-rearing pattern.

References

Berry, J.W., A cultural ecology of social behaviour. In L. Berkowitz (Ed.), *Advances in Experimental Social Psychology*. New York: Academic Press, 1979.

Sutton, Smith, B. and Roberts, J.M., "Play, Games and Sports," In H.C. Triandis and A. Heron (Eds.) *Handbook of cross cultural psychology: Developmental psychology*, Boston Mass;: Allyn and Bacon, 1980.

Triandis, H.C., Vassiliou, V. and Nassiakou, M., Three cross-cultural studies of subjective culture. *Journal of Personality and Social Psychology, Monographs, Suppl.*, 1968, *8*, No. 4, 1-42.

7

Cognitive Development Across Cultures

DR. JOHN W. BERRY

Abstract

The goal of cross-cultural psychology is to produce a more nearly universal set of principles that apply to all human populations. There is general agreement among researchers that cognitive processes are universal, but that its direction, level and organization may widely differ. The problems raised by these can be approached in four ways, namely, those of abilities, styles, stages and intelligence. These approaches permit comparative cross-cultural studies as well as studies of multicultural groups within cultures.

Researchers must adopt the position of the "cultural relativist" (understanding people from the people's own perspective) and avoid the imposition of their own standards. Cultural uniqueness and the integrity of the group should be granted even to ethnic groups within multicultural societies.

L'objectif de la psychologie comparée des milieux culturels est d'élaborer un ensemble de principes les plus universels possibles qui s'appliqueraient à toutes les populations humaines. Les chercheurs s'accordent généralement pour reconnaître que les processus cognitifs sont universels. L'auteur choisit quatre concepts dans le domaine du développement cognitif pour les étudier tant dans des cultures variées que dans des groupes pluriculturels au sein de milieux culturels.

L'auteur conseille aux chercheurs d'adopter la position de "relativiste culturel" (comprendre les gens à partir de leur propre point de vue) et d'éviter d'imposer à d'autres leurs propres normes. Il faut reconnaître, même aux groupes ethniques vivant au sein de sociétés pluriculturelles, l'intégrité et le caractère unique de la culture propre à un groupe.

In this review, *cognition* is conceived broadly to include many aspects, such as perception, thinking and remembering. All these areas of psychological life involve the basic problems of an organism interacting with, and adapting to, its environmental setting. However, they vary in their manner of direct contact with this environmental setting: perception involves the immediate apprehension, selection and coding of the environment; thinking involves manipulation of the perceived features of the environment; and remembering involves the storing and later retrieval of these features.

The goal of cross-cultural psychology is to produce a more nearly *universal* set of principles, which apply to all human populations. More specifically, the goals of a cross-cultural psychology of cognition are:

1. To transport our present hypotheses and laws to other settings to test their applicability or generalizability;
2. To explore new cultural systems to discover cognitive variations and differences we have not experienced within our own cultural context;
3. To compare our prior understanding with our newer knowledge within diverse cultures to generate more universal descriptions, hypotheses and laws of human cognitive functioning. (Berry and Dasen, 1974, p. 14.)

The goals of the cross-cultural study of cognitive development are (1) to describe and account for the changes which take place with age in cognitive behaviours in *all* human populations, and (2) to attempt to integrate them into universal principles of cognitive development.

There is general agreement among researchers in comparative cognition that cognitive *processes* are universal: that is, the way in which perception, thinking and remembering get done is common to all human organisms, regardless of the culture into which they are born.

From this common starting point, three other problems arise—problems of direction, level and organization. First the question of *direction* may be posed: Does the process of cognitive development take all people along the same road? Do all cultures nurture the same cognitive goals, harbour the same cognitive values? In more concrete terms, do adults in all cultures become quick, or do adults in some cultures become thoughtful? Do adults always become more analytic or more abstract, do some develop intuition, or do they develop practical, concrete cognitive behaviours? In short, although we all start with the same basic processes, do we all employ these processes to move us along the same developmental pathway?

A second problem is that of *level* or extent of development: Do some cultures push cognitive development further than do others? Do adults in some cultures become more competent, more generally able? Are some peoples more clever, others less so, on some universal scale? Of course, this question must be approached in relation to the previous one (that of *direction*), for if people are developing toward different goals, it may be impossible to assess how far they have progressed, at least by using any common yardstick.

Finally, the problem of *organization* must be considered. How are cognitive behaviours interrelated? Are they interrelated universally for all cultures? Or are they unrelated, or related in varying ways to each other? Put in other terms, is it possible to characterize cognitive development by a common single score, based upon a universal pattern of relationships, or are different kinds of scores needed (to take into account culturally variable relationships)?

APPROACHES TO THE CROSS-CULTURAL STUDY OF COGNITIVE DEVELOPMENT

One can incorporate treatments of all these problems into four distinct approaches to the comparative study of cognitive development: these are the approaches of abilities, styles, stages and intelligence.

Abilities

The *ability* or skills approach assumes universal *processes*, argues for variable *direction* in development, varies in the treatment of *level* of development, and does not usually consider whether or how single abilities are related to each other.

The ability approach is the most culturally relative, asking what abilities are important to do well in a particular culture (*direction*), examining how the culture nurtures that form of cognitive development to a satisfactory *level*, and tending to down-play the possibility of common patterns or interrelationships among the developed abilities.

Styles

The approach defined by cognitive *styles* generally follows the *ability* approach, but is additionally interested in the question of the structure or *organization* of abilities within each culture, and in the possibility that there may be some universality to these structures. Most workers adopt a culturally relative position, arguing that both *direction* and *level* of cognitive development will vary according to the cultural context. However, whether the *organization* will also be dependent upon cultural context, or whether it will be culturally invariant, is an unresolved issue.

Stages

The work of Piaget has established that cognitive development may best be conceptualized as a series of *stages*, each one superseding the earlier one. Once again, universal processes are assumed. A common course (*direction*) and rate (*levels* at particular times) are predicted, while abilities are thought to be *organized* within stages or *structures d'ensemble*.

The approach to the comparative study of cognitive development by way of stages has demonstrated some universality, but cultural factors do alter the *level* (that is, advance or delay the rate of development), affect the *organization* within a stage (but apparently does not alter the sequence of stages), and may affect *direction*, (at least at the level of formal operations). Continuing work will probably not alter this generalization, although it will almost certainly make more precise the specific effects to be expected from varying cultural influences.

Intelligence

The approach by way of the concept of intelligence is perhaps the most familiar one of all. It assumes universal *process, direction* and *organization*; however, cultural factors are considered to affect *level*. As such, it is the least culturally relative (that is, the most ethnocentric) of the four approaches.

Standard tests (assumed to measure constituent abilities) are applied to different cultural groups; the assumption is that the abilities are structured in a common way to exhibit "general ability" or intelligence. Variations in *levels* of intelligence are attributed to variations in culture (some smart, some not), rather than to peoples' pursuing differing goals (*direction*) or possessing differing cognitive structures (*organization*).

I have previously advocated a position of radical cultural relativism when employing the concept of intelligence cross-culturally, and I continue to reject that concept as a scientifically valid approach to the comparative study of cognition. Virtually all contemporary results of studies using intelligence tests across cultural groups can be explained most effectively by assuming ethnocentrism on the part of the researcher; if you think that there is only one race to be run (yours), people headed in a different direction will necessarily appear to be slow or even lost! However, if you realize that there are many races being run, by many people with different goals, then the pattern of results becomes understandable.

APPLICATION ACROSS CULTURES

The import of this observation is that psychologists and others, when working cross-culturally, must accept the position of cultural relativism; they must adopt a pluralistic point of view. That is, we must learn to understand people from their own perspectives (the so called *emic* approach) and avoid the imposition of the standards of the investigator's culture, (the *etic* approach).

In theory, this requirement is not difficult to accept, especially for educated people who may pride themselves on their lack of ethnocentrism and prejudice. But in practice such a requirement has proved to be exceedingly difficult. Although engaged in international research, we often see Western education, social services, industrialization, telecommunications, Christianity and the democratic process as universal values; however, we often fail to see that all these may be impositions on existing cultural systems which have been doing well without us.

APPLICATIONS IN MULTICULTURAL SOCIETIES

Most psychologists, physicians and social services workers do not engage in cross-cultural research or practice; however, the cultural dimension affects our work in meeting the needs of various ethnic groups within our multicultural societies.

Although the argument is a complicated one, I wish to assert that we should approach our work in multicultural societies from a position fully informed by the cross-cultural tradition, rather than from a position of uniculturalism. By this I mean that the existence of cultural variation in our societies should be approached as a microcosm of world-wide cultural variation, rather than simply as minor and troublesome variants to the so-called "mainstream."

This means that the cultural uniqueness and integrity of each group should be granted, and that the possibility of differing *direction* and *organization* of cognitive development be taken seriously. To be of any assistance, social institutions (and their professional workers) should accept individuals as they are now, and help them to get where they want to go. To do less is to impose an ethnocentric view, and to contribute further to the reduction of our greatest of human resources—that of cultural diversity.

References

Berry, J.W. and Dasen, P. (Eds.) *Culture and Cognition*. London: Methuen, 1974.

8

A Multinational Perspective on Child-Rearing Values

WALLACE E. LAMBERT

Abstract

An extensive study was completed in 1979 of parental attitudes to child-rearing practices in nine countries, in middle and working class families. The study allows us to see, among other things, how English and French Canadian parents deal with such issues as requests for help, displays of insolence, punishment, sex role differences, etc., in contrast to other national groups.

It appears that French Canadian, English Canadian and American parents form a North American set in their approach to child-rearing when compared to European samples from England, France, Belgium, Italy, Greece, and Portugal.

Of equal interest are child-rearing patterns among immigrant groups from these countries in North America, since the relocation of the families provides the opportunity to observe these values under cultural stress.

It appears that children are a major agent of change and that the values of immigrant parents move in the direction of the host nation norms.

In attempting to construct the global view offered here I shall draw upon a long, extensive and cross-national study of parents and their attitudes towards child-rearing made jointly by my colleagues and myself (Lambert, Hamers and Frasure Smith, 1979). Although the perspective is cross-national, in order to sharpen our perception I have decided to focus on Canada, which seems particularly appropriate because of the setting for this conference, and draw illustrations from English-speaking and French-speaking parents and their approaches to child-rearing. This study offers us a wide choice of national and cultural areas, for we could just as well focus on England, France, Belgium, Italy, Greece, Portugal, the United States, or Japan, since we conducted the study in each of these nations simultaneously. Near the end, I shall take the opportunity to broaden the perspective with illustrations from a series of national settings.

This was a complex, difficult to manage study. Parents of six-year-old children were interviewed in their homes. The interview procedure was novel in that each parent was asked to listen in private and then react spontaneously to tape-recordings representing episodes involving a child, one much like their own, in various types of everyday interactions with a parent, with a younger sibling, or with a playmate. What the child said and did in each episode was meant to evoke particular types of reactions from parents which could range from acquiesence, through ''laissez-faire'', to outright anger.[1] The parent's task then was to imagine himself or herself as the parental partner in these episodes, either in direct contact with the child or as an observer, and to give his or her first reactions.[2] This procedure, first tried out by Rothbart and Maccoby in California (1966), was used in a pilot study (Lambert, Yackley and Hein, 1971) where its effectiveness, reliability and interest value were tested. From previous research, then, we knew that parents get caught up with the taped episodes as though they are actually in interaction with their own children, only occasionally dropping out of the parental role to say ''Oh, no. My child would not go that far with me!'' or something similar. In fact, we feel that the procedure may be as evocative and natural, or more so than actual observations of family interactions. The pilot study also demonstrated that the results of an investigation of this sort are easily scored and analyzed, reliable, rich in terms of subgroup differences, and extremely suggestive, both theoretically and practically.

The results of our investigation permit us to say a good deal about how the process of socialization runs its course in each of the national settings. But at best we can only make tentative statements about this important and fascinating matter since our study deals with values and attitudes towards child-rearing, not with the actual observation of parent-child interactions. Furthermore, our study includes samples of parents only from large cities in each of the nations. We cannot, therefore, generalize about any nation as a whole. For instance, our English and French-speaking Canadian samples were collected in Montreal; this, obviously, does not allow generalizations about Canada as a whole.

As we shall see, what emerges from the results is that there are various types of parental values and attitudes toward child-rearing in vogue in each of the nations studied, and in general the single most important influence on parental reactions turns out to be the social class background of parents, not their ethnicity. In Canada, for instance, the effects of social class, in fact, are apparent in all but three of the ten value dimensions included in the study, and it also plays a role in various interactions. Although these social class comparisons in general hold as well for English as for French Canadian parents, this is not to say that the importance of social class is necessarily a distinctly Canadian phenomenon, for when comparisons are made with other national settings, it becomes clear that social class plays as important a role in all of the nations included in our study. What is instructive and interesting though is that Canada, one of the New World nations where social class distinctions are often said to be of little real significance, is characterized by pervasive and important differences in parent-child interactions which can be traced to social class background. One begins to wonder whether a powerful myth about a classless society has worked its way into our own belief systems. The truth is that the social class background of parents makes a good deal of difference in child-training value systems in Canada.

Three other factors play relatively less important roles: the English Canadian—French Canadian ethnicity of parents, the sex of the child, and the sex of the parent. Even so, each has its own distinctive and illuminating influence. We will consider first the role played by ethnicity, since that was the basic question that got the research started in the first place, and it is the question most parents, educators and social philosphers might ask first. Put simply, the question is this: How different or how similar are English and French Canadian parents in their approaches to child-rearing?

Ethnicity. Being French or English Canadian has a direct effect on how parents deal with children's requests for *help*, children's displays of *insolence*, and children's requests to have *guests* in to play. In each instance it is the English Canadian (EC) relative to French Canadian (FC) parents who hold back, in the sense that they are less spontaneous and less immediate in giving help, more controlling and harsh on insolence, and more restrictive in extending guest privileges. These contrasts make good social-psychological sense. For instance, EC parents may be more hesitant to extend help because they are anxious to have their children learn to help themselves, to be independent. Such an interpretation is consonant with the data available on independence training which, according to McClelland (1961), is emphasized more in the EC than FC communities, and, according to Rosen (1959), more in Anglo-American than Franco-American communities in the U.S.A.

Similarly, one might develop a convincing argument for the emphasis EC parents place on insolence. EC parents may well feel particularly vulnerable to what seems to be a tendency in the United States for children to break away from adult control and adult direction (see Bronfenbrenner, 1970).

That the FC parents have more of an open-door attitude toward guest privileges for playmates is a surprising and interesting phenomenon. One possible interpretation is that the French Canadian community, like most ethnic minority communities, may be more inclined to consider other members of the same minority group, including their own children's playmates, as extended family members. To have survived as an ethnic group, they perhaps have had to rely on one another to a great extent and to consider one another as co-habitants of a cultural island. It is also likely that, because of their need for strong ingroup ties, they may have learned to make sharp distinctions between members of the ingroup and members of the various outgroups that "surround" them. In contrast, EC parents may try to foster self-sufficiency by discouraging a dependence on playmates as agents of entertainment. Regardless of the interpretations, the major outcomes portray EC parents as less supportive and helpful when help is asked for, less permissive of insolence, and less open to guests than FC parents.

There are other more subtle comparisons that emerge through the various interactions. For instance, we found that EC mothers take a distinctively lenient and tolerant stance when a squabble breaks out between a child and a younger sibling, and when the child asks for comfort. The EC mothers thereby are at odds with their husbands, suggesting that there are more pronounced normative differences between the mother and father roles in the EC than the FC families. One wonders if there is some more superficial explanation for this tendency; for example, whether EC mothers may have some special source of influence (such as day time media inputs in the English language) that contributes to their distinctive degree of tolerance in these cases, or whether there is a deeper significance to the ways in which EC mothers fulfill the maternal role.

Of special interest is the flexibility and independence that characterizes the mother role in the EC families studied. EC mothers are as demanding and harsh as their husbands on matters of help withholding, insolence control and restrictiveness with regard to guest privileges, at the same time as they are tolerant and lenient in cases of squabbles between siblings, and comfort seeking. In one sense then, it is the EC mother who plays the more active or flexible role in socializing the child, since she, along with the EC father, plays the role of demanding parent in particular domains of interaction and, quite independent of the EC father, the softer, more comforting role in other domains.

The ramifications of this pattern could affect the EC child's interpersonal behaviour both within and beyond the family setting. For example, one could trace out an interesting link between the attitudes of EC mothers and fathers and the development of achievement motivation in EC children, following the research and theory of McClelland (1961); Rosen (1961); Rosen and D'Andrade (1959); Lambert, Yackley and Hein (1971); and De Koninck and Sirois-Berliss (1978).

There are also potentially important ethnic contrasts in how parents think about sex-role differences in the behaviour of boys and girls. As a group, FC middle class mothers are particularly attentive to boy-girl differences in styles of conduct, which suggests that these FC mothers may be especially concerned about recent social movements that tend to de-emphasize traditional models of comportment for boys and girls.

There is a parallel comparison at the social class level: working class parents of boys have much stronger expectations of sex-role differences than do middle class parents of boys. This contrast suggests to us that, in the eyes of working class Canadian parents, boys must be "boys" to succeed in life, whereas middle class parents are much more liberal on the issue, as though for them, the male's success in the middle class world calls for something more than "masculine" traits. At the same time we find that parents of girls from working class backgrounds are relatively less concerned about their daughters being similar to boys, suggesting that from their perspective girls would find it an advantage too to be able to cope with the harsher side of life. Middle class parents, in contrast, seem to want their daughters to be different from boys, as though for them femininity is relatively more important and valuable.

Social Class Background. The influence of social class background touches parents' relations with children on all the dimensions we examined except *help withholding, attention denial* and *comfort withholding*. On all other dimensions, it is the working class parents (both FC and EC) who are the harsher or more demanding in the socialization of children. In other words, relative to middle class parents, they are more inclined to side with the baby and against the child when a dispute breaks out; they control displays of temper, social temper, and insolence more severely; they restrict the child more on guest privileges, side more against the child when he argues with a playmate, control more his bids for autonomy, at the same time as they both expect and perceive greater degrees of sex-role differentiations in the comportment of boys and girls.   .

There are then only three dimensions that are not affected by social class, one concerned with a child's requests for parental aid, another with requests for comfort, and the third with a child's request for the attention or psychological presence of the parent. When a child asks for help, both working and middle class parents comply, whereas when a child asks for attention or comfort, both working and middle class parents deny the child. Thus, on matters where parents have to cope with requests for help or nurturance, social class background does not influence parents' reactions. It is, instead, specifically on matters calling for discipline and on bids for autonomy that working and middle class parents differ. The fact is that in these cases they differ to a substantial extent, indicating to us that we are dealing here with a major characteristic of Canadian child-rearing values, namely, that the social class background of parents overrides in importance ethnicity, sex of child or sex of parent.

The outstanding finding then is that Canadian parents of working class backgrounds are decidedly more demanding and more punitive than middle class parents in their child-rearing values. Their relative harshness is limited to provocations by the child that call for discipline and to signs of the child's early moves toward independence or autonomy. With the data available, we can only speculate about the reasons for these parental differences in outlook. It could well be that working class parents train their children with more severity and exigence, as a means of preparing them for the world these parents know well, a world where, because of one's lower status in society, one must be prepared to suffer, to be humiliated, and, especially, to be prepared to do what one is told. It is a world, too, where there is little room for free choice about matters of sex-role comportment. Young boys have to be trained to become men just as young girls must learn to take on the roles of women, although girls should learn to be able to take the bumps of life. Very early or precocious moves toward independence on the part of the child might well worry working class parents who could lose their child to outside influences before the childhood training has been completed. The training is not all harsh, however, for when aid and nurturance is called for, these discipline-oriented working class parents are as ready to help and comfort as anyone else.

The contrasts suggest that *middle* class parents use another world of experience as a reference point. They want their children to face experiences and to learn how to think for themselves, to become able to take care of themselves, and to learn to be prepared to tell others what to do rather than follow directives themselves. Early attempts at autonomy would be encouraged, and any standardized views of what constitutes manly and womanly comportment would be questioned. This contrast fits rather nicely with the developmental stages of achievement motivation found by McClelland (1961) and Rosen (1961). Strength of achievement motivation, these researchers have found, is clearly associated with social class and the middle class experience not only generates relatively more achievement motivation, but also seems to provide an earlier foundation for autonomy, for flexibility and for self-reliance.

The contrast between the middle and the working classes also takes on another type of significance if one thinks of the effects exerted on personality development of relatively harsh versus relatively lenient parental attitudes towards the socialization process. But we must be clear here about what we mean by the terms "harsh," "demanding," "soft," or "psychological," since we have been using these terms freely here to contrast the approaches of middle versus working class Canadian parents. As we see it, a strong case can be made from the Canadian findings that it is the working class parents who are *both* the more "strict" and the more "punitive", as Stanley Guterman (1970) defines these terms. It is the working class Canadian parents who, relative to the middle class, set more definite limits on what the child can or cannot do, and who put more pressure of a characteristically more punitive nature on obedience to rules and standards. These more clearly defined limits cover aggression or temper directed towards siblings, towards peers and towards parents. It is likely, then, that Canadian working class children face "disciplinary procedures" that are "more consistent and predictable" in Guterman's terms. To this extent the *stricter* socialization of the working class Canadian child may contribute to the development of a relatively strong conscience, in contrast to the development of a relatively weak conscience in the case of middle class children. If this conclusion seems odd to those who would be challenged to defend the middle class strategies, perhaps they can argue that this potential advantage of working class upbringing is offset by the more authoritarian and demanding models working class parents provide their children. Or it might be said that the advantage of parental firmness and strictness is offset by the greater degree of working class parental punitiveness. This last argument goes well with what we have seen throughout our study: Canadian working class parents are more inclined to use threat-of-punishment or punishment techniques, while middle class parents are more inclined to use "psychological'' and ''reasoning'' approaches to discipline, making them more lenient and ''soft'' or, in other words, less punitive. Of course, this non-punitive approach could be easily confused with a ''studied neglect'' of children, as Bronfenbrenner (1970) might argue.[3]

Parents of Boys versus Parents of Girls. There are three instances in the Canadian study where parents of girls differ in their reactions from parents of boys: in controlling *social temper* outbursts, denying the child *attention*, and *siding against* the child who quarrels with a playmate. In each instance, it is the parents of girls who are the harsher socializers, and there are no counterbalancing instances where parents of boys are the harsher. These three forms of conduct, then, are particularly annoying to Canadian parents when they originate from girls. When we take into consideration the fact that the taped episodes used in the study were precisely the same in the boy and girl versions, these differences in parental reactions to sons and daughters become doubly interesting. Thus, to the extent that Canadian girls are overdisciplined for social temper displays, for arguing with a playmate, and are more thwarted on requests for attention, one can by the same token argue that Canadian boys are relatively underdisciplined and underthwarted.

Apparently, we are dealing here with a broadly shared point of view in Canada, since no ethnic differences emerge in these cases, nor are there social class differences. Thus, Canadian parents in general appear to bring girls up so that they will not be socially aggressive or attention seekers. But while social aggressiveness and attention-seeking are negative characteristics for Canadian girls, the same characteristics are evidently considered positive ones for Canadian boys. One can look at this boy-girl contrast as society's way of developing a clear model of the differences expected in adult men and women. The more that adult sex-role models differ, the greater the basis there would be for complementariness in relationships involving men and women and the easier it might be to establish a natural division of socialization responsibilities between mothers and fathers.

There are, however, questions that this contrast brings to mind. Is it valuable or appropriate to differentiate between boys and girls in this fashion from childhood on? If social aggression is a bad trait for girls, how could it be a good trait for boys? It is this matter of training aggression *out* in one case and *in* in the other that becomes particularly interesting. If it were man's natural proclivity to be socially aggressive, then to discourage it in the case of girls would cause them biological and emotional harm. If it is not a natural tendency and if it is easy to control, why should boys be encouraged to be aggressive in this already very aggressive world? Apparently, Canadian parents feel that to survive in this aggressive world, boys must be given more opportunities than girls in order that they may learn to take care of themselves!

Mothers versus Fathers. There are two unambiguous instances in the Canadian study where being a mother rather than a father affects how one reacts to children: one involves attention seeking, the other, disputes between the child and a playmate. In the case of attention seeking, Canadian fathers are harsher in their reactions than mothers, while in the case of siding with the playmate and against the child, Canadian mothers are harsher than fathers. These contrasts suggest that in Canadian families, EC or FC, there is a division of socialization responsibilities, and apparently fathers are expected to take nagging or attention-getting ploys as their speciality, while mothers take on the task of training proper behavior in the child's relations with those outside the family. We have no explanation for why these two particular differences emerge or how the purported division of responsibilities develops. Nonetheless, it would be worthwhile exploring in further research other aspects of socialization to test this general notion—that Canadian fathers are more responsible for keeping peace within the family and Canadian mothers more responsible for smooth relationships with others in the community.

What is noteworthy in the Canadian study is the lack of evidence for "cross-sex permissiveness," that is, we have found no incidents where fathers are differentially harsh with sons and relatively supportive of daughters and where mothers favor sons and show biases against daughters. This is noteworthy because Rothbart and Maccoby (1966) in their study conducted in the U.S.A. found a large number of examples of cross-sex permissiveness. In the Canadian study not only have we found no cross-sex permissiveness, we have found examples of same-sex permissiveness instead.

The Canadian study we have just sketched out here was one of a number included in the overall investigation, and perhaps it is appropriate to conclude this report by placing these descriptions of English and French Canadian styles of children-rearing values into a broader, cross-national perspective. The overall investigation presented in Lambert, Hamers and Frasure Smith (1979) includes Canadian parents as two examples among some eleven national groups studied, and this broad background permits one to see which features, if any, hold generally, and which features of a particular group still stand out as distinctive when viewed in a broader perspective.

What actually happens is that many of those features that stood out as different and distinctive in the two- or three-nation comparisons level off or fade away on the "wider screen" of a ten-nation comparison. But what is fascinating is that not all narrow-screen contrasts fade away on the wide screen: some distinctive national characteristics hold up, and, what is just as important, some surprisingly stable cross-national trends stand out in sharper relief.

The parental groups included were: American, English Canadian, French Canadian, English, French, French Belgian, Dutch Belgian, Italian, Greek and Portuguese. In each case, information on both working and middle class subgroups of parents was available. [4] The question of interest here, then, is how distinctive English Canadian and French Canadian parents' values are in this broader context.

The French Canadian, English Canadian and American parents form a North American set. Although they differ from each other in distinctive ways in the degrees of harshness or leniency displayed in their approaches to child-rearing, they are alike in so many ways that the three groups form a sharp contrast with our European samples. For example, in contrast with European parents, they are much more prone to grant the six-year-old autonomy. Then, in each of the three North American settings, there is a sharp difference in approach to matters of discipline, depending upon the social class background of the family: middle class North American parents are much more permissive and lenient than working class parents when the child's behavior calls for discipline. In fact, North American middle class parents prefer to divert, distract or at the most scold rather than threaten or actually punish a child who misbehaves. Social class is less important on aid issues for North American families. Finally, parents in North America have relatively low sex-role expectations—they tend toward uni-sexism—and their perceptions of sex-role differences are generally in line with their expectations.

What we come to then is the intriguing conclusion that, if one takes a broad enough perspective, EC and FC parents are not all that distinctive in their approaches to child-rearing. They actually end up being pretty much North American and not nearly so "English" Canadian or "French" Canadian as those ethnic suffixes imply. In fact, our results indicate that EC and FC parents of the same social class background are more similar in their child-rearing values than either group is with parents of the same ethnic origin but of a different social class. Furthermore, it appears that EC and FC parents of a particular social class background are, in terms of these values, more like American, Greek, Portuguese, Italian or Belgian parents of the same social class background than they are like EC or FC parents of a different social class background. Thus, we come full circle here; now is the time to begin to wonder seriously how much "distinctiveness" is real and how much is a figment of the imagination of grown-ups who, in large measure, get the own group-other group contrasts started in the first place.

References

Aboud, F.E., & Taylor, D.M. Ethnic and role stereotypes: Their relative importance in person perception. *Journal of Social Psychology*, 1977, *85*, 17–21.

Bronfenbrenner, U. *Two worlds of childhood: U.S. and U.S.S.R.* New York: Russell Sage Foundation, 1970.

DeKoninch, J., & Sirois-Berliss, M. La motivation au rendement dans les rêves et durant l'éveil chez des étudiants canadiens-français et canadiens-anglais. *Canadian Journal of Behavioral Science*, 1978, 10, 329–338.

Guterman, S.S. *The Machiavellians*. Lincoln: University of Nebraska Press, 1970.

Lambert, W.E., Hamers, J.F., & Frasure Smith, N. *Child-rearing values: A Cross-national study*. New York: Praeger Publications, 1979.

Lambert, W.E., Yackley, A., & Hein, R. Child-training values of English Canadian and French Canadian parents. *Canadian Journal of Behavioural Science*, 1971, *3*, 217–236.

McClelland, D.C. *The achieving society*. New York: Van Nostrand, 1961.

Rosen, B.C. Race, ethnicity and the achievement syndrome. *American Sociological Review*, 1959, *24*, 47–60.

Rosen, B.C. Family structure and achievement motivation. *American Sociological Review*, 1961, *26*, 574–585.

Rosen, B.C., & D'Andrade, R.G. The psychosocial origins of achievement motivation. *Sociometry*, 1959, *22, 185*–218.

Rothbart, M.K. & Maccoby, E.E. Parents' differential reactions to sons and daughters. *Journal of Personality and Social Psychology*, 1966, *4*, 237–243.

Witkin, H.A. Studies in space orientation. *Journal of Experimental Psychology*, 1948, *38*, 762–782.

Witkin, H.A. Social influences in the development of cognitive style. *Handbook of socialization theory and research*, (Ed.), D.A. Goslin. New York: Rand McNally, 1969.

Witkin, H.A. Socialization and ecology in the development of cross cultural and sex differences in cognitive style. Paper presented at 21st International Congress of Psychology, Paris, 1976.

Witkin, H.A., & Berry, J.W. Psychological differentiation in cross cultural perspective. *Journal of Cross Cultural Psychology*, 1975, *6*, 4–87.

Notes

1. Two separate tapes were made for each national setting, one for mothers, one for fathers, with local language or dialect variations worked into the child's statements. The English version follows. (1) Mummy (Daddy) come look at my puzzle. (2) Mummy (Daddy), help me! (3) Does this piece go here? (4) Baby, you can't play with me, You're too little. (5) He can't play with my puzzle. It's mine! (6) Leave my puzzle alone or I'll hit you on the head! (7) I don't like this game. I'm gonna break it. (8) I don't like this game. It's a stupid game, and you're stupid, Mama (Daddy). (9) Ow-w! Baby stepped on my hand! (10) Mummy (Daddy), it hurts! (11) Mummy (Daddy), get me another puzzle. (12) It's not raining now. Can I go across the street and play? (13) Why can't I? I'm gonna go anyway. (14) Can Chris come in and play? (15) Chris, lemme put the pieces in myself. You watch me. (16) Don't touch the pieces. You don't know how to do it. (17) If you don't leave 'em alone, I'll beat you up.

   The parents' responses to each item were coded, and then items were congregated and combined to form one of the 10 separate scales or value dimensions. Since higher scores on these scales generally indicate more punitive or restrictive attitudes, the names assigned to the scales refer to the restrictive end; thus, it is a "Help Withholding" scale rather than a "Help Giving" scale. The scales are: *Help Withholding* (Items 1, 2, 3, and 11); *Comfort Withholding* (9, 10); *Temper Control* (7); *Social Temper Control* (6, 17); *Insolence Control* (8, 13); *Siding with Baby vs. Child* (4, 5, 6); *Attention Denial* (9); *Autonomy Control* (12); *Guest Restrictions* (14); *and Siding with Guest vs. Child* (15, 16, 17). For each scale, scores can range from a permissive reaction (assigned a low score), to a restrictive reaction, a moral reprimand, taking the baby's or the playmate's (rather than the child's) side in a dispute, or withholding assistance. For example, in response to the child's statement "Daddy, help me!" (item 2), a parent's reaction, "Let's see now, where would that piece go?" would be rated high in help giving, while another reaction, in the form, "Try it in different places and see how it works." would be rated more toward the help withholding limit, next to an outright refusal or a complete ignoring of the child's request for help. Again for item 8 ("I don't like this game. It's a stupid game, and you're stupid Mama!"), parental reaction could range from overlooking the insolence and trying to understand the child's frustration, to demanding an apology, to reprimanding the child, to physically punishing the child. In addition to responding to the taped episodes, parents were also asked to respond to two questionnaires, half completing them before and half after they had listened to the tape. The first questionnaire, referred to as *Perceived Differences in Sex-roles*, consisted of 40 items which probe for parents' perceptions of how similar or different boys and girls are in their typical behaviours or reactions, e.g., in assertiveness, persistence, or helpfulness. A second questionnaire, referred to as *Expected Differences in Sex-Roles*, measured parents' expectations about sex-role differences in behaviour, revealing, for example, whether they felt it is important or not for a boy or a girl to be bold and self-assertive.
2. The details of the procedure, the coding and the reliability of coding are given in Chapter 1 and the Appendices of Lambert, Hamers and Frasure Smith, 1979.
3. Our findings make contact as well with another extremely rich research domain, that of field independence—dependence, associated with Witkin (1948; 1969; 1976) and Witkin and Berry (1975). The relationship is presented in detail in Lambert, Hamers and Frasure Smith (1979), and there we see how parental child-rearing values can effect children's perceptual, cognitive and social development.
4. Data for middle class Japanese parents are also given in Lambert, Hamers and Frasure Smith (1979).

Principes d'éducation des enfants vus sous un angle multinational

L'auteur fait le compte rendu d'une étude dans laquelle on a examiné les attitudes
parentales face à l'éducation des enfants au sein des classes moyennes et ouvrières de
neuf pays différents. Il analyse plus particulièrement la façon dont les parents canadiens, d'origine anglaise et française, réagissent à certaines situations comme l'appel à
l'aide, les manifestations d'insolence, la punition, l'adoption de rôles sexuels
différents, et ainsi de suite, par comparaison avec d'autres groupes ethniques.

Il semble que les parents Canadiens-français, Canadiens-anglais et Américains
font partie d'un même ensemble nord-américain quant à leur attitude sur la façon
d'élever les enfants, si on les compare à des échantillons de parents européens provenant d'Angleterre, de France, de Belgique, d'Italie, de Grèce et du Portugal.

L'auteur étudie également les façons d'élever les enfants parmi des groupes immigrant de ces pays vers l'Amérique du Nord; cette dernière analyse permet d'observer
comment évoluent ces principes dans des conditions de stress culturel. Les enfants
font figure d'agents de changement importants alors que les principes des parents
immigrants évoluent dans la direction des normes du pays d'accueil.

La recherche à laquelle j'emprunte les données présentées ici est une longue et
vaste étude comparative de parents de nationalités diverses et de leurs attitudes
par rapport à la façon d'élever les enfants (Lambert, Hamers et Frasure Smith,
1979). Je me propose d'offrir une perspective plurinationale des parents, des
enfants et du processus d'éducation de ces derniers. Toutefois, afin de projeter
une structure bien nette, j'ai décidé de centrer mon exposé sur le Canada, ce qui
semble plutôt approprié étant donné le site de cette conférence, et de puiser mes
exemples auprès de parents anglophones et francophones et dans leurs attitudes
sur la façon d'élever les enfants. Nous avons heureusement, dans cette étude, le
loisir de faire un choix, car nous pourrions tout aussi bien porter plus particulièrement notre attention sur l'Angleterre, la France, la Belgique, l'Italie, la
Grèce, le Portugal, les Etats-Unis ou le Japon, puisque notre recherche s'est faite
dans chacun de ces pays simultanément. Vers la fin de mon exposé, je saisirai
l'occasion d'élargir cette perspective en apportant des exemples provenant d'un
nombre plus varié de milieux nationaux.

L'étude était complexe et difficile à contrôler. Il s'agissait de rencontrer dans
leur foyer et d'interviewer les pères et les mères d'enfants de six ans. La façon de

conduire l'interview était innovatrice dans ce sens que l'on demandait à chaque parent d'écouter, isolément, sur ruban magnétique des épisodes de la vie d'un enfant, assez semblables à celles de leur propre enfant, et de réagir spontanément à cette expérience. Les épisodes portaient sur des types divers d'interactions quotidiennes avec un des parents, avec un frère ou une soeur plus jeune, ou avec un petit compagnon invité à venir jouer avec lui. Les paroles et les gestes de l'enfant dans chacun des épisodes avaient pour objet de susciter chez les parents des types particuliers de réaction, qui pouvaient aller de l'acquiescement jusqu'à la colère franche, en passant par le laissez-faire.[1] Le parent devait alors s'imaginer qu'il était l'époux ou l'épouse du parent impliqué, par contact direct avec l'enfant ou comme observateur, dans chacun de ces trois épisodes et lui faire part de ses premières réactions.[2]

Cette technique, utilisée pour la première fois par Rothbart et Maccoby en Californie (1966), a été mise à l'épreuve au cours d'une pré-expérimentation (Lambert, Yackley et Hein, 1971) pour en vérifier l'efficacité, la fidélité et la validité. Nous savions donc, à partir de recherches antérieures, que les parents entraient dans le jeu des épisodes du ruban magnétique tout comme s'ils étaient de fait en interaction avec leurs propres enfants, n'abandonnant leur rôle parental qu'occasionnellement pour dire: ''Ah, non! Le mien n'irait pas jusque là avec moi,'' ou quelque chose de semblable. En réalité, nous croyons que la technique peut s'avérer aussi ou même plus évocatrice et naturelle que l'observation même d'interactions familiales. La pré-expérimentation a aussi servi à démontrer que les résultats d'une investigation de ce genre sont faciles à noter et analyser, qu'ils sont fiables, riches en ce qui a trait aux différences entre groupes et extrêmement suggestifs tant sur le plan théorique que pratique.

Les résultats de notre enquête nous permettent d'en dire beaucoup sur la façon dont le processus de socialisation se déroule dans chacun des milieux nationaux. Mais, au mieux, nous ne sommes en mesure de faire que des énoncés hypothétiques sur cette importante et fascinante question puisque notre étude porte sur les valeurs et les attitudes relatives à l'éducation des enfants et non pas sur des observations réelles d'interactions parents-enfants. De plus, notre recherche se limite à des échantillons de parents appartenant à de vastes milieux urbains dans chacun de ces pays; nous ne pouvons, par conséquent, faire de généralisation sur aucun des pays dans son ensemble. Par exemple, nos échantillons d'anglophones et de francophones ont été pris à Montréal.

Nous verrons que ce qui ressort des données c'est qu'il existe divers types de valeurs et d'attitudes à la mode relatives à l'éducation des enfants dans chacun des pays étudiés et que, en général, l'unique influence la plus importante sur les réactions parentales s'avère être les antécédents de niveau social des parents et non leur appartenance ethnique. Pour prendre le cas du Canada, on constate que l'influence provenant de la classe sociale est, en fait, apparente dans sept des dix dimensions de valeurs incluses dans l'étude et qu'elle joue également un rôle dans les diverses interactions. Bien que ces comparaisons de niveau social s'appliquent dans l'ensemble aux parents canadiens, tant anglophones que francophones, ceci ne veut pas dire que l'importance de la classe sociale serait nécessairement un phénomène distinctement canadien, car les comparaisons avec les autres pays montrent clairement que le niveau social joue un rôle aussi important dans tous les pays inclus dans l'étude. Fait intéressant et révélateur cependant, c'est que le Canada, l'un des pays du Nouveau-Monde où l'on prétend souvent que les distinctions de classes sociales ont peu d'importance réelle, soit caractérisé par des différences aussi profondes et marquées en ce qui a trait aux rapports parents-enfants, différences qui peuvent être reliées aux antécédents du niveau social. On en vient à se demander s'il ne se serait pas installé dans nos propres systèmes de croyance un mythe puissant de l'existence d'une société sans classes sociales. La réalité c'est que les antécédents de niveau social des parents ont une grande importance pour l'explication des différences de systèmes de valeurs relatifs à l'éducation des enfants au Canada.

Trois autres facteurs jouent un rôle relativement moins grand: l'origine ethnique des parents anglophones et francophones, le sexe de l'enfant et le sexe du parent. Quand même, chacun de ceux-ci exerce sa propre influence distincte et révélatrice. Nous allons d'abord considérer l'influence du facteur ethnique, puisque c'était là la question fondamentale à l'origine de cette recherche et parce que c'est l'interrogation que la plupart des parents, des éducateurs et des philosophes sociaux pourraient se poser en premier, à savoir: dans quelle mesure les parents canadiens d'origine anglaise et française diffèrent-ils dans leur façon d'aborder l'éducation des enfants?

Ethnie. Le fait d'être Canadien français ou Canadien anglais a des conséquences directes sur la façon dont les parents accueillent les appels à l'*aide* des enfants, leurs manifestations d'*insolence* et leurs demandes de faire entrer des *invités* pour jouer avec eux. Dans chacun de ces cas ce sont les Canadiens anglais (CA) qui hésitent, par comparaison avec les parents canadiens français (CF), dans ce sens que les premiers sont moins spontanés et moins disposés à aider sur le champ, plus répressifs et durs face à l'insolence et plus circonspects quand il s'agit d'ouvrir leur porte à des camarades de leur enfant. Ces contrastes peuvent s'expliquer sur le plan socio-psychologique. Les parents CA pourraient, par exemple, se montrer plus récalcitrants à se porter à l'aide de leurs enfants parce qu'ils sont plus préoccupés de les voir apprendre à pourvoir à leurs propres besoins, à devenir indépendants. Une telle interprétation est conforme aux données dont on dispose sur l'apprentissage de l'indépendance, apprentissage auquel, selon McClelland (1961), on attache plus d'importance dans les milieux CA que dans les milieux CF et plus aussi, d'après Rosen (1959) dans les milieux anglo-américains que dans le milieux franco-américains des Etats-Unis.

On pourrait, de la même façon, formuler une explication convaincante de l'importance que les parents CA attachent aux manifestations d'insolence. Il se pourrait fort que ces parents se sentent particulièrement menacés par la tendance, qui semble prévaloir chez les enfants des Etats-Unis, à se dégager du contrôle et des directives des adultes (voir Bronfenbrenner, 1970).

Il est à la fois surprenent et intéressant de constater que les parents CF manifestent une attitude plus ouverte envers les compagnons de jeu de leurs enfants. Une interprétation possible serait que le milieu Canadien français, comme la plupart des minorités ethniques, serait plus enclin à considérer les autres membres du même groupe minoritaire, y compris les compagnons de jeu de leurs propres enfants, comme faisant partie de leur plus vaste famille. Pour survivre comme groupe ethnique, ils ont peut-être dû, dans une grande mesure, compter les uns sur les autres et se considérer comme isolés dans un îlot culturel. Il est également vraisemblable que, vu leur besoin de liens solides au sein du groupe, ils aient appris à établir des distinctions nettes entre les membres de leur groupe et ceux des divers groupes étrangers qui les "encerclaient". Les parents CA par contre essaieraient peut-être de renforcer les attitudes d'indépendance en entraînant leurs enfants à ne pas compter sur des compagnons de jeu comme source de divertissement. Mais peu importe les interprétations, les principaux résultats dépeignent les parents CA comme étant moins disposés à apporter leur appui ou leur encouragement face aux demandes d'aide, moins tolérants devant l'insolence et moins accueillants vis-à-vis des invités que les parents CF.

Les diverses interactions font ressortir d'autres comparaison plus subtiles. Nous avons trouvé, par exemple, que les mères CA adoptent une attitude franchement indulgente et tolérante quand une querelle éclate entre un enfant et son frère ou sa soeur plus jeune et que le premier cherche à se faire consoler. Ce faisant les mères CA se placent en contradiction avec leurs maris, ce qui permet de supposer que les différences normatives entre les rôles paternel et maternel seraient plus prononcées chez les familles CA que chez les familles CF. On se demande s'il n'y aurait pas une explication plus superficielle de cette tendance, à savoir que les mères CA pourraient être l'objet de quelque source spéciale d'influence (comme des émissions de radio et de télévision en langue anglaise durant la journée) qui alimenterait leur niveau distinctif d'indépendance dans ces cas particuliers ou si encore il y aurait une signification plus profonde dans la façon dont les mères CA remplissent leur rôle maternel.

La souplesse et l'indépendance qui caractérisent le rôle de la mère dans les familles CA présentent un intérêt particulier. Les mères CA sont aussi exigeantes et dures que leurs maris sur les questions de refuser l'aide, de contrôler l'insolence et de fermer leur porte aux compagnons de jeu, mais pourtant elles se montrent généreuses et indulgentes dans les cas de disputes entre leurs enfants et de recherche de consolations. Dans un certain sens par conséquent, c'est la maman CA qui joue le rôle le plus actif et le plus souple dans la socialisation de l'enfant puisque, en même temps que le père, elle remplit le rôle du parent exigeant dans des domaines particuliers d'interaction et que, tout à fait indépendemment du père CA, elle adopte un rôle plus tendre et plus compatissant dans d'autres domaines.

Les ramifications de ce mode de répartition des attitudes pourraient avoir une influence sur le comportement de l'enfant dans ses rapports avec les autres tant à l'intérieur qu'à l'extérieur du milieu familial. On pourrait, par exemple, établir un lien intéressant entre les attitudes des mères et des pères CA et l'émergence d'une motivation de réussite chez les enfants CA, conformément aux recherches et à la théorie de McClelland (1961); Rosen (1961), Rosen et D'Andrade (1959); Lambert, Yackley et Hein (1971); et De Koninck et Sirois-Berliss (1978).

Il y a aussi des contrastes ethniques potentiellement importants dans la façon dont les parents conçoivent les différences attenant au rôle sexuel dans le comportement des garçons et des filles. Dans l'ensemble, les mères CF des classes moyennes sont particulièrement attentives aux différences dans la façon dont doivent se conduire garçons et filles, ce qui porterait à croire que ces mères CF auraient pu être amenées à s'inquiéter considérablement des mouvements sociaux récents tendant à réduire l'importance traditionnelle des modèles de comportement pour garçons et filles.

Une comparaison parallèle vaut pour le niveau de classe sociale: les parents de garçons de classes ouvrières attachent beaucoup plus d'importance aux différences attenant au rôle sexuel que les parents de garçons des classes moyennes. Ce contraste nous amène à penser que, aux yeux des parents canadiens des classes ouvrières, les garçons doivent se comporter comme des garçons pour réussir dans la vie, alors que les parents des classes moyennes se montrent beaucoup plus ouverts sur le sujet comme si, pour eux, le succès du mâle dans le monde bourgeois requérait quelque chose de plus que des traits ''masculins''. Par contre, nous découvrons que les parents de filles provenant des classes ouvrières s'inquiètent relativement moins de ce que leurs filles ressemblent à des garçons, laissant ainsi supposer que de leur point de vue il serait avantageux pour les filles d'être capables d'affronter les aspects les plus rudes de la vie. Les parents des classes moyennes, au contraire, semblent vouloir que leurs filles se montrent différentes des garçons, comme si pour eux la féminité était relativement plus importante et plus précieuse.

Classe sociale. L'influence du niveau social touche aux relations des parents avec leurs enfants sur toutes les dimensions que nous avons étudiées, sauf le refus d'aide, le refus d'attention et la *privation de marques de compassion*. Par rapport à tous les autres aspects, ce sont les parents des classes ouvrières (les CF comme les CA) qui sont les plus durs et les plus exigeants en ce qui a trait à la socialisation de l'enfant. Autrement dit, par comparaison avec les parents de classes moyennes, ils sont plus enclins à se ranger du côté du bébé, et contre l'enfant, quand une querelle éclate; ils exercent un contrôle plus sévère sur les manifestations de colère, de mauvaise humeur en groupe et d'insolence; ils imposent plus de limites au privilège d'inviter des amis, se prononcent plus souvent contre l'enfant quand il discute avec un compagnon de jeu, contrôlent plus rigoureusement ses prétentions à l'autonomie, tout en s'attendant à, et en percevant de fait, des degrés plus élevés de différenciation du rôle sexuel dans le comportement des garçons et des filles.

Trois dimensions seulement échappent donc à l'influence de la classe sociale: l'une se rapportant à la recherche par l'enfant du secours des parents, l'autre à sa demande d'être consolé et la troisième au besoin d'attention de l'enfant ou de la présence psychologique du parent. Lorsqu'un enfant demande qu'on l'aide, les parents des deux classes, moyenne et ouvrière, se conforment à ses désirs, alors que s'il cherche attention ou compassion, les parents des deux classes la lui refusent. Par conséquent, dans les domaines où les parents doivent faire face à des demandes d'aide ou de soins, le milieu social n'intervient pas dans les réactions des parents. C'est plutôt par rapport spécifique aux questions requérant de la discipline ou aux prétentions à l'autonomie que les parents des classes moyennes et ouvrières se distinguent. Il arrive que dans ces domaines ils présentent des différences considérables, ce qui indique que nous avons affaire ici à des caractéristiques importantes des principes d'éducation appliqués à l'enfant canadien; c'est-à-dire que le milieu social des parents a plus d'importance que le facteur ethnique, le sexe de l'enfant ou celui du parent.

Le résultat qui tranche, par conséquent, c'est que les parents canadiens des classes ouvrières sont nettement plus exigeants et plus répressifs que ceux des classes moyennes dans leurs principes quant à la façon d'élever les enfants. Leur sévérité relative se limite aux provocations de la part de l'enfant qui appellent des mesures de discipline et aux signes prémonitoires des premières tentatives de l'enfant en vue de l'indépendance ou de l'autonomie. Les données dont nous disposons ne nous permettent que des hypothèses sur les raisons de ces différentes façons de voir des parents. Il se pourrait fort bien que les parents des classes ouvrières se montrent plus sévères et plus exigeants dans l'éducation de leurs enfants afin de les préparer vis-à-vis d'un monde que ces parents connaissent bien, un monde où, à cause du niveau inférieur qui nous est dévolu dans la société, on doit s'attendre à souffrir, à subir l'humiliation et, surtout, à se montrer disposé à faire ce que l'on nous ordonne, Il s'agit également d'un monde où il y a peu de place pour l'arbitraire dans les questions de comportement relatif au rôle sexuel. On doit enseigner aux jeunes garçons à devenir des hommes tout comme les jeunes filles doivent apprendre à assumer les rôles de la femme, même si celles-ci doivent aussi acquérir la capacité de supporter les heurts de la vie. Les tous premiers gestes, précoces, que l'enfant ébauche vers l'indépendance peuvent fort bien être une source d'inquiétude pour les parents des classes ouvrières qui risquent de voir leur enfant leur échapper pour passer à des influences de l'extérieur avant que son éducation familiale ne soit complétée. Cette éducation n'est pas du tout rude, cependant, puisque, quand la situation exige de l'aide et des soins, ces parents des classes ouvrières portés à la discipline sont autant disposés à apporter secours et réconfort que n'importe qui.

Les contrastes laissent supposer que les parents de classes *moyennes* prennent comme point de référence un monde fait d'autres expériences. Ils veulent que leurs enfants confrontent la vie et apprennent à penser par eux-mêmes, qu'ils soient capables de prendre soin de leur personne et qu'ils soient préparés à dire aux autres quoi faire plutôt qu'à suivre des directives. Ils favorisent donc les premiers efforts vers l'autonomie et remettent en question toute attitude stéréotypée sur ce que devrait être un comportement masculin ou féminin. Ce contraste correspond plutôt bien avec les stades du développement de la motivation de réussite identifiés par McClelland (1961) et Rosen (1961). Ces chercheurs ont découvert que la force de la motivation de réussite était nettement associée au niveau social et il s'avère que l'expérience vécue par les classes moyennes a pour effet non seulement d'engendrer relativement plus de motivation de réussite mais apparemment aussi de procurer plus tôt dans le développement des bases à l'autonomie, à la souplesse et à la confiance en soi.

Ce contraste de la classe moyenne prend également un sens d'un autre genre si l'on songe aux effets que des attitudes parentales relativement sévères, par opposition à des attitudes relativement indulgentes, en ce qui a trait au processus de socialisation peuvent avoir sur le développement de la personnalité. Mais il faut bien préciser ici ce que nous entendons en utilisant les termes ''sévère'', ''exigeant'', ''indulgent'' ou ''psychologique'', termes auxquels nous avons eu recours pour établir un contraste entre les façons de faire des parents canadiens des classes moyennes par comparaison avec ceux des classes ouvrières.

A notre sens, on pourrait à partir des résultats canadiens défendre assez fermement le point de vue que ce sont les parents des classes ouvrières qui sont à la fois les plus ''stricts'' et les plus ''répressifs'', dans le sens que Stanley Guterman (1970) donne à ces termes. Ce sont ces parents canadiens qui, par comparaison avec ceux des classes moyennes, imposent plus de limites à l'enfant en fonction de ce qu'il lui est permis et pas permis de faire et qui exercent plus de contraintes (et d'un type plus violent) en ce qui a trait au respect des règles et des normes. Ces limites plus nettement définies recouvrent l'agressivité ou les manifestations de colères dirigées contre les frères et les soeurs, les compagnons et les parents. Les enfants des classes ouvrières canadiennes doivent, vraisemblablement, faire face à des ''mesures de discipline'' qui sont ''plus constantes et prévisibles'' selon le vocabulaire de Guterman. La socialisation *plus rigoureuse* de l'enfant de la classe ouvrière canadienne peut, dans cette mesure, contribuer, dans le cas des enfants de la classe moyenne, à la formation d'une conscience relativement faible. Si telle conclusion paraissait étrange à ceux qui se sentiraient poussés à défendre les stratégies de la classe moyenne, ils pourraient peut-être soutenir en contrepartie que l'avantage virtuel de l'éducation reçue par les enfants de la classe ouvrière se trouve annulé par les modèles plus autoritaires et plus exigeants que les parents de cette classe imposent à leurs enfants. Ou encore que l'aspect plus positif de la fermeté et de la sévérité des parents est contrebalancé par la plus grande propension à punir de ces mêmes parents des classes ouvrières. Ce dernier argument correspond bien à ce que nous avons constaté dans toute notre étude: les parents canadiens de la classe ouvrière sont plus portés à avoir recours à la menace-de-sévir ou à des moyens de punition et que les parents de la classe moyenne sont plus enclins à utiliser les moyens ''psychologiques'' et ''de raisonnement'' pour aborder la discipline, les rendant ainsi plus indulgents et tolérants ou, en d'autres mots, moins répressifs. Bien sûr, comme Bronfenbrenner (1970) pourrait le soutenir, cette attitude non-répressive risque d'être facilement confondue avec une ''indifférence préméditée'' à l'égard des enfants.[3]

Parents de garçons et parents de filles. Il se présente trois circonstances dans l'étude canadienne où les parents de filles donnent des réactions différentes de celles des parents de garçons: lorsqu'il s'agit de contrôler les *manifestations de colère publiques*, de refuser son *attention* à l'enfant et de *prendre parti contre* l'enfant qui se querelle avec un ou une camarade. Dans chaque cas, ce sont les parents des filles qui se montrent les plus durs comme ''socialisateurs'' et on ne trouve pas, pour compenser, d'exemples où les parents de garçons seraient plus intraitables. Les parents canadiens trouvent donc ces trois formes de conduites particulièrement agaçantes, quand elles sont le fait des filles. Si l'on tient compte du fait que les enregistrements d'épisodes utilisés dans cette étude étaient précisément les mêmes dans les versions se rapportant aux garçons et aux filles, ces différences de réactions parentales à l'égard de leurs fils et de leurs filles devient doublement intéressantes. Ainsi dans la mesure où les fillettes canadiennes sont soumises à une discipline excessive par rapport à leurs manifestations de colère en public, à leurs querelles avec un compagnon ou une compagne de jeu et sont plus rabrouées suite à leurs recherches d'attention, on pourrait dans le même ordre d'idée affirmer que les garçons canadiens sont relativement épargnés sur le plan de la discipline et de la frustration.

Apparemment il s'agit ici d'un point de vue populaire au Canada puisque dans ces cas on ne décèle aucunes différences ethniques, ni différences de niveau social. Ainsi, les parents canadiens semblent-ils, en général, élever leurs filles de façon à ce qu'elles ne se montrent pas agressives sur le plan social et à ce qu'elles ne cherchent pas à attirer l'attention. L'agressivité sociale et la recherche de l'attention sont, par contre, des traits d'autant plus positifs pour les garçons canadiens, que ce sont justement des traits négatifs pour les filles canadiennes. On peut voir dans ce contraste garçon-fille la façon dont la société élabore un modèle clair des différences qu'on s'attend de retrouver chez les adultes, hommes et femmes. Plus les modèles de rôle sexuel des adultes seront différenciés, plus l'existence d'une complémentarité dans les rapports entre hommes et femmes sera fondée et plus il devrait être facile d'établir un partage naturel des responsabilités de socialisation des mères et des pères.

Par ailleurs, ce contraste soulève des questions. Est-il profitable ou convenable de faire ce type de différenciation entre garçons et filles à partir de l'enfance et dans la suite? Comment l'agressivité, caractéristique négative chez les filles, peut-elle avoir une valeur positive chez les garçons? Ce fait de former à *réprimer* l'agressivité dans un cas et à l'*exprimer* dans l'autre devient particulièrement intéressant. S'il s'agissait d'une propension naturelle à se montrer agressif sur le plan social, le fait de réprimer cette tendance dans le cas des filles aurait pour elles des effets biologiques et affectifs nuisibles. S'il ne s'agit pas d'une tendance naturelle, facile à contrôler, pourquoi devrait-on encourager les garçons à se montrer agressif dans un monde où l'agressivité occupe déjà une si grande place? Apparemment les parents canadiens estiment que pour survivre dans ce monde de violence, on doit donner aux garçons plus qu'aux filles l'occasion d'apprendre à se défendre!

Les mères et les pères. Il y a deux cas clairs et nets dans l'étude canadienne où le fait d'être une mère plutôt qu'un père a une influence sur la réaction vis-à-vis des enfants: l'un porte sur la recherche de l'attention, l'autre sur les disputes entre l'enfant et un camarade. Dans le premier cas, les pères canadiens réagissent plus durement que les mères, alors que quand il s'agit de prendre la part du camarade contre l'enfant ce sont les mères qui se montrent les plus dures. Ces contrastes laissent supposer que dans les familles canadiennes, CA ou CF, les responsabilités de socialisation seraient divisées et, apparemment, on s'attendrait à ce que les pères s'occupent plus spécialement de contrer les stratagèmes de harcèlement et de recherche d'attention, alors que la tâche d'enseigner à l'enfant comment se conduire dans ses relations avec ceux qui ne sont pas de sa famille serait du ressort de la mère. Il nous est impossible d'expliquer l'apparition de ces deux différences particulières ni la façon dont cette tendance à une division des responsabilités s'établit. Il vaudrait néanmoins la peine d'explorer dans des recherches subséquentes d'autres aspects de la socialisation afin de vérifier cette opinion générale, à savoir que, au Canada, c'est plutôt aux pères qu'incombe la responsabilité de maintenir la paix au sein de la famille et plutôt aux mères celle d'entretenir de bons rapports avec l'entourage.

Ce qui mérite d'être souligné dans l'étude canadienne c'est l'absence de faits à l'appui du concept de "tolérance à l'endroit du sexe opposé";* en effet, nous n'avons trouvé aucune indication voulant que les pères soient plus durs avec leurs fils et offrent relativement plus d'appui à leurs filles, alors que les mères feraient preuve de favoritisme vis-à-vis de leurs garçons et de parti pris contre leurs filles. On peut s'en étonner car Rothbart et Maccoby (1966) dans une étude faite aux Etats-Unis rapportaient un grand nombre d'exemples de tolérance à l'endroit du sexe opposé. Non seulement ne trouvons-nous pas de cette tolérance croisée dans notre recherche canadienne, mais nous notons plutôt des exemples de tolérance à l'endroit de l'enfant du même sexe.

L'étude canadienne dont nous venons de tracer une esquisse n'était qu'une des recherches comprises dans le projet global; peut-être conviendrait-il donc, en conclusion, de situer ces descriptions des styles canadiens anglais et canadiens français d'éducation des enfants dans une perspective transnationale plus vaste. La série de recherches présentée dans le livre de Lambert, Hamers et Frasure Smith (1979) considère cette étude sur les parents canadiens comme deux exemples parmi quelque onze groupes nationaux analysés; ce cadre plus large permet de voir quelles sont les caractéristiques, s'il en est, qui s'appliquent universellement et quelles sont les caractéristiques d'un groupe particulier qui apparaissent toujours comme distinctives, quand on les replace dans une plus vaste perspective.

Ce qui se passe en réalité c'est que plusieurs des caractéristiques qui se présentaient comme différentes et distinctives dans les comparaisons entre deux ou trois pays s'émoussent ou s'estompent sur l'"écran plus vaste" d'une comparaison de dix pays. Mais le point fascinant c'est que ce ne sont pas tous les contrastes de l'écran plus étroit qui s'évanouissent sur l'écran global: certains traits nationaux caractéristiques persistent et, fait tout aussi important, certaines tendances transculturelles étrangement stables émergent en relief plus prononcé.

Les groupes de parents étudiés furent les suivants: Américains, Belges flamands, Belges français, Britanniques, Canadiens anglais, Canadiens français, Français, Grecs, Italiens et Portugais. Dans chaque cas on s'est intéressé aux deux classes, ouvrière et moyenne, de parents.[4] La question qui se pose donc, présentement, est de savoir dans quelle mesure les principes des parents canadiens anglais et canadiens français sont distinctifs dans ce contexte plus large.

Considérés ensemble, toutefois, les parents canadiens français, canadiens anglais et américains forment un groupe nord-américain. Bien qu'ils soient différents les uns des autres de façon distinctive quant aux degrés de sévérité et d'indulgence manifestés dans leurs attitudes vis-à-vis de l'éducation des enfants, ils se ressemblent sur tellement de points que les trois groupes font nettement contraste avec nos échantillons européens. Par comparaison avec ces derniers, par exemple, ils sont beaucoup plus enclins à accorder de l'autonomie à l'enfant de six ans. Dans chacun des trois milieux nord-américains, il existe donc une différence marquée dans la façon d'aborder les questions de discipline, selon les antécédents de niveau social de la famille: les parents nord-américains des classes moyennes sont beaucoup plus tolérants et indulgents que les parents des classes ouvrières lorsque le comportement de l'enfant demande à être discipliné. En fait, les parents nord-americains des classes moyennes préfèrent détourner, distraire ou, au pire, réprimander, plutôt que de menacer ou effectivement punir l'enfant qui n'est pas sage. Enfin, les parents nord-américains attachent relativement peu d'importance aux rôles sexuels—ils ont des tendances à l'unisexisme— et leur perception des différences de rôle attenant au sexe est généralement aussi peu définie que leur intérêt pour ces différences.

Nous arrivons donc à cette conclusion surprenante que, lorsqu'on se place dans une perspective assez large, les parents CA et CF ne se distinguent pas du tout dans leur façon d'aborder l'éducation des enfants. Dans les faits, ils se montrent plutôt nord-américains et ils sont loin de paraître aussi canadiens "anglais" ou "français" que ces épithètes ethniques le laissent entendre. Effectivement, nos résultats indiquent que les parents CA et CF qui ont les mêmes antécédents de niveau social se ressemblent plus dans leurs attitudes vis-à-vis l'éducation des enfants que l'un ou l'autre de ces groupes avec des parents de même origine ethnique, mais de classes sociales différentes. De plus, il ressort que les parents CA et CF issus d'une classe sociale particulière ont plus d'affinités, par rapport à ces attitudes, avec les parents américains, grecs, portugais, italiens ou belges de même niveau social qu'avec des parents CA et CF issus de classes sociales différentes. Nous en arrivons donc à fermer la boucle et nous commençons à nous demander sérieusement quelle proportion de "caractère distinctif" il convient d'attribuer à la réalité des choses et quelle proportion ne serait que le fruit de l'imagination d'adultes qui, dans une grande mesure, sont responsables en premier lieu de la formation de leurs propres contrastes entre groupes.

Bibliographie

Aboud, F.E., & Taylor, D.M. Ethnic and role stereotypes: Their relative importance in person perception. *Journal of Social Psychology*, 1977, *85*, 17−21.

Bronfenbrenner, U. *Two worlds of childhood: U.S. and U.S.S.R.* New York: Russell Sage Foundation, 1970.

DeKoninck, J., & Sirois-Berliss, M. La motivation au rendement dans les rêves et durant l'éveil chez des étudiants canadiens-français et canadiens-anglais. *Revue canadienne des Sciences du Comportement*, 1978, 10, 329−338.

Guterman, S.S. *The Machiavellians*. Lincoln: University of Nebraska Press, 1970.

Lambert, W.E., Hamers, J.F., & Frasure Smith, N. *Child-rearing values: A Cross-national study*. New York: Praeger Publications, 1979.

Lambert, W.E., Yackley, A., & Hein, R. Child training values of English Canadian and French Canadian parents. *Canadian Journal of Behavioural Science*, 1971, *3*, 217−236.

McClelland, D.C. *The achieving society*. New York: Van Nostrand, 1961.

Rosen, B.C. Race, ethnicity and the achievement syndrome. *American Sociological Review*, 1959, *24*, 47−60.

Rosen, B.C. Family structure and achievement motivation. *American Sociological Review*, 1961, *26*, 574−585.

Rosen, B.C., & D'Andrade, R.G. The psychosocial origins of achievement motivation. *Sociometry*, 1959, *22*, 185–218.

Rothbart, M.K. & Maccoby, E.E. Parents' differential reactions to sons and daughters. *Journal of Personality and Social Psychology*, 1966, *4*, 237–243.

Whitkin, H.A. Studies in space orientation. *Journal of Experimental Psychology*, 1948, *38*, 762–782.

Witkin, H.A. Social influences in the development of cognitive style. *Handbook of socialization theory and research*, (Ed.), D.A. Goslin. New York: Rand McNally, 1969.

Witkin, H.A. Socialization and ecology in the development of cross cultural and sex differences in cognitive style. Paper presented at 21st International Congress of Psychology, Paris, 1976.

Witkin, H.A., & Berry, J.W. Psychological differentiation in cross cultural perspective. *Journal of Cross Cultural Psychology*, 1975, *6*, 4–87.

Notes

1. On a préparé deux enregistrements distincts pour chaque milieu ethnique, un pour les mères, un pour les pères, en prenant soin de modifier les énoncés des enfants en fonction du langage ou des dialectes régionaux. Voici la version française. (1) Maman (papa) viens voir mon casse-tête (puzzle). (2) Maman (papa), aide-moi! (3) Ce morceau, est-ce qu'il va ici? (4) Bébé, tu peux pas jouer avec moi; t'es trop petit. (5) Il peut pas jouer avec mon casse-tête. C'est à moi! (6) Laisse mon casse-tête tranquille ou je te frappe sur la tête! (7) Je n'aime pas ce jeu-là. C'est un jeu stupide et tu es stupide, maman (papa). (9) Oh..h! Bébé m'a écrasé la main! (10) Maman (papa), ça fait mal! (11) Maman (papa), procure-moi un autre casse-tête. (12) Il ne pleut pas, là. Est-ce que je puis aller jouer de l'autre côté de la rue? (13) Pourquoi je peux pas? Je vais y aller quand même. (14) Est-ce que Chris peut entrer et jouer? (15) Chris, laisse-moi placer les morceaux moi-même. Toi tu me regardes. (16) Touche pas aux morceaux. Tu sais pas comment le faire. (17) Si tu les laisses pas tranquilles, je vais te battre.

   La réaction des parents à chacun des items a été mise en code et les items ont ensuite été regroupés et combinés pour former l'une des 10 échelles ou types de dimensions de valeurs distinctes. Etant donné que les scores les plus élevés de ces échelles représentent généralement des réactions plus sévères ou coercitives, les noms qu'on a donnés aux échelles se rapportent au pôle répressif de la gamme des réactions possibles; ainsi on parlera de "refus d'aider" plutôt que de "venir à l'aide". Les échelles sont: *Refus d'aider* (items 1, 2, 3 et 11); *Refus de réconfort* (9, 10); *Contrôle des manifestations de colère* (7); *Contrôle des gestes antisociaux* (6, 17); *Contrôle des expressions d'insolence* (8, 13); *Prendre la part du bébé contre l'enfant* (4, 5, 6); *Refus d'attention* (9); *Contrôle des gestes d'indépendance* (12); *Contraintes dans le choix des invités* (14); *Prendre la part de l'invité contre l'enfant* (15, 16, 17). Dans chaque échelle, les scores peuvent aller d'une réaction de grande tolérance (désignée par un score faible) jusqu'à une réaction répressive, une réprimande, le fait de se ranger du côté du bébé ou du compagnon de jeu (plutôt que de celui de l'enfant) lors d'une querelle, ou le refus de venir en aide. Par exemple en réponse à la demande de l'enfant: "Papa, aide-moi!" (item 2) la réaction suivante d'un parent: "Voyons donc où ce morceau peut bien aller" serait évaluée comme forte dans le sens de se porter à l'aide, tandis qu'une autre réaction de la forme suivante: "Essaie-le à plusieurs places pour voir si ça marche" se situerait plus vers le pôle négatif, tout près du refus explicite ou de l'indifférence totale vis-à-vis de la demande d'aide venant de l'enfant. De même dans le cas de l'item 7 ("Je n'aime pas ce jeu-là. C'est un jeu stupide et t'es stupide, maman!") la réaction parentale pourrait aller d'une attitude consistant à oublier le ton insolent pour essayer de comprendre la frustration de l'enfant, jusqu'à exiger qu'il s'excuse, à le réprimander, voire à le corriger physiquement. En plus de leurs réactions aux épisodes enregistrés, on demandait aussi aux parents de répondre à deux questionnaires qu'on présentait dans la moitié des cas avant et dans l'autre moitié après qu'ils avaient écouté les bandes magnétiques. Le premier de ces questionnaires, intitulé *Différences perçues, quant au rôle sexuel*, comprend 40 items qui sondent les perceptions des parents quant au degré de similitude et de différence manifesté par les garçons et les filles dans leurs comportements ou réactions typiques, v.g. dans leur capacité de s'affirmer, de faire preuve de persévérance ou de se montrer utile. Le second questionnaire, intitulé *Différences présumées, quant au rôle sexuel*, mesure ce à quoi les parents s'attendent quant aux différences que le rôle sexuel doit exercer sur le comportement: s'ils croient important ou non, par exemple, qu'un garçon ou une fille se montre audacieux et capable de s'affirmer.

2. Les détails sur la façon de procéder, le codage et la fidélité du code sont présentés dans le chapitre et dans les appendices du livre de Lambert, Hamers et Frasure Smith (1979).

3. Nos résultats se rapprochent également d'un autre domaine de recherche extrêmement riche en données, celui de la dépendance ou de l'indépendance vis-à-vis du champ perceptif, associé aux noms de Witkin (1948; 1969; 1976) et Witkin et Berry (1975). Le rapport entre les deux est décrit en détails dans le livre de Lambert, Hamers et Frasure Smith (1979); on y voit comment les principes des parents sur l'éducation des enfants peuvent influencer le développement perceptif, cognitif et social des enfants.

4. Le livre de Lambert, Hamers et Frasure Smith (1979) présente aussi des données sur les parents japonais des classes moyennes.

III. LONG-TERM STUDIES OF CHILDREN WITH LEARNING DISABILITIES

editor: John Crichton

9

Learning-Disabled Children Growing Up

OTFRIED SPREEN, PH.D.

Abstract

Two hundred and five severely learning-disabled children had been referred to the Neuropsychology Laboratory at the University of Victoria, in British Columbia between 1964 and 1973 when they were between the ages of eight and twelve. Recently, a long-term follow-up study was done on the subjects, approximately nine years after their initial referral when they reached their teens and early twenties.

Detailed student and parent interviews as well as Bell Inventory (adjustment scales) and student record cards were used to examine the problems that learning-disabled children have in adjusting in later life to their environment as late teenagers and adults.

Three distinct groups emerged: those with clear neurological signs called brain-damaged; those with soft signs called minimal brain-damaged, and those with no neurological signs called learning-disabled. Most of the dimensions studied, e.g., educational achievement, health and personal adjustment, group differences, and degree of difficulty, followed the pattern of the extent of neurological impairment. The pattern suggests a continuum of neurological impairment which is reflected in adult outcome.

L'auteur présente les résultats préliminaires d'une étude longitudinale de 205 enfants que l'on avait dirigé vers le Laboratoire de Neuropsychologie de l'Université de Victoria en Colombie Britannique entre 1964 et 1973 parce qu'ils montraient des troubles d'apprentissage sérieux; ces enfants avaient alors de huit à douze ans. Les mêmes sujets ont été vus environ neuf ans après leur premier examen, alors qu'ils étaient des adolescents.

On s'est servi d'interviews en profondeur auprès de ces étudiants et de leurs parents de même que de l'*Inventaire Bell* (échelles d'adaptation) et des résultats scolaires des étudiants pour étudier les problèmes que rencontrent, quand ils grandissent, les enfants qui ont des troubles d'apprentissage.

Trois groupes distincts sont apparus: ceux qui présentaient des symptômes neurologiques évidents et que l'on considérait comme atteints d'encéphalopathies congénitales ou néonatales; ceux qui présentaient des signes neurologiques légers et que l'on considérait comme atteints d'encéphalopathies bénignes; et ceux qui ne présentaient aucun signe neurologique et que l'on considérait comme des victimes de troubles d'apprentissage purs. Par rapport à la plupart des dimensions étudiées—à savoir la réussite d'une douzième année d'études, la délinquance et l'adaptation—les différences de groupes et le degré de difficulté se sont révélés proportionnels à l'importance de la détérioration neurologique.

This paper presents preliminary results of a long-term follow-up study conducted in Victoria and the western British Columbia area. The group of young people studied was not chosen from the school population at large, but consists of 205 children who had been referred to the neuropsychology laboratory of the University of Victoria because of learning problems. Since these children were second or even third-line referrals, they are perhaps more severely learning-disabled than children referred to an agency within the school system. Our study concentrated on the age group for which the largest number of referrals was available, namely, children between the ages of 8 and 12. Intake extended from 1964–1973.

On the average, follow-up took place approximately 9 years after the initial referral. At that time, the mean age was 19 years, although some subjects were as old as 25. Originally, more than 300 children had been studied; only 11 refused to participate in the follow-up for a variety of reasons; the remainder of the subjects not included in the follow-up had moved away. The remaining 203 clients participated in a very detailed 2-hour interview covering the personal, social, education, occupational and health adjustment areas. In addition, a separate interview by a different interviewer was conducted with one or both parents.

Hence, we have two independent sources of data, the "student interview" and the "parent interview." In addition, the Bell Inventory was completed by the students; the inventory deals primarily with various areas of adjustment that can be scored, i.e. emotional adjustment, social adjustment, home adjustment, and so on. The parents completed a behaviour rating scale dealing with the child's behaviour at the time in question, as it was seen retrospectively; and we also had a rating based on the interview behaviour prepared by the interviewers. In addition, we received permission from almost all of our subjects to obtain their permanent record cards from the schools.

Using this follow-up procedure, we addressed ourselves directly to the question of the outcomes of learning disabilities. The population studied consisted of 255 individuals who were in their late teens or were young adults at the time of the follow-up study. Of these, 52 were control subjects, chosen from school records after making sure that they were average learners at the target date and between the ages of 8 and 12. We wanted an average learner group without any reported learning or neurological problems during that time. The second aspect for classification within our total group was the neurological aspect. Since our neuropsychological laboratory has been collaborating with neurologists for many years, we have on file the neurological examination data on each individual in our sample. We recognised three groups: (1) those who had clear, indisputable neurological signs; (2) those who had so-called minimal brain dysfunction, i.e. neurological soft signs, which is often regarded as temporary maturational lag, and (3) a group in which the neurological examination had been negative. The first group, called B.D. (brain-damage) had 64 subjects, the M.B.D. (minimal brain-damage) group had 82, and the group of the learning-disabled without neurological impairment had 57 subjects.

According to some definitions the first two groups do not fit the generally accepted description of learning disabilities. There are some youngsters with relatively low I.Q.s, and some with physical handicaps. We therefore analyzed our data twice, once using the original referral groups, and once excluding those who did not meet the generally accepted definition of learning disabilities.

The average age of the group was 19 years and the mean original IQ's were 86, 95, and 100 for the three groups of learning-disabled children. For the reduced sample mean IQ's of 99.5, 100.5, and 107.5 were found. There were approximately 2½ times as many boys as girls. The parents came from all parts of society, judging by the occupational and educational level of the parents. Eighteen of these students had parents other than their natural ones and 23% of the learning-disabled children had experienced a divorce in the family (as compared with only 10% for the controls). The average family size was approximately four. The learning-disabled child was typically the second or third child in the family, not the oldest as is often claimed in the literature.

In an analysis of the "handedness variable," we found that there were more predominantly left-handed and bilateral subjects in the brain-damaged and minimally brain-damaged groups, as compared with the learning-disabled and control groups. However, when we eliminated those who had serious neurological impairment and low I.Q., the difference in handedness was no longer significant.

Generally speaking, factual information from the parent interview agreed very well with corresponding data from the student interview. On questions which called for an opinion, however, there were substantial differences. Parents reported that the student was much less happy than he thought himself to be. Students reported a degree of personal satisfaction which was far in excess of what the parents reported. On the other hand, when it came to remembering early events, (for example, whether behaviour problems had been present before initial contact or before the students were 8 to 12 years of age), the students did not think they had had many behaviour problems, while parents indicated that they had had quite a number. Students admitted to far more drug and alcohol use than the parents had reported.

With respect to reaching grade 12, almost 80% of the control group did, but a large proportion of the learning-disabled groups failed to achieve this level. The percentage reaching grade 12 was: group BD, about 15%, group MBD, 25%, group LD, approximately 33%; it seems, therefore, that the drop-out rate increases with the degree of neurological impairment.

Similarly, the percentages of children in the three groups who attended special programmes show higher values in the more impaired groups (group BD, 43%, group MBD, 32%, and group LD, 24%). The percentages reporting attendance at college or university showed a similar trend.

Figure 1 summarizes reports on the number of students who were expelled or suspended during their school years.

The bar marked "S" shows what the students reported, while bar "P" shows what the parents said. The disagreement is obvious. Almost 30 of the students in the BD group said that they had been suspended or expelled at least once. Again, the incidence is clearly related to the degree of neurological impairment. It might be expected that a student identified as brain-damaged would be relatively protected, and would receive a little more tolerance from the school system. Apparently that is not so. We should also note that the parents' report and the students' reports on suspension differ. This may reflect a protective attitude by the parents or they may have failed to remember a short suspension.

In inquiring about behaviour problems before initial referral, we had included as alternatives not only hyperactivity and discipline problems but such problems as severe anxiety and depression. Almost 20 of the control subjects reported problems; evidently problem behaviour is not as unique to the handicapped groups or the learning-disabled groups as might have been anticipated.

When we look at data on behaviour problems after the referral date, we find that many of the returnees viewed themselves as having had a problem primarily during the teenage years. The number goes up significantly in the follow-up groups but stays relatively stable for the control group. Again, group differences follow very clearly the pattern of increased neurological impairment.

With respect to delinquency, we asked for any type of problem that might have brought the student to the attention of the police.

On the whole, 50% or more of all four groups came to the attention of the police for various reasons. There was one substantial difference, one that concerned driving offenses. The learning-disabled and the control groups have large numbers of driving offenses. On ascertaining the penalties for the first offense, responses ranged from no charge and acquittal, all the way to imprisonment.

Again, all four groups show a similar number (about 23%) but the control group and the learning-disabled group without neurological impairment tend to show a relatively high frequency, particularly with respect to deprivation of privileges.

It is important to examine the severity of the penalties and to take into account subsequent offenses. Although in all groups the proportions of those committing offenses and those penalised are very similar, repeated offenses and serious offenses are less common in the control group. Similarly more serious penalties were incurred by the LD group without neurological dysfunction. However, these differences are not statistically significant and do not suggest the reported link between learning disabilities and delinquency (Spreen, 1981).

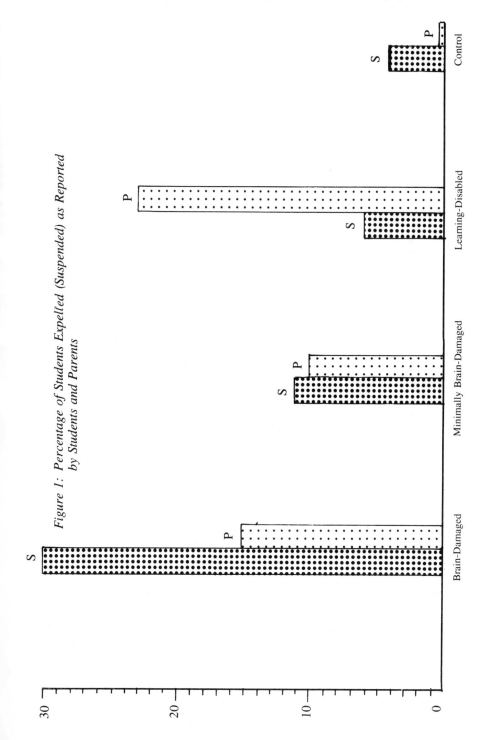

Figure 1: Percentage of Students Expelled (Suspended) as Reported by Students and Parents

In looking at the job and employment data for a reduced number of subjects (N=234), which excludes those with handicaps and low IQ's, there was a significant difference between the brain-damaged group and the learning-disabled groups. Employment was relatively low in the control group, probably because many of the controls were continuing school and did not have a job at the time of the interview.

The age when the first job was started was lower in the control group. They reported a mean age of 12.6, (the mean for parents' reported age was 13.2); whereas the other three groups clearly have started jobs at a later age (range 14.1−16.0). Very few of the controls (less than 4) reported that they had had difficulties in finding a job but 53 of the brain-damaged group reported difficulties of this kind. Obviously they were at a serious disadvantage.

In examining the present monthly income from all sources, the first two neurologically impaired groups differ from the learning-disabled group in being less successful. The control group does not make as high an average income as group 3 (learning-disabled), probably because they still hold only part-time and summer jobs. They tend to enter their vocation later than do the learning disabled group.

The evaluation of emotional adjustment is based on results from the Bell Inventory mentioned above. There were marked sex differences in all groups; emotional adjustment scores were lower for the female than for the male subjects. We often tend to say that having learning problems in school may not be all that serious for a girl. These data tend to contradict that statement (Peter and Spreen, 1979).

There is also a sex difference in regard to social adjustment. The difference exists also for the control group but it is much more striking for the three learning-disabled groups.

Social adjustment seems to be related to the degree of learning disability and to the degree of neurological impairment. The number of phone calls received per month was studied; the sex difference is not marked. This criterion seems to be significantly related to neurological impairment because the numbers increase steadily with decreased impairment, the number being highest in the control group.

Finally, we obtained information on the number of people who view him/her as "different." At the close of the interview, when we had established very good rapport with our subjects, we often went into more personal matters; the questions, however, were all phrased in a standard fashion. In this case, we asked, "Who sees you as different?" and then simply counted the number of people mentioned. By quantifying the replies, we found significant differences among the four groups. We also found a large difference again between what the student reported and what the parents said.

The mean student report was 1.4 persons for the first two groups and 0.7 for the third, which almost equalled the mean of 0.8 in the control group. Parents, however, reported very different figures. The parents felt that more people viewed the child as "different." Their reports were clearly related to the degree of handicap, particularly in the group with neurological impairment. For the control group, the parent-student differences were reversed. In that case the parents felt that nobody viewed them as different.

These findings are obviously related to parental attitudes. Even though their child is now 19, 20, 21 or 25 years old, they may still view him as somebody who is different from other people. Their son or daughter may have changed his/her perceptions. I think these data have implications concerning what we can tell parents. Another hypothesis is that brain-damaged children are not as aware of others' reactions to them as are their parents.

Obviously, we could analyze our data from a different viewpoint; we could now go back to look at the test results at the time when these students were between 8 and 12 years old and see if we could have predicted what happened to them later on. This would have been somewhat similar to what Dr. Satz was doing with his group in some of his earlier studies. This kind of prediction can be one of the more fascinating products of the study. Our preliminary analysis shows that only a few of our single tests have very high predictive value; but, in combination, they constitute a fairly good set of predictors, accounting for about 50% of the variance.

Our study currently continues with a second recall of all our former clients, who are now 25 years old on average. At this time, each returnee is re-examined neurologically, an update interview covering the last 6 years is given and a battery of psychological tests is administered. This phase of the study addresses not only the continuing success or failure in adjustment during early adulthood, but also examines the objectively tested abilities; moreover, the neurological examination will address the important question, namely, which neurological "signs" are persistent and which signs tend to disappear with age.

References

Peter, Barbara M. and Spreen Otfried, "Behaviour Rating and Personal Adjustment Scales of Neurologically and Learning Handicapped Children During Adolescence and Early Adulthood: Results of a Follow-up Study, *"J. Clinical Neuropsychology*, 1(1): 75−92, 1979.
Spreen, O., "The Relationship between Learning Disability, Neurological Impairment, and Delinquency," *J. Nervous and Mental Disease*, 169(12): 791−9, 1981.

10

Emotionally Disturbed Children and Adolescents and Their Learning Disorders

BRIAN J. McCONVILLE, M.B., Ch.B., F.R.C.P. (C)

AND

JAMES COTÉ, B.A. (HONS.)

Abstract

Significant information has been gained from a multidisciplinary approach to educational remediation and social emotional adjustment on a group of severely emotionally disturbed children and adolescents in a psychiatric inpatient and day care facility in Kingston, Ontario.

Three questions are posed: (1) Does this population show characteristics generally described for learning disordered children in other school settings? (2) Is remediation of their learning disorders possible? (3) How do emotional, familial and learning factors interact?

The treatment and follow-up results indicate that approximately 70 percent of these severely emotionally disturbed young people had learning problems which result in poor school performance, as compared to 10 to 15 percent in normal school population. The data obtained show that satisfactory remediation was possible using the multidisciplinary approach. Follow-up studies show that significant improvement in learning capacity and behavioural adjustment was maintained 6 months after discharge. However, such factors as family turmoil, psychopathology, hyperactivity and developmental delays have negative effects on overall outcome.

L'auteur analyse les résultats d'un effort pluridisciplinaire de correction pédagogique et d'adaptation sociale et émotionnelle tenté en milieu hospitalier psychiatrique à Kingston, en Ontario, auprès d'un groupe d'enfants et d'adolescents gravement perturbés sur le plan affectif.

Il se pose trois questions: 1) Est-ce que cette population présente les mêmes caractéristiques générales que les enfants manifestant des troubles d'apprentissage dans d'autres milieux scolaires? 2) Est-il possible de corriger leurs troubles d'apprentissage? 3) Comment les facteurs affectifs se rapportant à la famille et à l'apprentissage agissent-ils les uns sur les autres?

Les observations ultérieures révèlent que environ 70% de ces jeunes souffrant de perturbations affectives graves éprouvent des difficultés d'apprentissage qui entraînent un rendement scolaire médiocre, par comparaison avec 10 à 15% dans la population normale des écoles. Les données ont indiqué qu'on pouvait arriver à un redressement satisfaisant.

INTRODUCTION

Recent studies[1] have pointed out persistent deleterious effects for learning disorders and their associated behavioral difficulties. These effects continue into adolescence and affect not only overall learning, but also self-esteem and social skills. The Kauai[2] study showed the complex interaction of biological, family and sociological factors; the attitudes of parents and other child caretakers were shown to have pervasive affects.

Clinical multidisciplinary approaches are necessary, and in the Beechgrove Regional Children's Centre all disciplines are involved in the diagnosis and remediation of learning and behaviour disorders in children. A school is part of the Centre, and takes children from pre-kindergarten to grade 13; about half the pupils are adolescents.

We have previously reported[3] that learning difficulties were the most frequent presenting symptom in a psychiatric inpatient group of children. The present study reports on another such group, focusing on the association between learning, behavioural, organic and familial-social factors.

The particular questions adressed are:

1. Does this group of severely disturbed children and adolescents show the characteristics generally described for learning-disordered children in other school settings?
2. Is remediation of their learning disorders possible?
3. How do the emotional, familial and learning factors interact?*

The factors presented are:

1. A general description of the sample in terms of age, sex, length of stay, intelligence, behavioural and learning disorders, as well as neurologic abnormalities and use of medication.
2. The changes in learning disorders in this sample between admission and discharge.
3. The relationship between such antecedent variables as hyperactivity, fine and gross motor functions, laterality, pregnancy and birth problems, with subsequent learning and behaviour disorders.
4. The effect of psychiatric disorders, intelligence and family turmoil on the degree of remediation possible in learning disorders.
5. An assessment of follow-up data.

---

* Details as to methodology are available from the authors.

RESULTS

1. *General Characteristics of the Sample:*

There were 19 adolescents and 21 children in the group studied with more boys in the child group and more girls in the adolescent group. The day care and inpatient children were in treatment for a mean of 6.6 months, with a mean of 4.0 months for adolescents. The range of intelligence in the sample was between 53 and 120 with a full-scale WISC mean of 90 (Mean Performance I.Q. 93, S.D. 14; Mean Verbal I.Q., 89, S.D. 11.6).

2. *Neurological Abnormalities:*

Minor abnormalities, such as problems in laterality, fine motor and balance problems were found in 28 (70%) with moderate abnormalities, such as the full hyperkinetic syndrome. Fully established developmental delays and speech problems requiring remediation were found in 25 (63%). Major neurological abnormalities, such as aphasia and post-traumatic hemiparesis were found in 5 (13%).

3. *Use of Psychopharmacologic Agents:*

Methylphenidate was used in 15 (38%), all in children under 12. Major tranquillizers were used in 15 (38%), all in children over age 12. Anticonvulsants were used in 3 (8%), and other agents in 8 (20%) of the subjects.

4. *Learning and Behavioural Symptom Change:*

Prime symptoms in both behavioural and learning problems were chosen. For behaviour problems, we used the Achenbach[4] factors from the child behaviour profile of social skills. Social maturity, depressed-sad, aggressive-delinquent, hyperactive, anxious-phobic, schizoid, psychotic and overall symptoms were the scales selected. The Rutter (ICD-9)[5] classification indicated clinical psychiatric diagnoses. The learning symptoms selected, using the Ross classification employed by Sattler,[6] were those of hyperactivity, attention span, visual perception, auditory perception, planning ability, language function, fine motor coordination, gross motor coordination and higher thought processes. All differences quoted are beyond the .025 level of significance.

Most learning problems showed satisfactory change from time of admission to time of discharge. The overall grade improvements for reading, spelling, and arithmetic ranged from 0.5 to 1 year grade change for the period of intensive treatment, and the changes in perceptual and other "basic" learning processes are as shown in Table I. Children had a significantly greater number of identified learning problems than did adolescents, but also improved more, both in learning and behaviour.

TABLE I

Changes in Perceptual and Basic Learning Processes From Admission to Discharge as Reported by Teachers: Means, t-values, and Significance Levels

	ADMISSION	DISCHARGE	t-VALUE	SIGNIFICANCE LEVEL
1. Impulsivity	1.2	.77	4.0	.001
2. Attention span	1.3	.85	3.45	.001
3. Visual perception	.33	.28	1.43	ns
4. Auditory perception	.41	.23	1.86	.07
5. Planning ability	1.0	.67	2.97	.005
6. Language functions	.69	.62	1.36	ns
7. Fine motor coordination	.74	.62	2.36	.023
8. Gross motor coordination	.51	.36	2.63	.012
9. Higher thought processes	.67	.59	1.36	ns

5. *Associations Between Prime Symptoms and Paranatal Problems, Laterality, Visual-Motor Functions, and Developmental Hyperactivity:*

Those with more *pregnancy and birth complications* had more auditory-perceptual problems and greater hyperactivity, but also showed satisfactory behavioural and learning improvement.

Compared to those who were right dominant, those with *left dominance* averaged lower in verbal I.Q., arithmetic and global improvement, and showed more visual-motor integration problems. Those with *mixed dominance* also had more visual-motor integration problems and less global improvement.

Those who had more *visual-motor integration* problems did poorly in learning and behaviour, but those who had more *gross motor* problems showed satisfactory improvement, particularly in behaviour. Those with an early history of *developmental hyperactivity* had more learning and behavioural problems.

6. *Effect of Psychiatric Disorder, Intelligence and Family Turmoil on Learning:*

The more severe *psychiatric disorders*, such as psychosis or severe behaviour disorders, did significantly worse with treatment, both in terms of the learning variables, and also the behavioural disorders found in these children and adolescents. No clear differences in outcome were found between children and adolescents.

Those who had more *aggressive-delinquent behaviour* problems did worse in learning. (In contrast those with a larger number of behaviour problems on admission did better in both learning and behaviour. This seeming paradox is a

replication of an earlier finding; children presenting rather marked overt behavioural difficulties showed considerable later improvement, perhaps because of
the higher expressivity of early presenting symptoms, before antisocial rage factors have developed).

There was no significant association between *intelligence* and global ratings
by teachers on learning or behaviour change, although those with higher verbal
intelligence tended to do better in learning.

Those who showed the most variance in sub-test scores on the WISC showed
the most improvement in learning, and those with lower Wide Range Achievement Test scores showed less improvement in learning and behaviour; this was
true for spelling, word recognition and arithmetic.

Finally, those who had more family turmoil also learned less, and showed less
behaviour improvement at time of discharge.

7. Follow-up Results:

At follow-up generally satisfactory improvement was reported by the liaison
teacher in terms of global learning and global behaviour after six months re-
establishment at a regular school. The judgements were made in consultation
with the regular school teacher. Follow-up scores on learning correlated with
increased planning ability and higher thought function ability at discharge.
Improved behaviour at discharge was also associated with greater learning capacity at follow-up. More family turmoil and structural disorganization, as well as
more peer problems, correlated with less improvement at follow-up, both in
learning and behaviour.

Overall, those with a greater number of symptoms and greater symptom
severity showed less sustained improvement in learning. Finally, those with
higher Blishen[7] socio-economic status showed greater improvement on follow-
up, in both learning and behaviour.

DISCUSSION:

In terms of the particular questions addressed, this group of severely disturbed
children and adolescents show learning problems similar to other learning disordered groups. However, the prevalence of poor school performance symptoms in
this study and in our previous study (incidence of 70% and 68% respectively) is
much higher than in the 10−15% of learning disorders for the general population. Since the types of learning disorders were selected from a standard list, it is
not possible to say whether any new or unusual learning problems existed.

The study also indicates that it is possible to take severe disturbances of learning and behaviour in childhood and adolescence and show satisfactory remedia-

tion in a variety of areas, in a manner similar to results found for less disturbed groups.

Family turmoil and psychopathology can be predictive of poor success in this group and it also seems that earlier perinatal problems, hyperactivity, developmental delays in basic learning processes and psychiatric disorders tended to have negative effects on overall outcome. However, no clear pattern can be inferred from this small study.

"Pure" learning disabilities do not make up a large proportion of inpatient and day care practice in psychiatric settings. Although it is possible to focus particularly on children who have only identified "special learning" problems, there are also intrapsychic, familial, medical and other factors to be considered.

A directed multidisciplinary approach for a variety of learning and behaviour disorders, along with intensive remediation, seems to offer the best hope for the very large number of children who have both learning and behaviour difficulties. However, the number of multidisciplinary facilities for children with emotional and learning disorders is quite small. If it is not possible to establish such facilities, then a reasonable alternative is to put together a strong, multidisciplinary special education group which will then be available to the schools for planning and evaluating complex interventions for children and adolescents with learning and behaviour disorders.

References

1. Weiss, G., Minde, K., Werry, J.S., Douglas, V. and Nameth, E. Studies on the Hyperactive Child VII. Five Year Follow-up. *Arch. Gen. Psychiatry*. 24, 409−414, 1971.
2. Werner, E., and Smith, R.S. An epidemiologic perspective on some antecedents and consequences of childhood mental health problems and learning disabilities: A report from the Kauai longitudinal study. *J. Amer. Acad. Child Psychiatry*. 18 (2) 292−306, 1979.
3. McConville, B.J., and Purohit, A. Classifying Confusion: A study of inpatient treatment in a multi-disciplinary Children's Centre. *Amer. J. Orthopsychiat*. 43 (3) 411−417, 1973.
4. Achenbach, T.M. The child behaviour profile: In ages 6−11. *J. Cons. and Clin. Psychol*. 46 (3), 478−488, 1978.
5. Rutter, M.L., Shaffer, D., and Sturge, C. *A Guide to a Multiaxial Classification Scheme for Psychiatric Disorders in Childhood and Adolescence*. Institute of Psychiatry. London, 1976.

6. Sattler, J.M. *Assessment of Children's Intelligence*. Philadelphia, Saunders. pp. 332–333, 1974.
7. Blishen, B. A revised socio-economic index for occupations in Canada. *Can. Rev. Soc. Anthrop*. 13 (1) 1976.

11

Early Identification of Learning Disorders: Kindergarten to Grade 7

LINDA EAVES, Ph.D.

Abstract

In 1972, the Department of Paediatrics, University of British Columbia, began a study in Vancouver, attempting to identify early, children who appeared likely to have difficulties in school. In this study, a Modified Predictive Index (MPI) based on the de Hirsch model was used to identify kindergarten children at risk.

These same children were studied 3 years later in grade 3, and 4 years after that in grade 7. The data reveal a remarkable persistence of learning difficulties identified at kindergarten, regardless of the school's attempts to provide remedial assistance. Thus, while good prediction of problems now appears possible, new methods of intervention will be required before early identification can serve a useful purpose.

L'auteur rapporte une étude, commencée en 1972 à Vancouver en Colombie-Britannique, qui visait à l'identification, dès les premières années, des enfants susceptibles d'éprouver des difficultés à l'école. Dans cette recherche on a utilisé un test appelé "Modified Predictive Index (MPI)*, basé sur le modèle de de Hirsch, pour identifier les enfants des classes maternelles représentant un risque.

Les mêmes enfants ont été examinés, trois ans plus tard, en troisième année et, à nouveau, quatre ans plus tard, en septième année. Les résultats témoignent de la persistance remarquable des difficultés d'apprentissage décelées en classe maternelle, en dépit des efforts tentés à l'école pour y remédier. Par conséquent, même si on semble maintenant en mesure de prévoir les difficultés, il faudra trouver de nouvelles méthodes d'intervention avant que l'identification précoce puisse servir à quelque chose.

* On pourrait traduire par "Index prédictif modifié".

While interest in the field of learning disabilities is enormous and growing, the number of reports on the natural life-history of learning-disabled children is very small. This may change as others find themselves in the same position as we did. As part of a wave of researchers who published studies on the early identification of learning disabilities five to ten years ago, I and my colleagues in The Department of Paediatrics at the University of British Columbia now find that what was originally a three year study of learning-disabled children has turned into a seven year one. This expansion of our scope demands an updated report, a demand that this paper will set out to meet.

We began this study in 1972 in an effort to identify early, children who appeared likely to have difficulty in school. We first used the term minimal brain dysfunction (MBD) to describe children with certain difficulties and later shifted to the more general term "learning disabilities" (LD). The type of child we are talking about is described as having MBD by neurologists, as hyperkinetic or dyslexic by pediatricians and psychiatrists, as learning-disabled or perceptually handicapped by educators, as "all of the above" by psychologists, and simply as "difficult" by parents. These children, who comprise 5-15 percent of any school population, have normal intelligence, but with a pattern of unevenness in areas measured by the WISC, or with a verbal/performance discrepancy. They may be overactive, distractable, impulsive, and/or may have difficulty in concentrating, a short attention span, poor gross or fine motor skills, a lag in visual perceptual areas and difficulties in school learning even when instruction is adequate.

At the beginning of the study we felt we could not correctly call a child "learning-disabled" in kindergarten, since explicit in the definition of LD is the notion of school failure, at least 1-2 years behind grade level in academic (usually reading) achievement. Therefore, the term MBD implied being "at risk" for LD, later in school. To further complicate matters, we found a number of children who showed the characteristic syndrome of MBD only to a limited extent, and we called them "immature", assuming that they were showing a developmental immaturity which would later be outgrown.

The children we studied intensively were from a larger sample of more than 2000 K children who were screened with a modified version of the de Hirsch Predictive Index. De Hirsch and her colleagues in 1966 reported a simple, 20 minute screening test which, given in K, effectively identified 76−80 percent of the poor readers at the end of Grade 2. We modified the Predictive Index to include the draw-a-person test and name-printing and called it the Modified Predictive Index or MPI. It included tests of language, learning ability and memory, perceptual motor development, as well as the Wepman Auditory Discrimination Test.

Children scoring *3 or lower* on the MPI were designated as the "at-risk group". From the 316 "at-risk" children, we selected 74 by statified random sampling—to represent all social classes and with the sex ratio the same as in the total sample. Only children who spoke English before entering school were included. Thirty-one children who passed the MPI (scored 4 or higher) were picked as controls, selected in such a way as to make sure that they came from the same school as at least one of the at-risk children. In this way we attempted to control for both social class and teacher and school variations.

These 106 children were then observed between ages 6 and 6½ for intensive neurological and psychological examinations. These examinations led to diagnoses of 30 normal children, 33 MBD, 30 immature, 3 retarded and 5 emotionally disturbed.

Follow-up data on the children were obtained on two occasions: at the end of Grade 3 when 76 percent (81 children) were located; and four years later, at the end of Grade 7, when 69 children (65 percent of the sample) were located. The data consist of achievement test scores, a 36-item teacher's checklist on behaviour and school achievement and also, in Grade 7, a 44-item parent checklist in which parents described their child's behaviour, activities and any problems.

PREDICTIVE VALUE OF THE SCREENING TEST TO GRADE 3

A passing score on the MPI given in K predicted correctly for 76 percent (62 of 81) of the sample whether they would be passing or failing readers at the end of Grade 3. For the reading failures alone, 97 percent, or 38 of 39, had been identified as "at risk" in K, but almost one-third (17 of 55) of those diagnosed as "at risk" in K became passing readers. In other words, almost all Grade 3 reading failures were considered to be at-risk in K, but many at-risk children did improve by Grade 3 to become passing readers.

It had been expected that most of the improvement would be in the group classified as immature, because implicit in this classification was the assumption that they would "outgrow" their immaturity, but this prediction was only partially confirmed. In the MBD group only 24 percent (6 of 25) were passing readers, of the immatures almost 40 percent (10 of 26), while in the normal group 92% (23 out of 25) were passes.

THE NORMAL CHILDREN IN GRADE 3

Those diagnosed as normal at the beginning of Grade 1 progressed well in school and showed few problems. Eight children or 31 percent received some form of learning assistance, but only two had such help for more than one year. In this sample, then, all passed the K screening test; all had been considered normal on the psychological and neurological examinations; only one was reading below grade level and none had been held back in school.

THE IMMATURE CHILDREN IN GRADE 3

Most of the children in this group were performing below the Grade 3 level, but above the achievement level of the MBD's. The average reading comprehension score was Grade 3.25, compared with Grade 2.4 for the MBD's and Grade 4.7 for the normals. Almost 60 percent were reading at or below Grade 2.6 level and 10 of 26 (38 percent) had repeated at least one grade.

In all the areas we investigated those initially classified as immature were found to be performing at a level between the two other groups. Their mean IQ score was 100 compared with 113 for the normals and 94 for the MBD's. The number of teacher complaints per child was 8 for the immatures, 11.5 for the MBD's and only 2 for the normals. Three children were considered management problems in this group, while the number for normal children was 1, and for the MBD's, 7.

The immature group as a whole did not improve as much as we had expected. 16 of the 26 children were passing into Grade 4, but only 2 of these were having no difficulty in school.

THE MBD'S IN GRADE 3

This group of children was performing well below the two other groups. Almost three-quarters were reading below the Grade 2.6 level. Not surprisingly, 68 percent had either failed (13 of 25) or were in a special class (4 of 25). The teachers' estimates of the children's abilities in mathematics, reading, spelling and printing placed them below the normals and immatures, with more than half of them below the Grade 3 level in all areas. They also showed more unevenness in their abilities than did the normal children.

It was clear that the MBD children had received more extra help through learning assistance centres, special classes, counselling, etc., than had the other groups. Only 2 of these children had not received any extra help and both of them were reading above the Grade 4 level. One child scored well above average on all measures and was reading at the grade 7 level, but his severe gross motor problems had led to inclusion in this group. Only 5 children of this MBD group evidenced learning disabilities. Two of them, however, were repeating Grade 3 and had shown the classic syndrome of short attention span, hyperactivity, distractability, low frustration tolerance and emotional liability; yet they were reading at the high Grade 4 level.

RESULTS TO GRADE 7

Now that the children are turning 13, we find similar patterns as in the initial evaluation of the results. Since we are still in the process of collecting data, preliminary information is available on only 54 children, or about three-quarters of those we expect to follow up.

In the normal group of 23, 20 had made good progress in school. One boy had repeated Grade 6 and had shown mild behaviour problems, but his school work was average. Another had shown disturbed behaviour which was evident in a mild form in Grade 1, but his school work is above average. One boy is at the bottom of his class, showing a mild learning problem, but was 1 year behind in Grade 3. None of the normals have fallen behind since Grade 3.

In the immature group of 14 children, 4 had improved by Grade 3 to become average students and continued to make good progress to Grade 7. The 9 who still had school or behaviour problems were significantly behind by Grade 3 and continued to have difficulty. Two repeated a grade, and one was in a remedial class.

The group diagnosed as MBD in Grade 1 fared least well. Only 2 of 17 children had no difficulty either at school or at home. Over half have repeated a grade or are in a special class. They have shown a great variety of problems including problems with coordination, peer relations, attention span and self-confidence, as well as with academic subjects. Four children were doing well academically by Grade 3 (including the boy with reading scores at the Grade 7 level) and they continue to do so but have had difficulty getting along with others or have markedly poor coordination, which has interfered with sports and thus affected peer relationships.

One child was felt to have serious emotional problems as well as potential learning problems in Grade 1. These persist today. He is one year behind in school and his teacher feels that he should be placed in a special class in high school.

Twenty-seven children in the early grades had been described as showing two or more of the following cluster of behaviours: short attention span, overactivity, distractibility, low frustration tolerance or impulsiveness. This was 90 percent of the at-risk group (the MBD's and immatures combined). By Grade 7, only 7 of these children appear to have "outgrown" these traits. The remaining 74 percent, or 20 children, were still restless, distractable, or had a short attention span. In addition, the parents often describe them as tense and fidgety and as having difficulty going to sleep or simply as "difficult to live with."

Learning problems are not necessarily associated with this behaviour cluster. About a quarter of those who are still overactive have no learning problems, while half of those who appear to have outgrown the behaviour have no learning problems.

Only 5 children in the at-risk group were felt to have serious coordination problems at ages 6−8; none of these have outgrown these problems by age 13.

Another seven children (or 22 percent of the at-risk group) had difficulty in peer relations and were described as having a poor social sense and as being unable to recognize nonverbal communications. These tended to be teased and/or rejected by their classmates. None have improved by Grade 7. Only three of these also have learning problems.

In short, most of the at-risk children have not outgrown their difficulties. The most interesting finding is that in this group those who have caught up (which is only 19 percent, or 6 out of 31 children), had done so by Grade 3 and there are no children who show major improvements after that. It appears then from this sample that a few children will outgrow problems seen in Grade 1, but by Grade 3 achievement and behaviour patterns are set and little change occurs in the next 4 years. The next question is, of course, "Why do some improve?" and the answer to that awaits further analysis.

What can we conclude from this? First, it is possible from a relatively simple paper and pencil test given at the end of K to predict for more than 75 percent of the children whether they will be passing or failing readers by the end of Grade 3. Moreover, there was little change in the children's achievement patterns from Grade 3 to Grade 7. Prediction from the kindergarten test is much better for children who pass the test than for those who fail. Of the 15 percent of our sample who were identified as at-risk in K, half improved by Grade 3 to become passing readers.

When the children were examined individually and in detail, further distinctions based on the severity of their disorders were made. While some might prefer different labels than the ones we used (immature and MBD), it is clear that these at-risk children are clinically identifiable. However, after the children have been some years in school, these diagnoses do not distinguish very well among them. Those diagnosed immature are performing better than the MBD's, but both groups are far below the normal children. Perhaps, then, the distinction is artificial and we are dealing with a continuum. Only 6 of the at-risk children could be considered problem-free by Grade 7, so 80 percent of those identified in Grade 1 are still having difficulties six years later. The persistence of both behaviour and learning problems is remarkable. No children have "caught up" academically after Grade 3 and less than a quarter of those with behaviour problems have outgrown them.

These children have not gone unidentified in their schools. They have received, in varying degrees, all that the schools had to offer in the way of learning assistance, modified programmes, special classes, etc. Even with this expenditure of effort, most are still far behind their normal classmates and in some cases present substantial problems in classroom management.

For this sample any conclusions regarding the current treatment of the learning-disabled can only be pessimistic. Possibly not enough is known about the specific disorders, the ideal treatment for each, and the best child-teacher or child-method match. Thus, the treatment is haphazard and often discontinuous and inappropriate. Even more alarming is the possibility that the children themselves may not be capable of ever functioning in an average way in the present school system, regardless of treatment, and they will need learning assistance for their entire school careers. Those with motor or peer problems are, of course, even more difficult to help.

Years ago, we optimistically predicted that early identification of at-risk children would allow for early intervention and thus prevent many problems. Now we see that learning and behaviour problems in the early grades are persistent. The improvement that has occurred in some children seems to be independent of specific treatment and is probably due to maturation or some complex interaction of child, parents and school.

The early identification is not difficult. However, matching the treatment to disorder, defining goals for the learning-disabled, improving communication between clinicians and school, and finding the best time for intervention are all topics that must be examined by research if these children are to be helped more adequately.

Reference

de Hirsch, K., Jansky, J., and Langford, W.S. *Predicting Reading Failure*. New York Harper and Row, 1966.

12

Prevention of Disabilities:
Some Neurological Aspects of Learning Disorders

J. KEITH BROWN, M.B., F.R.C.P., D.C.H

Abstract

In this paper the author discusses the growth of the nervous system and the factors influencing this. He points out that the brain develops during the whole school period and that the brain can be regarded as a learning organ. Many factors including sex, asymmetry, dominance, genetic influences, environment, and brain damage may all affect the growth of the neurological system which results in slowing up of one or more areas of brain function. There need not be anything specific in how this shows in the child to allow one to say which factors are most important in each particular case. It is noted that many of these children have major schooling and behavioural problems.

It has been estimated that as many as 15% of all school children show some type of learning disorder. If this estimate is true, there could be 30,000 children with some form of schooling difficulty in a town of 200,000. The high incidence of learning disorders has given rise to a veritable learning industry. As with many other aspects of paediatrics, therapies and systems of management have abounded—often with no attempt being made at any scientific form of evaluation. Unfortunately, the medical aspects have been completely overshadowed by the concept of hyperkinesis and so-called minimal brain damage and by its treatment with sympathomimetic amines such as methylphenidate. The uncharitable view may be justified that the large numbers of children with learning disorders have provided a welcome guaranteed practice for some private paediatricians. There is no doubt that minimal brain damage does exist, possibly with an incidence in the region of 2−3/1,000 children, and that some of these children are helped by medication. In this article we shall briefly consider some of the other factors which may account for the problems in the other 14% of children with learning disorders.

We can consider the problem of learning disorder as arising from three main sources:—the parent, the teacher and the child. The parents' own education, interest in education (e.g. Parents' Association), their pre-school teaching of colours, numbers, etc., are obviously important. However, language is the basis of reading and writing skills; and the vocabulary and grammatical sophistication of the child will depend upon the language to which the child is exposed in the home, both in quantity and quality (open or restricted sentence construction). The parents' attitude toward reading bedtime stories to their children is culturally determined and so is the presence of books in the home and a persisting interest in reading. A stable home from the emotional point of view is also essential for motivation in school work. Anxiety is a potent cause of a disrupted attention span. The severely maladjusted child from the disrupted home is unlikely to see much point in education.

That there are bad teachers, just as there are bad doctors and bad lawyers, no one doubts; and colleagues know good and bad teachers in their own schools. A teacher's personal problems may make her more intolerant and affect her teaching. The organization of the classroom, (whether open or closed), the noise level and the use of new, often untried, "methods" have often been equated in the lay mind with causes of schooling difficulty. There is in fact little evidence that a qualified young teacher using a new teaching method in an open plan classroom has any more children with learning disorders than an old maid with a large stick in an old-fashioned and deadly quiet classroom, provided both are interested in their jobs and able to promote a sense of security in the children. It is the enthusiasm and interest of the teacher, rather than her "method" or classroom organization, which will motivate the children. Curriculum, however, must not be ignored. There are large regional differences in the United Kingdom relating to emphasis placed upon reading, arithmetic and spatial skills. Good teaching will result in more children doing well in exams and getting university scholarships. Good teaching also appears effective in developing certain character traits, as we see in the number of senior politicians, judges and bishops who come from a very restricted educational sector in the U.K. If a child fails to learn, it is easy to blame the teacher; yet, even with additional individual help by a remedial teacher, this child's progress may be very slow. We can alternatively blame the parents' child-rearing practices or the family dynamics.

NEUROPHYSIOLOGY OF LEARNING

Since this paper is chiefly related to the neurology of learning disorders, only brief mention will be made of a few other areas such as motivation, attention, learning strategies and codes (Luria 1973). Thought can be defined as the content of consciousness and anything which interferes with the level of alertness, such as drugs or insufficient sleep will make the child appear inattentive. Attention or concentration is associated with, but is not the same as, the level of arousal; it is the ability to "gate" significant from insignificant sensory inputs coming to the brain. The ability to switch off unwanted stimuli is thought possibly to be a function of the intralaminar thalamic nuclei, and damage to this area has been considered a cause of increased distractability and poor concentration, with resultant hyperactive behaviour. Since a child will not pay attention to incoming signals which are meaningless, the mentally handicapped child appears to pay no attention to what is said (does not listen rather than does not hear); his play lacks imagination, and he may wander around in an aimless manner. Since the child with specific learning difficulties finds certain lessons meaningless mumbo-jumbo, he will not pay attention to them. His failure of concentration is not the cause, but the effect, of his learning difficulty. The child who is anxious, maybe about events at home, will also appear more distractible.

Measurement of concentration span in children reported by teachers as inattentive often shows that these same children will concentrate for long periods on the most boring tasks as long as they are succeeding. Chronic failure, and the anxiety it produces, may also disrupt attention. Although a few brain-damaged children certainly have a short concentration span and this can be markedly disrupted by drugs (such as Phenobarbitone or Clonazepam), and although decrease in levels of arousal (due to metabolic diseases or impaired consciousness due to drugs) may also impair concentration, these are not common causes of learning difficulty, even in epileptic children.

Motivation to learn has already been mentioned in considering the parent and teacher role. This is a large and important area but will not be considered further in this brief review.

There are several ways in which behaviours can appear and although we often say that the child learned to walk or eat, this may not be strictly true. Pure reflex behaviours are seen in the rooting, sucking, swallowing reflexes and respiratory control we call feeding behaviour. The walking, stepping, crawling and Bauer reflexes are part of coordinated swimming which is necessary *in utero* in order for the infant to assume the vertex position for delivery, i.e. a form of human hatching behaviour. The primitive postural reflexes such as A.T.N.R. have to be inhibited before sitting, crawling and walking can appear. This depends upon neurological maturation and, although we certainly learn through walking, we do not learn to walk in the sense of having to practice it. We are only now beginning to realize, e.g., from studies of identical twins reared from early life in separate environments, how even very complex behaviour patterns can be genetically imprinted in the developing brain and do not depend solely upon environmental experience. As a new ability develops there is often a behavioural pattern which develops with it to ensure its usage (prior to the child's being able to voluntarily select its usage in the light of experience). We see this with forced visual pursuit, forced grasping, forced utterances and forced exploration which occur when visual fixation and following, development of hand function, voluntary control of voice, or walking, respectively develop. The brain is therefore to some extent pre-programmed.

The next level of "learning" is that of a simple memory response when the same sound, visual cue, sensation etc. consistently triggers the same learned memory response, i.e., conditioned reflex learning as opposed to innate reflex behaviours. This stage may persist for life in the severely mentally handicapped child, but can be used as the basis for conditioning in social training, e.g., toileting, feeding and dressing. Stereotyped behavioural responses occur in language as seen with naming, the recitation of nursery rhymes and the singing of simple tunes which are simply learned memory sequences which never vary and need not have any meaning.

The types of learning which concern us in the school age child require cognition or understanding; this requires that many differing memory experiences on a similar subject can be grouped together, i.e., a concept is formed. It is one thing to point to an orange and have the child say 'orange'; it is totally different to say "What do you understand by an orange?" and have the child respond in terms of the colour, consistency, size, feel, usage, and such scientific information as "a source of Vitamin C" gained from experience which allows one to give "meaning" to the word. Concept development necessitates a system of coding memories and classifying them, allowing recalled experiences to aid in reasoning and thinking. Language is, in essence, this coding system; it depends upon different symbols organized together in all areas of the brain.

Most of us use a phonemic code of words as our predominant symbol system. A musician, mathematician, chemist, electronics engineer, will use different codes and will be able to think, reason and express himself in this language system, i.e., we should not restrict ourselves to thinking of a system of symbols only in terms of, for example, the English, French or German languages. Since the mentally handicapped child has global delay in cognitive learning, he/she will have difficulty in all symbol systems. (Brown, 1978).

IS LEARNING LOCALIZED WITHIN THE BRAIN?

Does the brain store learned memories in localized areas? Is the symbol system used in learning determined by whether it is primarily auditory, visual or tactile? If so, does this determine the site of storage?

If we believe that the brain has to do with learning and that memories are stored in a physical sense, then the memory has got to be stored in a particular place and cannot be in a diffuse store in a vague mass of jelly, as the black box approach to the psychology of learning often suggests. The brain has a definite structure. The eyeball is connected to the occipital cortex, the hand to the motor strip, the ear to the superior temporal gyrus. These are primary areas and represent the basic wiring of the brain. We often hear that the brain is "plastic" in the child, with the implication that any form of therapy therefore is justified as the brain will rewire. *Primary* areas are fixed and nothing will connect the eye to the frontal lobe for vision. Only 5% of the cortex represents primary areas; but cerebral palsy, blindness or deafness is permanent if these areas, their connections or end organs are irrevocably destroyed. However, 95% of the cerebral cortex constitutes the so-called *association* areas which are often confused with the primary areas. The brain is asymmetrical and there may be some pre-programmed preference for language on the left side, nevertheless, if these areas are damaged the child will use the corresponding area on the opposite side. If both areas are damaged, then he cannot store visual material in a totally foreign area, e.g., in an auditory association area.

It does appear that, in the young child, who has not developed dominance, the brain behaves as two brains and may store conflicting mirror image material. Later, the left hemisphere normally develops as predominantly the language hemisphere and the right hemisphere as the visual. The reason that one side is eventually suppressed for certain modalities is not because the other may not be able to process language or visual stimuli equally well but that without asymmetry, confusion may result from the interference of conflicting information. Although the right hemisphere is perfectly capable of becoming the major language hemisphere, e.g., after damage to the left by a stroke or traffic accident, the child still puts auditory stores in auditory (i.e., Wernicke's) areas and motor skills relating to the mouth in Broca's area, not in some foreign area. Learning is plastic inasmuch as the child can change to a corresponding area in a different hemisphere. We cannot change primary areas as we cannot make new association areas long distances from the primary area subserving that symbol system.

Whether learned material is stored in a particular area or is diffusely non-localized, was one of the issues which has caused conflict between neurologists and psychologists; from what has been said above, both views are now compatible. Memories can be fixed in a particular region but the "language" to link these together for concept formation must involve widespread areas of the brain on both sides. The neurologist who sees strokes, tumours, abscesses and focal trauma, has always had a strictly focal approach to neurology. That a left-sided cerebral infarct and not a right-sided one causes dysphasia cannot be disputed, but in the case of tumours and head injuries, complicated by raised intracranial pressure, brain damage from the focal lesion is common. Penfield's research on the effects of focal cortical stimulation has been one of our mainstays in studying cortical localization. Studies of a vast number of gunshot wounds, as by Luria (1973), has added further evidence but, again from the study of pathological brains. Recent studies to show the local disappearance of the alpha wave, anticipation waves and more recently the beautiful radioactive tracer studies of regional cerebral blood flow, have all helped to confirm that in the mature normal non-pathological brain, learning is indeed fixed in the areas classically taught. Not only is learning therefore stored in a particular way but it can be switched on and off as shown by changes in local blood flow. Suppression of mirror learning on the opposite side is what we mean by the acquisition of dominance and it is not the same as laterality (see later). The connections between the two hemispheres which allow this, and within a single hemisphere, which allow different learning areas to be linked together, continue to develop through childhood and can be demonstrated as defined fibre tracts, not just as a vague concept.

SPECIFIC LEARNING DISORDERS

If there is a certain structure to the brain subserving learning of specific sensory modalities, and if these are under genetic control, it may be possible to lose them in isolation as a result of either brain damage or genetic disorder. We accept in conventional neurology the apraxias such as constructional apraxia, articulatory apraxia or specific visual agnosia for objects, faces or words. We may get tactile agnosias with loss of sensation of objects or astereognosis, loss of textures or body image. One may get alexia without dysgraphia, or a whole combination of what are in effect losses of specific learning abilities.

In children we may also see these disorders, but in a different way, because the child has not learned and then lost an ability, as does the injured adult, but has difficulty learning it in the first place. Hence, although we talk about aphasia in children, it would not be expected to be exactly the same as in the adult in whom islands of previously learned material may remain.

We can think in terms of dysphasia, dyslexia, dysgraphia, dysmusia, articulatory dyspraxia, specific visuo-spatial difficulties (visual agnosia), dyscalculia, all of which may occur as specific difficulties in otherwise normal children.

FACTORS INFLUENCING BRAIN DEVELOPMENT

We shall now turn to a consideration of factors which influence brain development to see if these will also influence learning. We can consider the various factors under several headings: (a) sex, (b) lateralization, (c) genetics, (d) environmental factors, (e) hormones and vitamins, (f) brain damage.

Sex—The adult male brain is heavier than the female brain, but the girl's brain is, at all ages up to puberty, heavier than the boy's. The Y chromosome appears to slow up the rate of brain maturation; so disorders such as intraventricular haemorrhage in the preterm newborn, which is peculiar to a particular stage of maturation, is much more common in boys than in girls. If the male brain develops more slowly than the female, we would expect all developmental disorders to be more common in the male and this is certainly the case, e.g., 66 out of 82 cases of reading retardation are in boys. (Mason, 1967). If there is an additional Y chromosome, as in the XYY Syndrome, there are even more schooling and developmental problems. The male is taller and more aggressive than the female which, again, appears to be a direct effect of the Y chromosome, which must therefore modify brain function as well as development. A further effect of sex is the effect of hormones. The male gonad secretes testosterone about 6 weeks after conception and this changes the female brain (with which all foetuses start) to a male brain, i.e., from a cyclical hypothalamic rhythm to a tonic one. This may also influence limbic development and facilitate fight versus flight, i.e., aggression versus anxiety.

Lateralization and Brain Asymmetry

The brain is not symmetrical, and asymmetry of gyral pattern can be seen from the last trimester of pregnancy. Asymmetry of alpha rhythm, asymmetry of cortex on *CT* scan, together with the known asymmetry in storage of learned material, suggests that the asymmetry is innate. Behaviour *in utero* is also asymmetrical, most infants being born in the L.O.A. position, which must be due to the foetus' adopting an asymmetrical posture. After birth, the infant more often continues with head rotation to the right. Although at 6 months a left-handed approach is common, after the grasp reflexes have disappeared by 10 months, definite right preference is noted in most infants.

If we look at children's gait, using polarized light goniometry or footprint patterns, we again see a persistent asymmetry. Studies with techniques such as dichotic listening show left-earedness is more significant than left-handedness as an association with learning difficulty. Whether a child is right-eyed, right-handed, or right-footed, a bilateral or crossed lateral pattern has always been a debatable contentious association with learning disorder; statistical analyses yield conflicting results. The gene for right-handedness may induce brain asymmetry and cause the two hemispheres to develop at a different rate. It is thought that absence of this induced asymmetry means that there is a random chance for right or left-handedness and possibly also for the siting of speech. Among left-handed children, speech is still in the left hemisphere in 60% of cases and on the right side in 40%. Normally, therefore, the brain has an induced asymmetry, a predilection for speech to be on the left side, and for the right and left sides to mature at different rates. The suggestion that there is some built-in pre-programming for speech to develop with certain basic processes already laid down, as suggested by Chomsky, is becoming a more attractive proposition. At any given age, more boys than girls are strongly left-handed, and the left hemisphere appears to develop more slowly in boys (Cohen, 1976). This suggests that learned hand skills are slower to develop on the right and postural (non-learned) skills on the left hand side of the body.

Genetics

The blueprint for brain development is coded in the DNA and readout of this must continue long after birth as development continues. If an abnormality is present in the information governing the early stages of brain development then, obviously, a much more profound effect will result than if an abnormality affects an aspect which is late in the maturation cycle.. Total absence of brain differentiation (as in the cortical dysplasias), we would accept as diseases because we can see a structural abnormality. Many of the specific learning disorders affecting speech, reading and writing, are also inherited in a dominant manner, but for reasons given above, they may more severely affect males. In true word-blindness, or severe dyslexia, the person can name letters and has no difficulty with speech or visuo-spatial concepts; but he cannot make T.R.E.E. into tree, no matter how much remedial reading help is given. In the true severe genetic form, progress is very poor as if in trying to make a colour blind person see a tree as green. We could regard this severe form of dyslexia as a disease.

There is a normal distribution curve for the age of acquisition of all abilities, e.g., most children walk between the ages of 10 and 14 months. The 10% of the population which is below the 10th percentile will appear slower than the majority (90%); yct they aic normal people. The brain may be slower in maturation only in certain fields, so that one may have delayed visual fixation, delayed toilet training (enuresis), delayed postural development (slow walkers and shufflers), or slow speech development. If 10% of any normal population may be regarded as slow in maturation and 3% as very slow (below 3rd percentile), then statistics showing 12% of children with slow speech, and 4% with very slow speech, development must be interpreted against this background. Only 1 or 2% may actually be slow as the result of some pathological disorder. Developmental slowness in speech and in the acquisition of dominance are the two areas most likely to cause schooling difficulty and, in the past, were the ones often misdiagnosed as minimal brain damage.

Speech and language must always be differentiated from each other. Children with delay in speech development require a full battery of tests of hearing amplitude, hearing frequency range, auditory discrimination, auditory memory, comprehension, active vocabulary, passive vocabulary, syntax and articulation. In the typical developmental pattern, articulation is delayed most, then syntax, and comprehension least of all. If the reverse is the case, then mental handicap or dysphasia is suspected. The child will omit, substitute, reverse the sounds he cannot make for ones he can.

In acquisition of any motor task, we first learn the parts of the task in isolation, then sequence them, increasing in speed and efficiency; finally, the act becomes subconscious. Whether one is learning to drive a car or to speak, the parts are learned and then sequenced; so the child may make sounds such as 's' in isolation before putting them into certain consonant blends as in 'spoon'. Sentence length will be shorter and grammar, especially in tenses and pronoun usage, will be retarded. Certain families (e.g., the Campbells, Kerrs) with an increased incidence of left-handedness, have shown marked retardation in their speech development, especially the boys, but by the age of 7 years, speech has improved and is subsequently normal. A percentage of these children will also have slow reading and spelling problems and may remain dysgraphic until secondary school entrance (Mason 1967). When confined to articulation without any syntactical or semantic component, this syndrome is in essence a motor learning disorder and no different from a developmental dyspraxia. In some children there is a more severe disruption of motor learning in relation to speech, i.e., a true articulatory dyspraxia, and this may have a much more severe long term disruption of communication. In others, syntax and semantics are involved and the child has a developmental dysphasia. It can be seen that there is a grey area between children who are at the lower end of the normal distribution curve (slow developers) and those with a true genetic disorder affecting a particular area of brain development. (Ingram 1959).

The acquisition of dominance is a gradual process. Up to this time, the brain behaves as a "split" brain or two separate brains. Dominance, as far as this article is concerned, is defined as the permanent fixation of learning of particular symbol systems to one hemisphere, which is mainly by the suppression of conflicting information from the corresponding module on the opposite side. It may be achieved in some way by the development of circuits which are seen as the alpha rhythm on the EEG. Dominance is genetically slow in developing in certain families in boys more often than girls. Clinically, we see certain interference phenomena such as reversals in speech, reversals in reading, reversals in writing, reversals in block design, reversals in figure perception as in Raven's matrices, right-left confusion, difficulty with crossed commands, finger agnosia, mirror movements, associated movements, difficulty with graphaesthesia. It is easy to see how an adult-oriented neurologist could interpret these as abnormal signs the same as those seen in parietal lobe damage or angular gyrus lesions in adults; hence, the so-called soft neurological signs of brain damage are confused with developmental signs. These usually resolve in normal children around 7 years of age but may persist to 10+ years in children with delayed dominance; these are associated with learning difficulty and apparent clumsiness.

Environmental Factors

No matter how advanced the computer, if the programme is faulty then the saying "put rubbish in and you get rubbish out" applies to the human as well as the electronic computer. Certain behaviours and responses may be preprogrammed, e.g., the mechanisms of speech. However, without environmental stimulation, speech cannot develop. The topic of environmental factors is too enormous to consider here except to point out that social and cultural factors obviously have a profound effect on learning. In this particular article we are considering the brain's contribution to learning disorders. Nevertheless, the importance of the environmental experience of the child is seen if we consider the fact that, in normal children age 7−8 years, the mean intelligence quotient in social class 1 is 113 and in social class 4 is 86. In spelling and numbers, the contrasts are even greater with 60% of social class 1 classed as ''good at numbers'' and less than one tenth as many in social class 5.

We do not, however, want to dwell on the effects of environment in programming the brain so much as the effect of environment upon brain development. If a child is exposed to severe psychosocial deprivation then he will cease to grow; and if that deprivation is prolonged, he may never catch up, i.e., the result is ''deprivation dwarfism''. He may develop secondary deficiencies of growth hormone and ACTH and develop aberrant behaviour. He will also have arrested cerebral development and will become disinterested, apparently deaf and blind, insensitive to pain, as well as developmentally retarded. Love and stimulation may reverse this pattern so that many months' developmental spurt may occur in a few weeks, as there may be dramatic catch-ups in somatic growth. The brain has, however, been arrested in development, in spite of adequate nutrition and a normal genetic background. Catch-up brain growth may show as an increase in head size, splayed sutures on X-ray, as well as the clinical increase in abilities. Experiments upon cats during the phase of rapid brain growth have shown that, at the time dendritic connections between cells are forming, stimulation of these pathways is essential if development is to progress normally (Blakemore 1974). Purpura (1964) has shown that in some cases of mental handicap, the dendrites have no spines to connect to other neurones. In the young infant the dendritic spines develop and if a connection is made they become plump and healthy; if not, they become long and straggly and may atrophy. This evidence suggests that long periods of sensory deprivation at critical periods during rapid brain growth could lead to a permanent disorder of brain development.

Hormones and Vitamins

The effect of male sex hormones on the developing brain has already been discussed. Progestational hormones are thought possibly to hasten brain maturation as when given to mothers in early pregnancy. Thyroid hormone is vital for normal brain maturation, and if deficient during the phase of rapid brain growth, the brain will be permanently retarded. Nutrition must also be adequate from the point of view of the balance of amino-acids, vitamins etc., and malnutrition during the vital period of rapid brain growth, especially from 28 weeks gestation to 6 months postnatally, may permanently affect brain growth.

Brain Damage

Brain damage in the sense of destruction of nervous tissue and its replacement by glial scar tissue (or else a hole, as in porencephaly), can be recognized readily at autopsy as "brain damage". It can be seen on a CT scan and clinically shows as mental handicap, cerebral palsy, epilepsy (e.g., infantile spasms or Lennox-Gastaut syndrome), cortical blindness or organic psychosis. Less severe grades of brain damage may affect smaller and more focal areas; and if these do not cause a motor handicap, diagnosis may be more difficult unless abnormalities show on EEG, CT scan or more detailed neurological or neuropsychological examination. This may show as very minor types of cerebral palsy, clumsy children, milder forms of epilepsy, slow speech development, behaviour disturbance, verbal-performance discrepancy on the W.I.S.C., poor performance on the Bender-Gestalt test, visuo-spatial difficulty or learning disorder. If we follow up children who were asphyxiated at birth and then showed abnormal cerebral behaviour, and if we exclude overt cerebral palsy, etc., as defined above, we find that these children tend to be clumsy (50%), behaviourally more difficult than sibs to rear (70%), speech retarded (26%) and have learning difficulties when they get into school (Brown and Burt, 1980). "Minimal brain damage" does exist, but as discussed earlier, it is *not* common.

A concept which has not always been considered in the past is that disease need not cause overt damage but could influence the actual rate of brain development, so that a child who would normally have walked at one year, now walks at two years, but eventually walks normally. If we look at children with hydrocephalus we find that, compared with normal children, they have clumsy hands (P 0.001) but this is not due to clumsiness, ataxia, involuntary movements or spasticity. It is, in effect, a developmental dyspraxia. The children perform worst of all in those abilities which they should be learning at that age, so that the rate of learning of handskills has not been destroyed but slowed down (Minns *et al*, 1977). Similarly a child who after perinatal asphyxia cannot draw a diamond at 7 years, may well be able to do it at 10 years. Brain damage which affects overt behaviour is easy to diagnose. But how do we differentiate slow development of speech in a premature infant (25% of infants with a birth weight of less than 2,000 gm have retarded speech development) when brain damage is a more likely effect from a genetic cause? In the same way, some social class 5 families may be in social class 5 because of genetically poor intelligence, or a familial disease such as tuberous sclerosis, rather than because of environmental reasons. A slow-witted mother who drinks and smokes during pregnancy, does not attend for antenatal care, goes into premature labour with a breech presentation, mixes up the infant's feeding schedule, is not hygienic so that the child gets diarrhoeal illnesses as a baby, will not breast feed, does not speak to the infant, cannot read bedtime stories, does not understand contraception and has more children than she can cope with, maybe batters them—the child will have major schooling and behaviour problems. Do the child's learning difficulties result from genetic factors, brain damage, or environmental factors, or most likely from all three?

Learning disorders as a result of brain damage, without necessarily hard neurological signs but with signs of immaturity, may arise especially after perinatal asphyxia and prematurity. (In both of these groups, 25% have been found to be slow in speech and of the premature 20% are found to be slow in reading.) In 60% of cases, the epileptic child has learning difficulties which may be related to the frequency of fits, drugs, loss of time from school, but most significantly, these difficulties are especially likely in a boy with a left-sided epileptic focus. Difficulty with numbers is also especially common in epileptic boys.

Thus it appears that although none of the above factors may be acting alone, they may all result in some degree of environmental delay. It is this delay which causes the learning difficulties we see in school, as the child attempts tasks his age-mates accomplish easily, but that are beyond his level of neurological maturity.

Further expansion of Dr. Brown's views may be found in:

Brown, J. K. 1978. *Mental Handicap and Degenerative Encephelopathies. Textbook of Paediatrics*. Edit. Forfar and Arneil. Churchill, Livingston, Edinburgh.

Brown, J. K. 1980. A Neurologist's View of Learning Disorders. Sonia Machanick Memorial Lecture. *Transactions of the College of Medicine of South Africa*.

Complete references for this article are on p. 116.

La Prévention des infirmités:
Quelques aspects des troubles d'apprentissage

J. KEITH BROWN

Sommaire

L'auteur discute ici de la croissance du système nerveux et des facteurs qui l'influencent. Il fait remarquer que le cerveau se développe durant toute la période scolaire et qu'on peut le considérer comme un organe d'apprentissage. Plusieurs facteurs, y inclus le sexe, l'asymétrie, la dominance, les influences génétiques, le milieu et les encéphalopathies, peuvent exercer une influence sur la croissance du système neurologique pour ralentir l'action d'un ou plusieurs domaines de fonctionnement cérébral. Il n'est pas nécessaire de connaître rien de précis quant à la façon dont ceci se manifeste chez l'enfant pour être autorisé à déterminer quels sont les facteurs les plus importants dans chaque cas particulier. On constate que plusieurs de ces enfants rencontrent des problèms considérables à l'école et dans leur comportement.

On a estimé que le nombre des écoliers susceptibles de présenter des troubles d'apprentissage d'un genre ou un autre pouvait aller jusqu'à 15%. Si ce calcul est juste, il s'ensuit que dans la moyenne des grandes villes il y aurait environ 30,000 enfants qui présenteraient une forme quelconque de difficulté scolaire. Cette situation a donné naissance à une véritable industrie d'apprentissage. Comme dans le cas de plusieurs autres problèmes de pédiatrie, les thérapies et les stratégies se sont développées à foison—souvent sans aucune tentative pour un arriver à une forme quelconque d'évaluation scientifique. Malheureusement les aspects médicaux ont été complétement relégués dans l'ombre par le concept d'hypercinésie et de présumée "encéphalopathie congénitale minimale" avec traitement par des amines sympathomimétiques, comme le méthylphénidate. On ne peut s'empêcher de manquer de charité et de penser que, en certains milieux, le grand nombre des enfants présentant des troubles d'apprentissage a fourni une clientèle opportune, assurée, à certains pédiatres de pratique privée. Il est difficile de supposer, même un moment, que 15% des enfants puissent être victimes d'une forme quelconque d'encéphalopathie. Il ne fait aucun doute qu'il existe des cas d'encéphalopathie congénitale minimale, possiblement à un taux d'environ 2 à 3 par 1000 enfants, et que certaines de ces victimes peuvent bénéficier de médication. Dans cet article, nous considérerons brièvement quelques uns des autres facteurs qui peuvent expliquer les problèmes, dans le cas de l'autre 14% des enfants qui présentent des troubles d'apprentissage.

Nous pouvons supposer que le problème des troubles d'apprentissage a trois sources principales: les parents, les enseignants et l'enfant. L'éducation des parents eux-mêmes, l'intérêt qu'ils portent à l'éducation (les associations de parents, par exemple), l'enseignement pré-scolaire qu'ils font des couleurs, des nombres, etc., sont évidemment importants, mais c'est le langage qui est à la base des compétences en lecture et en écriture, et les connaissances grammaticales et de vocabulaire de l'enfant dépendront du langage auquel il est exposé à la maison, tant de sa quantité (800 mots à l'heure) que de sa qualité (construction des phrases ouvertes ou fermées). L'attitude des parents en ce qui a trait à la lecture de comptines à leurs enfants au moment de les mettre au lit est dictée par le milieu culturel, de même que la présence des livres dans la maison et un intérêt persistant dans la lecture. Un foyer stable sur le plan émotionnel est également essentiel à la motivation pour le travail scolaire. L'anxiété est une cause importante des troubles de l'attention. Il est peu probable que l'enfant sérieusement inadapté, issu d'un foyer brisé, attache beaucoup de poids à l'éducation. Qu'il existe de mauvais professeurs, comme il y a de mauvais médecins et de mauvais avocats, personne n'en doute et nos collègues connaissent de bons et de mauvais maîtres dans leurs propres écoles. Les problèmes domestiques et conjugaux que connait une éducatrice dans son propre foyer peuvent accroître son intolérance et avoir un effet néfaste sur son enseignement. L'organisation de la salle de classe, qu'elle soit ouverte ou fermée, le bruit s'ajoutant à l'emploi de nouvelles ''méthodes'', qui souvent n'ont pas été mises à l'épreuve, ont souvent été considérés, dans l'esprit du profane, comme des causes de difficultés d'enseignement. Pourtant il y a peu de faits pour indiquer que la jeune maîtresse, fraîche émoulue, qui utilise une nouvelle méthode pédagogique dans une salle de classe de type ouvert, rencontrerait plus d'enfants présentant de vrais troubles d'apprentissage, que la vieille fille brandissant férule, dans une salle de classe antique, fermée, où règne un silence funèbre, pourvu bien sûr que ces deux éducatrices s'intéressent à leur travail et qu'elles soient capables d'inspirer aux enfants un sentiment de sécurité. C'est l'enthousiasme et l'intérêt de l'institutrice, plutôt que sa ''méthode'' ou l'organisation de sa classe, qui motiveront l'enfant. Toutefois, on doit tenir compte du programme. Au Royaume-Uni il existe de grandes différences régionales dans l'importance relative accordée au développement des capacités de lecture, d'arithmétique et d'organisation spatiale. Un bon enseignement donnera des enfants qui réussiront mieux aux examens et qui récolteront plus de bourses universitaires. Il semble aussi capable de développer certains traits de caractère, comme on le constate par le nombre d'hommes politiques importants, de juges et d'évêques qui proviennent d'un secteur d'enseignement très précis et très restreint au Royaume-Uni. Il est facile de blâmer le professeur quand un enfant n'arrive pas à apprendre et pourtant, même avec une aide individuelle additionnelle de la part d'un spécialiste de la rééducation, le progrès se fait souvent très lent. On pourrait retourner la balle et s'en prendre aux méthodes d'éducation des parents ou trouver des failles dans la dynamique familiale.

LA NEUROPHYSIOLOGIE DE L'APPRENTISSAGE

Cette communication porte surtout sur la neurologie des troubles de l'apprentissage; c'est pourquoi certains domaines comme la motivation, l'attention, les stratégies et codes d'apprentissage (Luria, 1973) ne feront l'objet que d'une brève mention. La pensée peut se définir comme le contenu de la conscience et tout ce qui vient modifier le niveau d'activation ou d'éveil, tels les drogues ou le manque de sommeil, peut faire que l'enfant paraisse inattentif. L'attention ou la concentration est reliée au niveau d'activation, mais différente de celle-ci: c'est la capacité de "filtrer" les influx sensoriels significatifs et non significatifs qui arrivent au cerveau. On croit que la capacité d'éliminer les stimuli non désirés serait une fonction des noyaux intralaminaires; les atteintes à cette région du thalamus ont été considérées comme l'une des causes de la propension plus grande à la distraction et à une mauvaise concentration et du comportement hyperactif qui en résulte. Par contre, l'enfant ne porte pas normalement attention aux signaux dépourvus de sens, ce qui fait que l'enfant mentalement handicapé a l'air de ne pas faire attention à ce qui se dit (ce n'est pas qu'il n'entende pas, c'est qu'il n'écoute pas); ses jeux manquent d'imagination et il peut errer un peu partout, sans but apparent. L'enfant qui éprouve des difficultés d'apprentissage particulières peut trouver que certaines leçons sont un charabia dénué de sens et, par conséquent, il ne s'y intéressera pas. Son manque de concentration n'est pas la cause, mais la conséquence de sa difficulté d'apprentissage. L'enfant qui est angoissé, peut-être à cause de ce qui se passe dans son foyer, paraîtra lui aussi plus enclin à être distrait. La mesure de la capacité de concentration d'enfants que les professeurs disent inattentifs montre souvent que ces mêmes élèves se concentreront vraiment durant de longues périodes de temps sur les tâches les plus fastidieuses, pourvu qu'ils rencontrent des succès. Les échecs chroniques et l'anxiété qui en résulte peuvent également troubler l'attention. Bien que certains enfants souffrant d'encéphalopathies congénitales aient, de toute évidence, une faible capacité (empan) de concentration et que celle-ci puisse être considérablement affectée par les drogues (tels le phénobarbital et le clonazépam) et bien que les chutes du niveau d'activation (dues à des maladies du métabolisme ou à une conscience diminuée par l'action de stupéfiants) puissent également nuire à la concentration, ce ne sont pas là des causes ordinaires de difficultés d'apprentissage, même chez les enfants épileptiques.

Nous avons déjà, en traitant du rôle des parents et des instituteurs, parlé de la motivation à apprendre. C'est un vaste et important domaine que nous ne pourrons étudier plus à fond dans ce bref exposé.

Il y a plusieurs façons possibles pour les comportements de se manifester et, même si l'on dit souvent que l'enfant a appris à faire une chose, marcher par exemple, ce n'est pas strictement vrai. Certains comportements sont purement réflexes, comme les réflexes des points cardinaux, de succion, de déglutition (palatin) et le contrôle de la respiration qui font partie de la réaction d'alimentation. Il y a un comportement réflexe opposé qui consiste à éviter, à faire la moue, à rejeter, à avoir des haut-le-coeur et à vomir, de telle sorte que, en réaction à la faim et à la soif, un comportement se trouve facilité par rapport à l'autre. Les réflexes de marcher, de se traîner à quatre pattes et le réflexe de Bauer font partie d'un comportement coordonné de natation qui est nécessaire *in utero* pour que le foetus prenne la position de présentation de sommet au moment de l'accouchement, c'est-à-dire que c'est une sorte de comportement humain d'éclosion. Avant que les comportements de s'asseoir, de se traîner à quatre pattes et de marcher puissent se manifester, il est nécessaire que les réflexes primitifs de posture soient inhibés. Ceci dépend de la maturation neurologique et, bien que nous apprenions sûrement quelque chose grâce à la marche, nous n'apprenons pas à marcher dans le sens où il nous faut en faire l'expérience et nous y exercer. Nous commençons à peine à comprendre aujourd'hui, à partir, par exemple, d'études sur des jumeaux identiques élevés dès le début de la vie dans des milieux séparés, comment les ensembles de comportement, même très compliqués, peuvent être le résultat d'une "empreinte" génétique dans le cerveau en voie de développement et ne dépendent pas de l'expérience puisée dans l'environnement. Au fur et à mesure qu'une nouvelle compétence se dégage, on constate souvent le développement simultané d'un pattern de comportement pour assurer son utilisation (avant que l'enfant soit capable de choisir volontairement, à la lumière de l'expérience, de l'utiliser). On observe ce phénomène dans le cas des comportements forcés de poursuite oculaire, de préhension, d'émission de mots et d'exploration, comportements qui apparaissent quand se développent les compétences respectives de fixation et poursuite visuelles, de manipulation, de contrôle volontaire de la voix et de locomotion. Le cerveau est donc, dans une certaine mesure, pré-programmé. Le niveau d'"apprentissage" qui suit est celui d'une simple réponse mnémonique quand le même son, le même indice visuel, la même sensation, déclenchent toujours la même réponse mnémonique apprise, c'est-à-dire l'apprentissage par réflexe conditionnel, au lieu de comportements réflexes innés. Ce stade peut persister durant toute la vie chez l'enfant gravement handicapé sur le plan mental, mais on peut aussi s'en servir comme base de conditionnement pour l'apprentissage social: par exemple, apprendre à faire sa toilette, à se nourrir et à s'habiller. Des réactions stéréotypées se présentent dans le langage, comme dans le comportement de nommer personnes et objets (c'est-à-dire le vocabulaire passif ou, d'une façon plus poussée, le type de l'habitué des réceptions mondaines), dans la récitation des comptines et la répétition des mélodies simples, qui ne sont que des suites mnémoniques apprises par coeur; elles ne varient jamais, ne sont pas modifiées non plus et n'ont pas besoin d'avoir de sens.

Les sortes d'apprentissage qui sont en cause chez l'enfant d'âge scolaire font appel à ses capacités de connaître et de comprendre, ceci exige le regroupement de plusieurs expériences mnémoniques portant sur un sujet semblable et provenant de différentes modalités sensorielles, c'est-à-dire la formation d'un concept.

Ce qu'on demande d'un enfant en l'amenant à désigner une orange du doigt et à prononcer le mot "orange" est tout-à-fait différent de ce qu'il doit faire quand on lui dit "Qu'est-ce que tu entends par orange?", alors que c'est la couleur, la dimension, la sensation, l'usage, l'information scientifique (v.g. vitamine C, fruit de citrus, etc.) qui permettent de donner une "signification" au mot. Ce processus exige un système pour le codage des souvenirs et leur classification en prévision du rappel, ce qui rend possible le raisonnement et la pensée. C'est le langage qui constitue essentiellement ce système de codage et il dépend de symboles différents qui intègrent ensemble l'activité de toutes les régions du cerveau. Nous utilisons, la plupart d'entre nous, un code phonémique de mots comme système prédominant de symboles. Par ailleurs, le musicien, le mathématicien, le chimiste, l'électronicien utilisent différents codes et ils sont en mesure de penser, de raisonner et de s'exprimer dans leur système de langage, c'est donc dire que nous ne devrions pas limiter notre conception d'un système de symboles aux langues française, anglaise ou allemande, par exemple. L'enfant qui souffre d'un handicap mental est sujet à un retard global dans l'apprentissage cognitif et éprouvera par conséquent des difficultés avec tous les systèmes de symbole (Brown, 1978).

L'APPRENTISSAGE EST-IL LOCALISÉ À L'INTÉRIEUR DU CERVEAU?

Le cerveau garde-t-il les souvenirs appris dans des régions précises et fixes, le système de symboles qui sert à l'apprentissage est-il déterminé en fonction de son caractère prédominant auditif, visuel ou tactile; est-ce que c'est cet aspect qui décide du site de l'entreposage? Si l'on croit que le cerveau est impliqué dans l'apprentissage et que les stocks mnémoniques sont conservés d'une façon physique, il s'ensuit que le souvenir doit être gardé dans un endroit précis et ne saurait être répandu de façon diffuse dans une masse gélatineuse vague, comme l'interprétation du type "boîte noire" de la psychologie de l'apprentissage le laisse souvent entendre. Le cerveau est doté d'une structure définie. Le globe oculaire est rattaché au cortex occipital, la main à la bande motrice, l'oreille à la première circonvolution temporale. Ce sont là des régions primaires qui sont les canalisations électriques fondamentales du cerveau. On dit souvent que le cerveau de l'enfant est "plastique", ce qui porterait à conclure que toute forme de thérapie serait justifiée, puisque le cerveau referait ses canalisations. Pourtant, les aires primaires sont fixes et rien ne pourra faire que l'oeil relié au lobe frontal soit jamais capable de voir. Malgré le fait que les aires primaires ne représentent que 5% du cerveau, la parésie cérébrale, la cécité et la surdité sont permanentes quand ces régions, leurs connexions, ou leurs organes terminaux sont irrévocablement détruits. Malgré le fait que le cerveau est, comme nous le verrons plus loin, asymétrique et qu'il puisse y avoir une certaine préférence pré-programmée pour le langage du côté gauche, il n'en reste pas moins que, advenant des dommages à ces régions, l'enfant utilisera les régions correspondantes, du côté opposé. Mais si les deux régions sont endommagées, il ne peut alors entreposer le matériel visuel dans une région totalement étrangère, dans la deuxième circonvolution temporale, par exemple, qui est une aire d'association consacrée aux symboles auditifs et non visuels. Il semble bien que chez le jeune enfant, avant que la dominance ne soit établie, le cerveau se comporte comme deux cerveaux et peut alors entreposer des matériaux incompatibles, disposés en images en miroir. La raison pour laquelle un côté finit par être inaccessible à certaines modalités (à savoir que l'hémisphère gauche devient normalement l'hémisphère prédominant du langage et le droit, celui de la vision) n'est pas que l'autre serait peut-être incapable de traiter le langage ou la vision également, mais que, sans asymétrie, il pourrait y avoir confusion due à l'interférence d'informations incompatibles. Même si l'hémisphère droit est parfaitement capable de devenir l'hémisphère principal du langage (dans le cas de dommages à l'hémisphère gauche à la suite d'une attaque ou d'un accident de la route, par exemple), l'enfant n'en continue pas moins à stocker les données auditives dans une région auditive (les champs de Wernicke) et à conserver les habitudes motrices relatives à la bouche dans le centre moteur de Broca, et non pas dans quelque région étrangère. L'apprentissage est plastique dans la mesure où l'on peut changer de côté. Nous ne pouvons intervertir les aires ou les champs primaires, de même que nous ne pouvons développer de nouvelles aires d'association à de grandes distances de l'aire primaire desservant ce système de symbole. La question de savoir si le matériel appris est entreposé dans une région précise ou s'il se trouve disséminé sans localisation possible est l'une de celles qui, dans le passé, a été cause de conflits entre neurologues et psychologues; si on se base sur ce que nous avons dit plus haut, une fois encore, les deux positions s'avèrent compatibles. Les souvenirs peuvent être logés dans une région déterminée, mais le ''langage'' qui les rattache ensemble pour la formation des concepts doit impliquer des régions éparses du cerveau, des deux côtés. Le neurologue, familier avec les attaques, les tumeurs, les abcès et les traumatismes en foyer, a toujours entretenu une attitude strictement localisatrice. On ne saurait mettre en doute le fait que c'est l'infarctus de côté gauche, et non celui du côté droit, qui entraîne de la dysphasie, mais dans le cas de tumeurs ou de blessures à la tête, se compliquant de pressions intracrâniennes accrues, on a souvent des dommages cérébraux provenant de la lésion focale. Les études de Penfield sur les effets de la stimulation corticale focale ont été l'un des arguments principaux en faveur de la localisation corticale. Les études sur des nombres considérables de blessures faites par des balles de fusil, comme celles de Luria, ont donné un poids additionnel à cette position, mais, là encore, il s'agissait de cerveaux pathologiques. Les travaux récents portant sur la disparition locale des ondes alpha, les ondes d'anticipation et, maintenant, les belles expériences avec les marqueurs radioactifs pour retracer le flot de sang dans les régions du cerveau ont tous contribué à démontrer que, dans le cas du cerveau normal arrivé à maturité, l'apprentissage est vraiment fixé dans les régions que l'on avait traditionnellement identifiées. Par conséquent, non seulement l'apprentissage est-il entreposé de façon particulière, mais il peut être activé et déactivé comme on le constate par les changements dans le flot sanguin local. La suppression de l'apprentissage en miroir du côté opposé, voilà ce que nous entendons par l'acquisition d'une dominance et ce n'est pas la même chose que la latéralité (voir plus loin). Les connexions entre les deux hémisphères qui permettent cette suppression et celles au sein d'un seul hémisphère qui permettent de relier ensemble différentes régions d'apprentissage continuent à se développer durant toute l'enfance et on peut démontrer qu'il s'agit de faisceaux de fibres précis et non pas d'un vague concept.

TROUBLES D'APPRENTISSAGE SPÉCIFIQUES

S'il existe dans le cerveau certaines structures dans lesquelles se fait l'apprentissage des modalités sensorielles et si ces structures sont sous contrôle génétique, il se peut qu'on les perde sélectivement comme conséquence de lésions cérébrales ou de désordres génétiques. En neurologie conventionnelle, on reconnait l'existence d'apraxies, comme l'apraxie constructive, l'apraxie articulatoire ou l'agnosie visuelle spécifique des objets, des visages ou des mots. On peut avoir des agnosies tactiles avec perte de sensation des objets (astéréognosie), des textures ou de l'image du corps. Il y a aussi des cas d'alexie sans dysgraphie, ou toute une combinaison de perturbations qui sont, effectivement, des pertes d'aptitudes d'apprentissage spécifiques.

Ces troubles peuvent se présenter également chez les enfants, mais d'une façon différente, parce que l'enfant n'acquiert pas une compétence pour la perdre ensuite; il éprouve de la difficulté à l'apprendre tout d'abord. C'est pourquoi on ne doit pas s'attendre, même si on parle d'aphasie chez les enfants, à ce que celle-ci soit identique à celle des adultes chez lesquels des îlots de matériel appris dans le passé peuvent émerger.

Nous pouvons penser en termes de dysphasie, dyslexie, dysgraphie, dysmusie, dyspraxie articulatoire, de difficultés visuo-spatiales spécifiques (agnosie visuelle), de dyscalculie, toutes des malfonctions qui peuvent se présenter comme des troubles spécifiques chez des enfants par ailleurs normaux.

FACTEURS QUI INFLUENCENT LE DÉVELOPPEMENT
DU CERVEAU

Nous allons maintenant nous tourner vers la considération des facteurs qui influencent le développement du cerveau, pour voir s'ils ont également des effets sur l'apprentissage. Nous pouvons étudier ces divers facteurs sous plusieurs rubriques: A—Sexe; B—Latéralisation; C—Génétique; D—Environnement; E—Hormones et vitamines; F—Lésions cérébrales.

Sexe

Le cerveau de l'homme moyen a une masse plus grande que celui de la femme, mais le cerveau d'une fillette est, à tous les âges jusqu'à la puberté, plus lourd que ce-lui d'un garçon. Le chromosome Y semble ralentir la vitesse de maturation du cerveau, ce qui fait que les troubles, comme l'hémorragie intra-ventriculaire chez le nouveau-né arrivé avant terme, qui est typique d'un stade particulier de la maturation, sont beaucoup plus fréquents chez les garçons que chez les filles. Si le cerveau de l'homme se développe plus lentement que celui de la femme, il faut s'attendre à ce que tous les troubles de développement soient plus fréquents chez le garçon et c'est sûrement ce qui arrive, 66 sur 82 cas de retard dans l'acquisition de la lecture se présentant chez des garçons (Mason, 1967). Quand il y a un chromosome Y additionnel, comme dans le syndrome XYY, on constate encore plus de difficultés à l'école et dans le développement. L'homme est plus grand et plus agressif que la femme, ce qui encore semble être un effet direct du chromosome Y, qui doit donc agir sur le développement cérébral aussi bien que sur la croissance. Un effet additionnel lié au sexe est celui des hormones. La gonade mâle sécrète la testostérone environ six semaines après la conception et ceci change le cerveau femelle (qui est celui de tous les foetus au départ) en cerveau mâle, c'est-à-dire qu'il passe d'un rythme cyclique hypothala-mique à un rythme tonique. Il se peut également que cette transformation influence le développement limbique et facilite la lutte, au détriment de la fuite, c'est à-dire l'agression, par opposition à l'anxiété.

Latéralisation et asymétrie cérébrale

Le cerveau n'est pas symétrique et l'asymétrie du pattern des circonvolutions fait son apparition à partir du dernier trimestre de la grossesse. L'asymétrie du rythme alpha, l'asymétrie du cortex au scintillogramme CT, de même que l'asymétrie observée dans le stockage du matériel appris portent à croire que l'asymétrie serait innée. Le comportement *in utero* est également asymétrique, la plupart des enfants naissant dans la position oblique antérieure gauche, fait pro-bablement dû à ce que le foetus, et non pas la mère, adopte une posture asymétri-que. Après la naissance, le nouveau-né continue le plus souvent avec une rota-tion de la tête vers la droite. Bien que, à six mois, l'attaque de la main gauche soit la plus fréquente, une fois que les réflexes de préhension sont disparus vers le dixième mois, on observe une préférence pour la droite chez la plupart des bébés. A douze ans, l'asymétrie de posture est souvent apparente sur la gauche, c'est-à-dire que le côté gauche du corps se développe plus lentement que le côté droit. Lorsqu'on étudie la démarche des enfants, au moyen de la goniométrie à lumière polarisée ou des patterns tracés par les empreintes des pieds, on constate encore une asymétrie persistante. Les techniques comme l'écoute dichotique montrent que la prédominance de l'oreille gauche est plus importante que celle de la main gauche, en tant que signe accompagnateur des difficultés d'apprentissage. Qu'un enfant soit droitier de l'oeil, de la main ou du pied, une préférence bilatérale ou latérale croisée a toujours été un signe accompagnateur de troubles d'apprentissages controversé et les preuves statistiques sont contradictoires. Il est possible que le gène responsable de la préférence pour la main droite provoque une asymétrie du cerveau et fasse que les deux hémisphères se développent à des vitesses différentes. On croit que, en l'absence de cette influence pour produire l'asymétrie, il y a des chances égales d'être droitier ou gaucher et qu'il en est peut-être ainsi pour la localisation de la parole. Dans 60% des cas de gaucher (manualité), la parole est quand même située dans l'hémisphère gauche et chez 40%, du côté droit du cerveau. Le cerveau est donc doté d'une asymétrie déterminée génétiquement: une plus grande probabilité que la parole soit du côté gauche et que les côtés droit et gauche se développent à des vitesses différentes. L'hypothèse de l'existence d'une certaine pré-programmation innée de la parole, basée sur des processus fondamentaux déjà en place, comme le propose Chomsky, devient de plus en plus attrayante. A tout âge, les garçons se révèlent plus gauchers que les filles et l'hémisphère gauche semble se développer plus lentement chez les garçons (Cohen, 1976). Ceci laisse supposer que le développement des habiletés manuelles serait plus lent du côté droit du corps et la maturation des aptitudes posturales (qui ne sont pas apprises) serait plus lente du côté gauche.

Génétique

Le plan du développement cérébral est inscrit en code dans l'ADN et les programmes qui en émanent doivent continuer longtemps avec la maturation, après la naissance. Il est évident par conséquent que, s'il se présente une anomalie dans l'information relative aux premiers stades du développement, il en résultera des effets beaucoup plus profonds que dans le cas d'une anomalie apparaissant plus tard durant le cycle de maturation. L'absence totale de différenciation cérébrale, comme dans l'anencéphalie, ou les perturbations plus circonscrites des structures cérébrales, comme dans le cas de dysplasies corticales, sont facilement reconnues comme des maladies, car l'anomalie structurale est visible. Plusieurs des troubles spécifiques d'apprentissage affectant la parole, la lecture et l'écriture sont également héréditaires et dominants, mais, pour les raisons que nous avons indiquées plus haut, il peut arriver qu'ils aient des manifestations plus graves chez les hommes. Dans le cas d'une alexie verbale authentique (cécité verbale pure) ou d'une dyslexie sérieuse, l'individu peut nommer les lettres et il n'éprouve pas de difficulté avec la parole ou les concepts visuo-spatiaux, mais il ne peut pas construire "robe" avec R-O-B-E, peu importe combien d'aide en rééducation de la lecture on lui apporte. Dans les véritables cas génétiques graves, le progrès est très lent, comme s'il s'agissait de forcer un daltonien de percevoir un arbre comme étant vert. On pourrait considérer des conditions aussi sérieuses comme étant des maladies.

L'acquisition de toutes les habiletés se fait selon une courbe normale de distribution; par exemple, la plupart des enfants commencent à marcher entre le dixième et le quatorzième mois. Six pour cent de la population générale des enfants se situeront sous le dixième percentile; ces derniers se montreront donc plus lents que la majorité (90%), tout en étant normaux. Il peut arriver que le cerveau présente une maturation plus lente dans certains domaines seulement, de telle sorte qu'un enfant montrera du retard dans l'entraînement à la propreté (énurésie) par exemple, ou dans son développement postural (ceux qui commencent à marcher plus tard et ceux qui se traînent les pieds) ou dans l'acquisition de la parole. Puisque 10% des membres de toute population normale peuvent être considérés de maturation lente et 3% de maturation très lente (situés sous le troisième percentile), il faut évaluer ces chiffres à partir de cet arrière-plan. Il pourra se trouver que seulement 1 ou 2% des enfants soient vraiment retardés à cause d'un désordre pathologique.

La lenteur dans le développement de la parole et dans l'acquisition de la dominance sont les deux domaines les plus susceptibles d'entraîner des difficultés scolaires et, dans le passé, ce sont ceux qui ont été souvent diagnostiqués erronément comme résultant d'encéphalopathies congénitales minimales.

La parole et le langage doivent toujours être différenciés l'un par rapport à l'autre. Il faut soumettre les enfants qui présentent des retards dans l'apparition de la parole à une batterie complète de tests se rapportant à l'amplitude auditive, l'étendue des fréquences perçues, la discrimination des sons, la mémoire auditive, la compréhension, le vocabulaire actif, le vocabulaire passif, la syntaxe et l'articulation. Dans le profil de développement typique, c'est l'articulation qui est la plus retardée, puis la syntaxe; la compréhension l'est le moins ou ne l'est pas du tout. Quand le contraire se présente, on soupçonne la présence d'un handicap mental ou de dysphasie. L'enfant omettra, substituera et inversera les sons qu'il ne peut faire, les remplaçant par ceux qu'il maîtrise. Dans l'acquisition de toute compétence motrice, nous apprenons d'abord les parties de la tâche isolément, puis nous les mettons dans l'ordre, accroissant vitesse et efficacité et, finalement, l'acte devient subconscient. Qu'il s'agisse de l'apprentissage de la conduite d'une automobile ou de la parole, on fait la même chose; par conséquent, l'enfant pourra faire des sons comme "s" isolément, avant de les réunir dans une suite de consonnes et voyelles, comme dans "statue". Les phrases seront plus courtes et la grammaire, surtout en ce qui touche l'usage des pronoms et des temps des verbes, sera retardée. Certaines familles (les Campbell et les Kerr, par exemple) chez lesquelles l'on trouve un plus grand nombre de gauchers présentent des retards accrus dans le développement de la parole, plus particulièrement chez les garçons, mais dès l'âge de 7 ans la situation s'est améliorée et le parler est normal dans la suite. Un pourcentage de ces enfants auront également des problèmes de lenteur de lecture et d'épellation et ils pourront présenter de la dysgraphie jusqu'à l'entrée à l'école secondaire (Mason, 1967). Quand il se limite à l'articulation, sans aucune composante syntactique ni sémantique, ce syndrome est essentiellement un trouble d'apprentissage moteur et n'est pas différent d'une dyspraxie associée à la croissance. Chez certains enfants on observe une perturbation plus grave de l'apprentissage moteur en relation avec la parole, c'est-à-dire une véritable dyspraxie articulatoire, et ceci peut représenter un désordre de la communication beaucoup plus sérieux et plus prolongé. Chez d'autres, la syntaxe et la sémantique sont en cause et l'enfant présente une dysphasie associée au développement. On peut constater l'existence d'une région grise entre les enfants situés à l'extrémité inférieure de la courbe normale de distribution (ceux qui se développent lentement) et ceux qui souffrent d'un authentique trouble génétique affectant une sphère particulière du développement cérébral (Ingram, 1959).

L'acquisition de la dominance est un processus graduel. Avant elle, le cerveau se comporte comme un cerveau "dédoublé" ou deux cerveaux séparés. Pour les fins de cet article, nous définissons la dominance comme la fixation permanente dans un hémisphère de l'apprentissage de systèmes particuliers de symboles, ce qui se fait surtout par la suppression d'informations incompatibles en provenance de l'organisation fonctionnelle correspondante du côté opposé. Elle peut se réaliser d'une certaine façon grâce à l'élaboration de circuits prenant l'apparence de rythme alpha sur l'électroencéphalogramme. Dans certaines familles la dominance est hériditairement lente à s'installer et chez les garçons plus que chez les filles. Sur le plan clinique, on constate certains phénomènes d'interférence comme des renversements dans la parole, dans la lecture, dans l'écriture, dans la construction de dessins avec blocs, dans la perception de figures comme les matrices de Raven, de la confusion droite-gauche, de la difficulté avec les ordres d'exécution simultanée de tâches différentes, de l'agnosie digitale, des mouvements "en miroir", des mouvements associés, de la difficulté avec la graphesthésie (dermolexie). Il est facile de comprendre pourquoi un neurologue habitué aux adultes pourrait y voir des signes anormaux semblables à ceux qui apparaissent suite à des dommages subis au lobe pariétal ou à des lésions du gyrus angulaire (pli courbe) chez des adultes et pourquoi les présumés signes neurologiques légers de dommage cérébral ont été confondus avec des signes de croissance. Ces derniers s'estompent habituellement, chez l'enfant normal, vers l'âge de 7 ans, mais ils peuvent persister jusqu'à 10 ans et plus chez des enfants chez qui l'installation de la dominance retarde; ils s'accompagnent alors de difficultés d'apprentissage et d'une apparente maladresse.

Environnement

Peu importe la qualité de l'ordinateur, si le programme est défectueux le dicton, ''mettez-y de la guenille et il en sortira de la guenille'', s'applique tant à l'être humain qu'à la machine électronique. Certains comportements et certaines réactions sont capables de pré-programmation, les mécanismes de la parole, par exemple. Sans stimulation provenant de l'environnement, cela ne peut se produire cependant. Nous avons abordé cette question brièvement à propos du rôle des parents et le sujet est trop vaste pour tenter de faire quoi que ce soit en si peu de temps, si ce n'est de souligner le fait que des facteurs sociaux et culturels exercent évidemment une influence profonde sur l'apprentissage; notre propos dans le présent article est la contribution du cerveau aux troubles d'apprentissage. Néanmoins on peut comprendre l'importance de l'expérience que l'enfant tire de son milieu, si l'on considère que, chez les enfants normaux âgés de 7 à 8 ans, le quotient intellectuel moyen est de 113 dans la classe sociale I et de 86 dans la classe sociale IV. L'épellation et la connaissance des chiffres sont encore plus anormales, alors que ceux qui sont considérés bons dans les chiffres représentent 60% des enfants de la classe I et moins d'un dizième de ce nombre chez les enfants de la classe sociale V.

Nous ne voulons pas nous attarder, cependant, tant sur l'influence de l'environnement sur la programmation du cerveau que sur son influence sur le développement de celui-ci. L'enfant qui est victime d'une carence psychosociale grave subira un arrêt de croissance et si cette carence se prolonge, il pourra ne jamais se rattraper, c'est-à-dire que l'on aura du nanisme d'insuffisance. Il peut contracter des déficiences secondaires de croissance hormonale et de corticotrophine (ACTH) et en arriver à des comportements aberrants. Son développement cérébral va également s'arrêter et il deviendra veule, désintéressé, apparemment sourd, aveugle, insensible à la douleur, en plus d'être retardé sur le plan du développement. L'amour et la stimulation peuvent renverser cette condition, de telle sorte qu'une poussée de développement de plusieurs mois peut se produire en quelques semaines, de même qu'un rattrapage dramatique de croissance somatique. Pourtant le développement du cerveau s'est arrêté, en dépit d'une nutrition adéquate et d'un arrière-plan génétique normal. Le rattrapage dans la croissance du cerveau peut se manifester par une augmentation du volume de la tête, par des engrenures du crâne évasées, de même que par l'accroissement clinique des compétences. Des expériences faites sur des chats durant la phase de croissance cérébrale rapide ont montré que, au moment où se forment les jonctions dendritiques entre cellules, la stimulation de ces voies est essentielle au progrès normal du développement (Blakemore, 1974). Purpura (1964) a démontré que, dans certains cas de handicap mental, les dendrites n'ont pas de tige pour entrer en connexion avec d'autres neurones. Ces tiges dendritiques poussent chez le nouveau-né et, quand une jonction s'établit, elles deviennent dodues et saines; en l'absence de connexions, elles se font longues et éparses et il peut arriver qu'elles s'atrophient. Ces faits laissent supposer que de longues périodes de privation sensorielle survenant à des périodes critiques au cours de la croissance rapide du cerveau pourraient amener un trouble permanent du développement cérébral.

Hormones et vitamines

Nous avons déjà parlé de l'influence des hormones sexuelles mâles sur le cerveau en voie de développement. On croit que les hormones progestinogènes viendraient peut-être hâter la maturation cérébrale, ce qui arriverait quand on les administre aux mamans au début de la grossesse. L'hormone thyroïdienne est essentielle à la maturation normale du cerveau et, s'il ne s'en trouve pas assez durant la phase de croissance rapide du cerveau, celui-ci sera retardé de façon permanente. L'alimentation doit également être adéquate du point de vue de l'équilibre des acides aminés, des vitamines, et ainsi de suite, et, là encore, la malnutrition durant la période vitale de la croissance rapide du cerveau, plus particulièrement de la vingt-huitième semaine de la gestation jusqu'au sixième mois après la naissance, peut affecter la croissance du cerveau de façon permanente.

Lésions cérébrales

A l'autopsie on peut identifier facilement les "lésions cérébrales", soit les dommages subis par le cerveau dans le sens d'une destruction du tissu nerveux et de son remplacement par des tissus cicatriciels névrogliques ou encore par un trou, comme dans la porencéphalie. On peut les détecter sur un scintillogramme CT et, cliniquement, elles se présentent sous la forme de handicaps mentaux, de parésie cérébrale, d'épilepsie (par exemple, des spasmes infantiles ou le syndrome de Lennox-Gastaut), de cécité corticale ou de psychose organique. Des lésions cérébrales moins graves peuvent affecter des régions plus restreintes et plus focales et si ces lésions n'entraînent pas de handicap moteur, le diagnostic peut être plus difficile, à moins que des anomalies apparaissent à l'électroencéphalogramme, au scintillogramme, ou à un examen neurologique ou neuropsychologique plus poussé. Celles-ci peuvent prendre l'apparence de types très bénins de parésie cérébrale, de maladresses enfantines, de formes plus légères d'épilepsie, de lenteur dans l'apparition de la parole, de trouble du comportement, de décalage entre les deux échelles "verbale" et "performance" au test WISC (Wechsler Intelligence Scale for Children)*, de mauvais rendement au test Bender-Gestalt, de difficultés visuospatiales ou de troubles d'apprentissage. Si nous étudions le développement ultérieur d'enfants asphyxiés à la naissance qui ont ensuite manifesté des comportements cérébraux anormaux et, si nous excluons la parésie cérébrale franche, etc., comme nous l'avons indiqué plus haut, nous trouvons des enfants qui sont maladroits (50%), plus difficiles à élever sur le plan du comportement que leurs frères et soeurs (70%), retardés dans le parler (26%) et qui éprouvent des difficultés d'apprentissage quand ils entrent à l'école (Brown et Burt, 1980). L'"encéphalopathie congénitale minimale" existe vraiment, comme nous l'avons dit au début de cet article, mais elle n'est pas fréquente. Un concept dont on n'a pas toujours tenu compte dans le passé c'est que, sans nécessairement causer de dommages manifestes, une maladie peut exercer une influence sur la vitesse même du développement cérébral, avec ce résultat qu'un enfant qui aurait normalement commencé à marcher à un an, le fait plutôt à deux ans, pour en arriver à un moment donné à marcher tout à fait normalement. Si nous examinons les enfants souffrant d'hydrocéphalie, nous constatons que, par comparaison avec les enfants normaux, ils ont des mains maladroites (P<0,001), mais cela n'est pas attribuable à la gaucherie, à l'ataxie, aux mouvements involontaires ou à la spasticité. C'est la conséquence d'une dyspraxie du développement. Ces enfants se montrent le plus malhabiles dans les choses qu'ils devraient normalement être en train d'apprendre à cet âge, ce qui fait que la vitesse d'apprentissage des habiletés manuelles n'a pas été détruite, mais ralentie (Minns *et al.*, 1977). De même l'enfant qui, comme conséquence d'une asphyxie périnatale, est incapable de dessiner un losange à l'âge de 7 ans, peut très bien être en mesure de le faire à 10 ans. Il apparaîtra sur-le-champ que la lésion cérébrale manifeste est facile à diagnostiquer, mais comment distinguons-nous la lenteur du développement du langage chez un prématuré (25% des nouveaux-nés qui, à la naissance, pèsent moins de 2,000 g présentent des retards dans l'acquisition de la parole), quand la lésion cérébrale découle plus probablement d'une cause génétique? De la même façon, la famille de classe sociale V peut se trouver dans cette classe à cause d'une intelligence génétiquement médiocre, ou d'une maladie familiale comme la sclérose tubéreuse (de Bourneville), plutôt que pour des raisons d'environnement. Une mère lourde d'esprit, qui boit et fume durant la gestation, qui n'assiste pas aux séances d'hygiène de la grossesse, qui entre en travail prématurément avec une présentation du siège, qui se mélange dans l'horaire d'alimentation du bébé, qui ne prend pas de précautions hygiéniques de sorte que l'enfant contracte des maladies diarrhéiques, qui refuse de le nourrir au sein, qui ne parle pas au poupon, qui se montre incapable de lui lire des comptines pour l'endormir, qui n'entend rien à la contraception et a plus de rejetons qu'elle est capable de s'en occuper, qui les maltraite peut-être—voilà qui donne un enfant qui aura des difficultés scolaires et des problèmes de comportement sérieux. S'agit-il alors de l'hérédité, de lésions cérébrales ou du milieu; ou plus vraisemblablement des trois?

Les troubles d'apprentissage résultant de lésions cérébrales, pas nécessairement accompagnées de signes neurologiques graves, mais plutôt de signes d'immaturité, peuvent surgir surtout après asphyxie périnatale, ou dans le cas de prématurés; chez ces deux types d'enfants, 25% présentent des lenteurs dans le développement de la parole et, dans le cas des prématurés, 20% sont lents en lecture. L'enfant épileptique éprouve des difficultés d'apprentissage dans 60% des cas, ce qui peut être associé à la fréquence des crises, aux médicaments, aux absences de l'école, mais ce qui paraît plus important, ces difficultés sont plus particulièrement susceptibles de se présenter chez le garçon qui a une épilepsie focale du côté gauche. La difficulté avec les chiffres est particulièrement fréquente chez les garçons épileptiques.

Il semble donc que même si aucun des facteurs mentionnés ci-haut n'agit isolément, ces derniers sont tous capables d'entraîner un certain retard dans le développement. C'est ce retard qui est responsable des difficultés d'apprentissage que nous observons à l'école, alors que l'enfant s'attaque à des tâches que ceux de son âge réussissent sans difficulté mais qui se situent au-delà de son propre niveau de maturité neurale.

* Test Wechsler pour les enfants

References

1. Blakemore C. and Van Sluyter R.C., 1974. Reversal of the physiological effect of monocular deprivation in kittens.*J. Physiol.* 237, 195–216

2. Brown, J.K., 1978. *Mental Handicap and Degenerative Encephalopathies. Textbook of Paediatrics*, Edit. Forfar and Arneil. Churchill Livingston, Edinburgh.

3. Brown, J.K., 1980. A Neurologist's View of Learning Disorders. Sonia Machanick Memorial Lecture. *Transactions of the College of Medicine of South Africa.*

4. Brown, J.K. and Burt, A., 1980. *Cerebral Palsy and Perinatal Asphyxia. Sydney Israel's Memorial Lecture.* Published by University of British Columbia.

5. Cohen, J., 1976. Handedness, speech pathology and hemispheric asymmetry. *Triangle*, Vol. 15, No. 4, 93–101.

6. Holder Hyden, 1964. R.N.A. a functional characteristic of neuron and glia in learning. In *R.N.A. and brain function in learning.* Edit. Brazier M. Berkeley and Los Angeles.

7. Ingram T.T.S., 1959. Specific developmental disorders of speech in childhood. *Brain*, Vol. 82, Part 3, 450–467.

8. Luria, A.R., 1973. *The Working Brain.* Penguin Press London.

9. Mason A.W., 1967. Specific Developmental Dyslexia. *Developmental Medicine and Child Neurology*, 9, 2, 183–190.

10. Minns R.A. *et al.*, 1977. Upper limb function in spina bifida. *Zeitschrift fur Kinderchirurgie* 22.4, 493–506.

11. Purpura D.P., Shofer R.J., Housepian E.M., Noback C.R., 1964. Comparative ontogenesis of structure-function relations in cerebral and cerebellar cortex. *Progress in Brain Research* 4, 187−221.

IV. PREVENTION OF
DEVELOPMENTAL DISABILITIES

editor: Bluma Tischler

13

Biological and Environmental Determinants of Developmental Disabilities

DR. JANET HARDY, M.D., C.M.

Abstract

In order to better understand the determinants of developmental disabilities, the basic developmental process must be understood. Some of the factors which influence developmental outcome are summarized and examples of the complex outcome are discussed. Special references are made to the environmental determinants of the long-range outcome of hearing-impaired "rubella" children and to the delayed language development of the children of adolescent mothers.

Pour mieux comprendre les causes déterminantes des défectuosités du développement, il faut connaître le processus fondamental du développement. L'auteur présente un aperçu de certains des facteurs qui influencent l'issue du développement et il donne des exemples de dénouements complexes. Il traite plus spécifiquement des influences de l'environnement sur l'évolution à long terme des enfants dont l'ouïe a été atteinte par la rubéole et du retard dans le développement du langage des enfants issus de mères adolescentes.

INTRODUCTION

More than 100 years ago, Little,[6] a British physician, described the importance of prematurity and low birthweight as precursors of cerebral palsy and similar neurological deficits related to the birth process. In the early 1960's, another British physician, M.C. Drillien,[1] made an important observation with respect to the long-term outcomes for small premature infants. In her longitudinal study of a large group of infants in Edinburgh, she found that, in the absence of severe neurological handicaps, the school performance of premature children raised in upper and middle class families differed little, on the average, from that of their normal birthweight sibs. On the other hand, the performance of similar premature children growing up in lower class families was, on the average, considerably below that of their normal weight sibs. Drillien's findings and those of other studies underlie the current concept of the 'vulnerable child,' i.e., the child who, because of biological factors, is at risk of developmental handicaps.

An ecological and "whole child" approach is needed for understanding the relative contributions of biological and environmental factors to the determination of the developmental outcome at any particular stage in the life cycle. The 'whole' child approach obviously entails consideration of the psycho-social and behavioural aspects as well as the physical and cognitive aspects of development.

THE DEVELOPMENTAL PROCESS

In Figure 1, an attempt is made to illustrate in simple, diagrammatic fashion the process of development and some of the biological and environmental influences which interact at various points in time to determine the final level of performance. The union of the genetic material supplied from each parent initiates the sequence of events for the new individual and sets the potential for further development. It is important to realize that this genetic material has a very long history stretching back through many generations. While it may establish the potential for highly successful development along all parameters, it may bear genes for conditions which cause serious developmental problems. In any event, the genetic material probably establishes a ceiling on developmental capability, a potential beyond which we cannot go and, almost certainly, a potential which very few of us even reach. Later events interact with the developing organism to nurture the potential or to reduce its realization.

From the point of conception, and even long before, environmental factors begin to impinge upon the developing fetus. It is important to realize that during pregnancy the developmental process depends upon interaction between the fetus and the intrauterine environment and that outside environmental influences are mediated through the maternal oganism. Some of the biological and environmental influences are summarized in Figure 1 and Table 2.

BIOLOGICAL INFLUENCES ON DEVELOPMENT

In Table 1, biological factors which have been demonstrated to affect development are listed. These factors are important because much can be done to prevent or minimize their effect. For example, many prenatal infections can be screened for, diagnosed and treated, as for example, syphilis and gonorrhea. Others such as rubella can be prevented by appropriate innoculation before pregnancy; or in the event of a confirmed diagnosis during pregnancy, the birth of a compromised infant can be prevented by abortion, should the parents so desire.

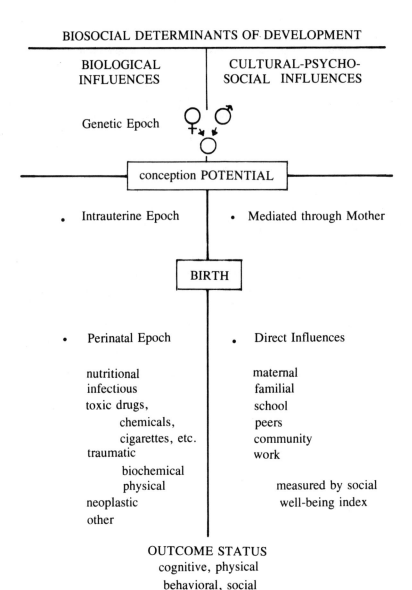

Figure 1: The Biosocial Determinants of Development and the Epochs During Which They are Operative

The use of toxic and abusive substances can be controlled during pregnancy by the physician and/or the patient. The use of cigarettes during pregnancy makes a major contribution to the problem of low birthweight;[3, 4] the frequency of low birthweight and the accompanying developmental problems would be greatly reduced if women would stop smoking during pregnancy. As the potential of certain drugs for causing fetal damage has become more clearly understood, physicians and their patients have become more discriminating in their use. The harmful effects of X-radiation during pregnancy is now well recognized and its use in obstetrics has been largely replaced by other techniques such as ultra sonography. Physical trauma during birth bears a strong relationship to subsequent cerebral palsy and neurological handicap. Improved obstetrics, particularly the judicious use of caesarean section, has materially reduced this risk in developed countries. Unfortunately, however, birth injuries are still commonplace in less developed populations.

Nutritional factors are extremely important. The relationships between maternal pre-pregnant weight and weight gain in pregnancy and subsequent infant birthweight and risk of perinatal death were clearly demonstrated in the Collaborative Perinatal Study[8] which showed that an average weight gain of 25–30 pounds was optimal. This is an amount well in excess of the old rule that a pregnant woman should not gain more than 16 pounds. The belief that prenatal nutrition is of importance is demonstrated by the widespread use of the WIC programme (Women, Infants, and Children) which provides nutritional supplements to many thousands of poor pregnant women across the United States.

Table 1. *Biological influences on development: Prenatal and postnatal*

> Genetic
> Infectious
> Toxic substances (drugs, cigarettes, alcohol)
> Traumatic—particularly during the birth process
> Nutritional
> Neoplastic

ENVIRONMENTAL INFLUENCES ON DEVELOPMENT

Let us turn now to consider the impact of the environment on the developing fetus and child. The mother provides the prenatal environment, and such factors as nutrition, infection and toxic substances in her environment obviously affect the fetus. However, I would like to discuss the environment in a more traditional context. Table 2 provides a summary of some of the environmental factors which influence the development of the child after birth. This list has grown from experience in a multidisciplinary, prospective longitudinal study of a large population of mothers and children living in the inner-city in East Baltimore. This study was designed to elucidate etiological factors responsible for perinatal wastage and the continuum of neurological, neurosensory and intellectual deficits associated with perinatal injury.

Approximately 4750 pregnancies were enrolled in the Child Development Study (between 1959 and 1966) at the time of the first visit for prenatal care in the Woman's Clinic of The Johns Hopkins Hospital. These pregnancies were followed with a standardized protocol during pregnancy, labor and delivery and 88% of the mothers and surviving children were followed through the age of 8 years. A representative subsample of almost 500 were followed until the children were 12 years of age. Approximately 77% of the mothers were black and most came from the lower middle and lower socio-economic levels in Baltimore. There were high rates of prematurity, perinatal and infant death, neurological impairment and mental retardation in this population of children. Additional outcome measures included intellectual functioning during childhood and school achievement.

I wish to comment on two aspects of this longitudinal study to illustrate the importance of environmental influences in determining the developmental outcome for the high risk or 'vulnerable' child.

Table 2. *Environmental influences on development*

>Family structure and stability
>Education of parents
>Quality of parenting
>Coping ability
>Resources
>>socio-economic
>>informational
>>helping networks—extended family
>>community resources

I. THE LONG-RANGE OUTCOME OF HEARING IMPAIRED CHILDREN:

In 1963−64, Baltimore experienced an epidemic of rubella, a part of the pandemic which devastated the United States between 1963 and 1965. With the assistance of Dr. John Sever and the staff of the Perinatal Infectious Disease Laboratory (National Institutes of Health), we were able to carry out a definitive study to determine the long-range effects of rubella identified during the prenatal period in this population.

II. LONG-RANGE OUTCOME OF ADOLESCENT PREGNANCY:

As we studied the antecedent relationships to outcome data in various categories, such as perinatal loss, mental retardation, neurological abnormality and school failure and maladjustment, we discovered that the children of adolescent mothers appeared in the adverse outcome groups out of proportion to their frequency in the study population. Thus, the children of mothers 17 years and below were at high risk of a number of adverse outcomes, as were their mothers. This finding has led us to: (a) a number of ongoing studies to document the adverse biological and social outcomes of adolescent pregnancy;[4] and (b) an attempt to identify some of the environmental factors which contribute to the generally poor outcome of adolescent pregnancy in this inner city population.

OBSERVATIONS

In all, about 330 documented cases of prenatal rubella were studied prospectively; 130 were enrolled in the Child Development Study, the remainder were enrolled at birth or shortly thereafter and followed according to the Study protocol. The additional cases were, in many instances, from more affluent, middle class families with greater resources for meeting the problem and thus provided a broader perspective of the importance of environmental influences.

The outcomes for these children have been described in detail elsewhere.[2, 3] Over 60% were hearing-impaired and almost one-third were mentally retarded (i.e., IQ below 70). There were many learning and information processing problems among those with relatively normal IQ scores. The observation that I wish to discuss here pertains to the hearing-impaired children who were not severely impaired intellectually or visually. It was those who had the benefit of considerable parental concern and stimulation who learned oral language, who had adequate school performance and who are likely to have reasonably productive lives. These parents used their resources and those of the community to keep hearing aids in order and to obtain early and special education for their children. They were those who made every effort to provide maximal language stimulation. The children, with approximately equal degrees of handicap, who did not learn oral communication were those in an unstimulating environment whose parents were unable to cope. These were children whose special needs had not been met, who had not had proper maintenance of their hearing aids. These children attended schools where signing was emphasized and they displayed generally poor performance academically over the years. They did not learn oral communication. Their outlook for employment is not encouraging. The parents and the environments which they provided played a dominant role in determining outcomes.

The children of adolescent mothers in our study, as indicated, had generally lower intellectual performance and a greater frequency of school failure than the children of older mothers. We hypothesize that this also reflects inadequate maternal stimulation of the child. In recent years, we have provided a comprehensive intervention programme to lessen the adverse consequences of adolescent pregnancy. This programme emphasizes psycho-social and health related education, in addition to medical care. The programme extends from the first prenatal visit to three years after the birth of the child, with mothers and children receiving service in the same comprehensive follow-up clinic. We have achieved success in many important areas. The health of the mothers and babies has been improved as compared with controls. Repeated pregnancy, school drop-out and welfare dependency have been significantly decreased. However, in following the developmental status of the children at 12, 24 and 36 months, we have become aware of a high frequency of delayed language development, a delay which is suspected by 12 months and progressively increases by the age of 36 months. We hypothesize that this progressive delay in language development may underlie the later poor intellectual functioning and inadequate school performance manifested by the children of adolescent mothers. On the basis of these findings we have begun to emphasize language stimulation in the parenting education programme provided and we are examining the parenting practices of the adolescent mother to identify reasons for the delay in the language development of her child.

DISCUSSION

Two other studies have provided insights with respect to the importance of environmental factors in determining developmental outcome. One of those, summarized by Werner and Smith (1977)[9] in a fascinating book entitled *Kauai's Children Come of Age*, describes an 18 year follow-up study of all the children born on the island of Kauai, in 1955. Among the over 600 children followed through age 18, 2% suffered severe perinatal stress. In this stressed group, four out of 5 (80%) had serious behavioural, learning and/or physical problems. The frequency of mental retardation in this group was 10 times, that of mental health problems was 5 times, and that of serious physical problems more than twice the number found among the total cohort of 18 year olds. Among those with moderate perinatal stress, the frequencies of mental retardation, mental health problems and teenaged pregnancies were also greater than those in the cohort as a whole but only by a factor of two to three times. Among the children diagnosed as learning disabled at age ten years, most had had serious problems which persisted through adolescence.

About a dozen variables—biological, psychological or sociological—showed significant relationships across time with outcomes, i.e., they were predictors of later problems. These are listed in Table 3. The last three variables, low maternal education, low standard of living and low family stability, all reflect the poor quality of the environment in which these particular children were growing up. These authors stress the inter-relationships between the biological and social variables which result in vulnerability, particularly in respect to the high risks of teenaged pregnancy.

The second study, the Milwaukee Study, of a disadvantaged segment of the population was reported by Heber and Garber.[5] They found that the infants of mothers whose IQs were below 80, had themselves an extremely high likelihood (80%) of testing below 80 at 6 years of age. It was postulated that cultural and environmental factors played a large role in the developmental failure of these children.

In conclusion, there is a large body of evidence, from many studies, only a few of which have been mentioned here, that indicates that developmental disabilities may result from complex interactions between biological and environmental influences upon the course of development. Much is already being done in terms of the primary and secondary prevention of developmental disabilities. However, more is needed and changes in life style that include the prevention of maternal smoking during pregnancy and attention to proper parenting and infant stimulation could have a major impact on the prevention of some of these problems.

Table 3. *Key predictors of serious problems*

1. Moderate to marked degree of perinatal stress;
2. Presence of congenital defects;
3. Very high or very low levels of infant activity;
4. Cattell IQ score below 80 by age 2;
5. Low PMA IQ score;
6. Moderate to marked degree of physical handicap by age 10;
7. Recognized need for placement in a learning disability class by age 10;
8. Recognized need for more than six months of mental health services by age 10;
9. Low level of maternal education;
10. Low standard of living at birth, age 2, or age 10;
11. Low family stability at age 2.

Note: From Werner and Smith,[9] page 12.

References

1. Drillien, M.C. and Ellis, R.: *The growth and development of the prematurely born infant*. Williams and Wilkins, Baltimore, 1964.
2. Hardy, J.B.: Clinical and developmental aspects of congenital rubella. *Archives of Otolaryngology,* Vol. 98, page 230−236, October, 1973.
3. Hardy, M.P., Haskins, H.L., Hardy, W.G. and Shimizu, H.: Rubella audiologic evaluation and follow-up. *Archives of Otolaryngology*, Vol. 98, page 237−245, October, 1973.
4. Hardy, J.B., Welcher, D.W., Stanley, J. and Dallas, J.R.: Long-range outcome of adolescent pregnancy. *Clinical Obstetrics and Gynecology*, Vol. 21, No. 4, December, 1978.
5. Heber, R. and Garber, H.: Prevention of cultural familial mental retardation. To be published as Chapter 14 in *Community Mental Health: A Behavioral-Ecological Perspective*. Edited by A. Jager and R. Slotnick, Plenum Press.
6. Little, W.J.: On the influence of abnormal parturition, difficult labours, premature births and asphyxia neonatorum on the mental and physical condition of the child, especially in relation to deformities. *Lancet*, 2:378, 1861.
7. Meyer, M.B.: Effects of maternal smoking and altitude on birth weight and gestation. *The Epidemiology of Prematurity*. Edited by D.M. Reed and F.J. Stanley, Urban & Schwarzenberg, Baltimore-Munich, page 81−104, 1977.
8. Niswander, K.R. and Gordon, M.: *The Women and Their Pregnancies: The Collaborative Perinatal Study of the National Institutes of Neurological Diseases and Stroke*. Philadelphia: Saunders, 1972.
9. Werner, E.E. and Smith, R.S.: *Kauai's Children Come of Age*. University Press of Hawaii, 1977.

14

Genetic Aspects of Mental Retardation

PATRICK M. MACLEOD, M.D., F.R.C.P. (C), F.C.C.M.G.

Abstract

Recent population studies show that 1 out of 30 babies is born with some recognizable congenital malformation. Chromosomal abnormalities are the most prevalent, with an incidence of 1 out of 200. Down's syndrome is the most commonly seen human chromosomal abnormality in the live born population. Approximately 1 out of 700 children is delivered with a defect in the closure of the neural tube—anencephaly—meningomyelocoele. The risks of recurrence in the extended family is high, in the order of 1 to 3 per cent. These two malformations are detectable by amniocentesis. The third commonest genetic cause of mental retardation is some inborn error of either hormone or amino acid metabolism. The incidence of these inborn errors approximates 1 out of 5000 live births. Although most are associated with some degree of mental retardation, it can be prevented by early treatment. For this reason neonatal screening is an integral part of good perinatal medicine.

Des études démographiques récentes révèlent qu'un bébé sur trente manifeste à la naissance une malformation visible quelconque. Les anomalies chromosomiques prédominent, avec un taux de 1/200. La trisomie 21 (syndrome de Down) représente l'anomalie chromosomique humaine la plus généralement répandue chez les nouveaux-nés vivants. Environ un enfant sur sept cents naît avec un défaut de fermeture du tube neural—anencéphalie—méningo-myélocèle. Les risques de récurrence dans la famille plus vaste sont décelables par amniocentèse. La troisième cause la plus commune d'arriération mentale est une erreur innée quelconque du métabolisme, soit des hormones, soit de l'acide aminé. Le taux de ces erreurs innées est d'environ une sur cinq mille naissances vivantes. Bien que la plupart de ces cas s'accompagnent d'un certain degré d'arriération mentale, ils peuvent être prévenus par un traitement précoce. C'est pourquoi le dépistage néonatal est partie intégrante d'une bonne médecine périnatale.

It has been estimated that 1 out of 30 babies is born with some recognizable congenital abnormality. Normally the child is born with 46 chromosomes; 44 of these are termed autosomes and two are the sex chromosomes. The normal male then has a 46, XY karyotype, and the normal female a 46, XX karyotype. The most common chromosomal abnormality is a Trisomy or a triplication of one of the autosomes. Approximately 1 out of 600 newborns has Trisomy 21 or Down's syndrome. The biological consequences of this extra chromosome begin shortly after conception and affect, for the most part, the central nervous system, leading to mental retardation, which is the hallmark of most chromosomal abnormalities. While it is true that any chromosome can be triplicated, the vast majority of such pregnancies are spontaneously aborted by 12 weeks. Occasionally a child will survive with a Trisomy of a larger chromosome, but few of them survive more than one year.

Disorders of sex chromosomes are the next most common group, with approximately 1 out of 600 males being born with an additional X-chromosome so that his karyotype is now a 47, XXY or Klinefelter's syndrome. About 1 out of 3000 girls is born with a missing X-chromosome, her karyotype being a 45, XO, or Turner syndrome. To a lesser extent, mental retardation is a feature in this syndrome.

These children are short in stature and, in later years, evidence disorders of secondary sexual differentiation.

Portions of chromosomes can be missing. These are termed deletion syndromes. For the most part they are all associated with significant mental retardation. Collectively, then, disorders of chromosomal number or constitution are seen in .5% of the newborn population.

The vast majority of chromosomal abnormalities are not familial, the patient usually being the only example of the chromosomal abnormality in a large kinship group. Recurrence of such a chromosomal abnormality is low, in the order of 1% or less. A possible exception is in the case of translocation. Here, a portion of a chromosome has been transferred to an otherwise normal chromosome. A parent may be a carrier of a balanced translocation and produce unbalanced eggs or sperm which produce children with significant triplications of portions of chromosomes and, as a consequence, mental retardation. Familial translocations are rare and the recurrence risk within a family is in the order of 2 to 10%.

Defects in the closure of the neural tube constitute the second most common recognizable syndrome of mental retardation. Approximately 1 out of 700 children is delivered with a defect in the closure of the neural tube. These range in severity from anencephaly, which is usually fatal early in the neonatal period, through the various types of spina bifida—including encephalocoele, meningomyelocoele and myelocoeles. They range in severity, so that for some this is a major handicapping condition, and for others it is not. Defects in the closure of the neural tube are familial. They are seen at a higher frequency in close relatives than chance alone would predict. Those who have had one affected child have an increased risk of about 2 per cent for producing a second similarly affected child. Incidence of the disease varies from a high of 1 out of 250 in parts of the northern British Isles, to a low of 1 out of 700 in British Columbia. It is more common among families with British heritage but seldom seen in native Indian communities. Analysis of the family histories of patients with a neural tube defect reveals that cousins are from 2 to 7 times more likely to be born with a similar defect than children taken from the general population. These observations have acquired a non-Mendelian explanation for the familial occurence of neural tube defect. The term "multifactorial inheritance" applies to this example. It has been estimated that at least four genes from both the mother and the father contribute to the genetic predisposition of the fetus. There may also be an environmental contribution occuring early in the pregnancy. Despite numerous studies, no single environmental agent has been identified.

The third cause of a genetically determined form of mental retardation is found in the so-called inborn errors of metabolism. These children suffer from congenital hypothyroidism which, if undetected, leads to significant irreversible mental retardation by 3 months. Approximately 1 out of 5000 children is born with an inborn error of amino-acid metabolism. An example of the latter would be phenylketonuria. It, too, is associated with significant mental retardation if not treated within the first few months of life. Because these disorders are relatively common and treatable, most communities now routinely screen the newborn population for these diseases.

Inborn errors are inherited in a simple Mendelian recessive mode of inheritance. Each of us carries approximately 6 genes which are potentially harmful to our children. If a child receives a double dose of one of these particular genes, one from his mother and one from his father, the child will be affected. Such a carrier couple has a 25% chance of having a second similarly affected child. Genes which produce recessively inherited disorders operate at the level of enzymes. In the case of classical phenylketonuria, the liver enzyme, phenylalaninehydroxylase is absent and, as a consequence, phenylalanine accumulates in the circulation and has direct and indirect harmful effects on the nervous system.

In the past decade, a number of strategies have emerged to monitor pregnancies at risk for chromosomal, multifactorial or autosomal recessive disorders.

It is technically feasible to perform an amniocentesis at about 16 weeks into a pregnancy and draw off a small amount of amniotic fluid. This permits a detailed chromosomal analysis of cells in the fluid and a detailed biochemical analysis of the fluid or, again, cultured cells. The diagnonis of Trisomy 21 can be made from an examination of the karyotype while the diagnosis of a neural tube malformation can be made from an analysis of the amniotic fluid alpha fetoprotein. A more detailed biochemical analysis of enzymes in the tissue culture of the cells obtained by amniocentesis can diagnose approximately 120 inborn errors of metabolism.

Amniocentesis is reserved for the monitoring of pregnancies at risk for one of these disorders. Pregnancies to women beyond the age of 35 are considered to be at risk for producing a child with a chromosomal abnormality. Women who have previously given birth to a child with a chromosomal abnormality are perceived to have a risk of approximately 1% of producing a second similarly affected child. Women who have previously produced a child with a defect in the closure of the neural tube have a 2% risk and their sisters may have a risk as high as 1%.

Pregnancies to couples who have produced a child with an inborn error of metabolism have a 25% risk of recurrence. Most of them can now be detected by amniocentesis. Finally, there are disorders of the nervous system which are caused by a genetic rearrangement of an X-chromosome. Amniocentesis can serve to establish the fetal sex in cases where only males are at risk for the particular disease.

These remarks are meant to represent an overview of some of the genetic aspects of mental retardation and some of the techniques available to establish a diagnosis early in the pregnancy.

15

Screening for Inborn Errors of Metabolism

DR. DAVID F. HARDWICK, M.D., F.R.C.P. (C)

Abstract

Screening newborn babies for inborn metabolic disorders is an accepted routine in most areas of North America and Europe. In British Columbia an integrated Screening, Diagnostic, and Treatment Programme has been evolved over the last decade, which permits prompt initiation of therapy following identification and diagnosis of the child at risk for metabolic disease. Screening consists currently of traditional blood-dot processing for phenylketonuria and urine specimens screening for a wide variety of aminoacidopathies and glycosurias. To date (1971–1978), 85,000 urine specimens have been processed. The mean age of infants screened was 4.4 weeks. Two per cent of infants screened were considered at risk, due to an unusual pattern of amino acids chromatographically. A persistent abnormality was identified in 0.22 per cent of urines screened. In about one quarter of these (0.06 per cent) a definite metabolic abnormality was confirmed. Treatment was instituted after diagnosis in the Biochemical Diseases Laboratory. Clinical investigation in collaboration with laboratory personnel was essential for prompt and cost-effective investigation.

Le dépistage des erreurs innées du métabolisme auprès des nouveaux-nés est une pratique admise et routinière dans la plupart des régions de l'Amérique du Nord et de l'Europe. En Colombie Britannique on a élaboré au cours des dix dernières années un programme intégré de dépistage, diagnostic et traitement qui permet une prompte mise en marche d'une thérapie, suite à l'identification et au diagnostic de l'enfant qui risque d'être atteint d'une maladie métabolique. Présentement le dépistage consiste dans l'analyse traditionnelle des taches de sang pour l'identification de phénylcétonurie et celle de spécimens d'urine pour une grande variété d'aminoacidopathies et de glycosuries. Jusqu'à la date de préparation de ce compte rendu (de 1971 à 1978), on avait traité 85,000 spécimens d'urine. L'âge moyen des nouveaux nés examinés était de 4,4 semaines. Deux pour cent des bébés étudiés étaient considérés comme représentant des risques à cause de la présence d'une disposition chromatographique inhabituelle d'acides aminés. On a identifié une anomalie persistante de 0,22% des urines analysées. Dans à peu près un quart (0,06%) de ceux-ci, on a confirmé la présence d'une anomalie métabolique précise. Après ce diagnostic dans le Laboratoire des Maladies Biochimiques le traitement fut entrepris. La recherche clinique faite en collaboration avec les membres du laboratoire s'est avérée essentielle pour une action prompte et économique.

I will begin by putting biochemical diseases into the context of cellular processes related to chromosomal abnormalities, themselves related directly to DNA. Abnormalities of chromosomal material (DNA) are translated into abnormal polypeptides or proteins via RNA which then alter a variety of cellular and metabolic processes. One type of abnormality is an abnormal circulating protein polypeptide; an example is the antihemophiliac factor required to clot blood, as in hemophilia. A second example is at the cell membrane level (1) where materials cannot be transported into cells. There may be an absence of an enzyme (2) which leads to a failure of the production of the next product in a chain of reactions and precursor materials may accumulate. Similar to this is the failure of mechanisms requiring the cooperative action of enzymes and vitamins (3) or other co-factors. A last process (4) is the absence or inactivity of degradative enzymes found in digestive sacs called lysosomes.

All cellular processes are determined by enzymes; necessarily, an enormous number of enzymes are present in the body, any one of which may be abnormal, leading to the possibility of a large number of rare diseases. In the process of screening for these diseases, we look to see where abnormal products develop. For example, we can measure the lack of function of abnormal proteins which fail to clot blood normally. We can measure materials in blood and urine samples which cannot be transported across cell membranes and are either accumulated in the blood or lost in the urine. In other disorders there may be an excessive accumulation of a side product that we can measure, or a deficiency of some material that should be produced but is not because the mechanism is blocked. In some situations we can screen for lysosomal or storage diseases (where an enzyme that should exist in the membrane of these digestive sacs inside the cell is missing), either by measuring the accumulation of material that is not degraded, or the lack of activity of the abnormal or missing enzyme.

SCREENING

In British Columbia more than 33,000 children are born annually; within this group we attempt to detect those who have some biochemical abnormality. Techniques of detection that we use in the laboratory are those that show the abnormal build-up products or the lack of functioning products in these diseased children. These diseases are indentifiable by screening tests before the full-blown clinical disease develops. Bear in mind that these diseases occur with a frequency of somewhere between 1:5000 to 1:150,000 so that tests have to fulfill criteria that will allow us, on an economic basis, to search for these children. Presented below is a series of criteria that can be applied to screening, specifically to screening in the newborn period. Several of the criteria are obvious and require no explanation.

Criteria for Screening

1. Is the disease a threat to life or does it cause disability?
2. Is the disease present in a fair frequency in the population under study? Frequency is "fair," only if the cost of screening is less than the cost of not screening and allowing the disease to develop. If one looks at certain population groupings, one can find increased frequency of disorders within certain enclaves; it therefore becomes economical to screen, even with relatively costly tests, those identified "at risk" populations.
3. Can the disease be treated effectively? This is important and was one of the original criteria applied to screening tests. Diseases were at one time screened for because of the possibility of effective treatment. Now this is no longer the only reason for screening (see #7).
4. Can the disease be identified during the newborn period or during gestation? Screening in the newborn period is inappropriate for diseases that are not manifest in the newborn unless significant morbidity can be prevented in later life. Screening for lipid disorders leading to atherosclerosis is one such possibility that is being considered currently.
5. Is the test simple, economical, medically acceptable, and practical for laboratory use? This may seem obvious but there are those of us who have been involved in screening programmes for a decade or more who have done inappropriate things, such as asking mothers to bring their babies back to the doctor's office at 6 weeks and then seating the mother and baby in an office full of people who are smoking, coughing or are obviously ill. That particular programme foundered on the basis of unacceptability.
6. Is there reliable confirmation available? I would point out that this is one of the most important criteria. From a planning point of view, there is little point in finding evidence of a disease through screening if nothing material can be done to confirm the diagnosis and treat it. In order to provide effective help, the disease must be diagnosed, treated and monitored for improvement. In a number of these disorders the treatment is roughly as bad as the disease, sometimes creating an artificial deficiency state with severe symptoms and signs. One must be absolutely certain that a definite diagnosis of the disease can be made before a screening programme is initiated.
7. If the disease is not treatable, is there some other significant benefit of early identification? Genetic counselling and termination of pregnancy are possibilities, depending upon the judgement of the parent. Improvement of treatment modes and diagnostic regimens are also significant reasons for screening.

The programme that exists in British Columbia fulfils these criteria. It is based to a large extent on that of the Massachusetts screening programme. We have in existence in the Children's Hospital a "Biochemical Diseases Programme" that was funded initially through the Children's Hospital and later by the government. The Biochemical Diseases Programme itself is a unified programme of screening, diagnosis and treatment. In many areas in North America, screening is conducted by a public health agency, the diagnostic and treatment facilities being run by hospitals. In our jurisdiction we have a combined programme which includes the screening function. There is also an "investigational strategy" or "diagnostic" laboratory function that allows confirmation of the disease after the abnormality has been detected in the screening programme. This ensures that when we treat the patient we are treating the disease. Treatment of the disease occurs in the community in the form of in-hospital and ambulatory programmes.

Screening Programme

At the present time a drop of blood is taken by heel prick from all babies in British Columbia. The heel-prick specimens are put on to filter paper, the blood dots dried and mailed to the Programme. These are tested for hypothyroidism by screening for T4 with radioimmune assay, and also for phenylketonuria (PKU) which is tested by the standard Guthrie inhibition assay. Another dimension of the screening programme is a screen of urine for aminoacidurias and glycosurias.

RESULTS

The data from the PKU programme shows that the incidence of PKU in British Columbia is relatively consistent with that for other populations largely of European origin. Although the screening for hypothyroidism has not continued long enough here to generate reliable statistics, it is expected to yield an incidence of about 1:4,000 to 5,000 cases, or two to three times the incidence of phenylketonuria. The data from the urine screening programme show a variety of different diseases. Over the past eight years we have screened about 100,000 patients, of whom about 0.25% have had abnormalities. If there were larger numbers we would be concerned that we would be worrying parents unnecessarily for non-existent diseases; if it were too much lower than that, we would consider the possibility of having missed diseases. The diseases that we have found include a number of biochemical disorders, such as heterozygous cystinuria, Hartnup disorder, hyperglycinemia and galactosuria. One patient with diabetes mellitus was found. Individuals with galactosuria requiring treatment have been identified. Aminoglycinuria, in which proline is excreted in the urine, is a curious disease present in a reasonably high frequency in some of our North American Indian enclaves. Those patients who are treatable and have in the past required treatment seem to be doing well currently.

Regarding checks and balances on the screening process itself, screening is an interesting technical phenomenon, in which the techniques, as pointed out earlier, are simple and economical, generally costing a few cents to about a dollar per specimen. From a social perspective, however, when one of these diseases is found, significant problems may develop in the family. The family is challenged with the knowledge that an abnormal child has to be treated, often with an unusual diet or therapeutic regimen. The parents are burdened with the knowledge that they have transmitted a defect to their infant—hardly a pleasant thought. Since the possibilities of family disruption, divorce and other problems are great, one has to consider not only the technical aspect of the screening but also its social propriety. In addition to the impact on the family, one has to consider the legality of the process, the morality of abortion, the prospects of stigmatization of the abnormal child, to identify a few obvious problems. The ethics and social consequences are societal in scale far beyond the province of a technical screener or indeed, of any one or two scientists or physicians involved in such a screening programme.

It has been our view, one held firmly in British Columbia, that government and governmental agencies should have a major input into deciding which types of diseases are to be screened for and the way in which the screening is to be handled. We therefore requested, and have secured the government's agreement to a supervisory committee for inborn errors of metabolism, which will review the screening programme annually and will also determine the social propriety of the screening mechanisms themselves. Individuals with legal, medical, theological and other backgrounds will review the screening process with respect to its ethics and socio-economic consequences. This is in addition to other governmental regulations which monitor the purely technical part of the process to make sure that the quality of the testing is adequate.

In conclusion, screening for inborn metabolic diseases is technically feasible and should be performed according to the criteria outlined. The technical screeners should continue to identify and proffer for screening, anything that can be screened economically. Governmental or other appropriate social agencies should have the opportunity of reviewing the non-technical aspect of screening in terms of their ethical and social propriety.

NOTE: Dr. Hardwick's research collaborators are: M.G. Norman, M.D., F.R.C.P. (C); L.T. Kirby, Ph.D.; L.K. Wong, M.D., F.R.C.P. (C)

V: THE MANAGEMENT OF CHILDREN WITH MULTIPLE HANDICAPS

editor: Donald McEachern

16

Meeting the Needs of Multiply Handicapped Children

MARTIN BAX, M.D.

Abstract

The needs of multiply handicapped children are seldom effectively met because services available for them are generally inadequate, and professionals are not usually trained to work with the complex problems they present.

In ensuring better help, both primary prevention, such as genetic counselling, and secondary prevention procedures to avoid behaviour disorders are primary tasks. Early diagnosis, as soon after birth as possible, and continuous assessment will help in the child's management. Care for such children must be addressed to such important problems as those of measuring the effectiveness of treatment, giving good advice to parents and other caretakers, and finding the right people to work with these children.

L'auteur fait observer que les services offerts aux enfants à handicaps multiples sont en général inadéquats, que les professionnels ne sont pas préparés pour faire face aux problèmes complexes en cause et que cette situation mène à des résultats médiocres.

Il considère qu'il faut commencer tant avec des méthodes de prévention primaire, tel le counseling génétique, qu'avec des méthodes de prévention secondaire, pour éviter les troubles de comportement. Une fois qu'on est en présence d'un nouveau-né à handicaps multiples, toutefois, un diagnostic rapide et une évaluation continue aideront à prendre soin de l'enfant. Il attire l'attention sur des problèmes importants liés à la mesure de l'efficacité du traitement, aux conseils à donner aux parents et à ceux qui s'occupent des enfants et au recrutement d'individus compétents pour travailler avec ces enfants.

Though cultures from ancient and sophisticated ones to those of the contemporary world have adopted brusque attitudes towards multiply handicapped children, most of the developed Western countries have provided services for them for many years. The question is whether these services are satisfactory. Most professionals in this field regularly see children whom the present services have failed to help, as well as some whose condition have worsened. A colleague reported about a child whom I had referred to his longstay unit some years ago:

> During his six years stay in the unit, John made little progress. His self-help skills improved, but he remained an isolated, withdrawn, self-

pre-occupied boy who made little contact with his environment. At times he had temper tantrums which were extremely difficult to eradicate and control. Diagnosis: blindness, sub-normality, behaviour disorder of child-hood.

Why the result was so unsatisfactory is a matter of speculation. However, this child initially was only under the care of an opthalmic surgeon and had no early support from an experienced handicapped children's unit; hence the opportunity was missed to prevent some of the behaviour disorders and subnormality which are now a feature of this child's condition. The early services that the child and the family had were inadequate and it is possible that his later difficulties stem from these early failures.

Oswin (1978) has recently chronicled the outcome for children living in long-stay hospitals in the United Kingdom. Her account shows that the care provided for multiply handicapped children has been incompetent and often unkind. All of us in the field can cite supporting evidence.

WHAT NEEDS TO BE DONE?

1. *Prevention*. Those working with the multiply handicapped child often for-get that many handicaps are preventable. Primary prevention means adequate genetic counselling, and ante-natal and perinatal services to prevent congenital causes of multiple handicap. But many children are handicapped postnatally by accidents and preventable illnesses which occur in the early years of life. Great strides have been made in the United Kingdom by confidential inquiries into the reasons for maternal mortality. The aim of these inquiries is to pinpoint what went wrong in specific cases in order to see that such errors to not recur. Similar inquiries into possible causes of multiple handicap, distressing as they might be to the parents involved, might help to lower their incidence. How many of the medical staff who are sometimes responsible for the failure of preventative ser-vices see these multiply handicapped children years later?

Secondary prevention means the prevention of other handicaps which may arise as a result of the first. The studies of Rutter and his colleagues show that many children who are handicapped also have behaviour disturbances. The fact that these behaviours are similar to those occuring in the non-handicapped sug-gests that they are not so much a function of the handicap as of the way we han-dle these children. Other handicaps, such as some of the secondary deformities of cerebral palsy, are quite clearly the result of inadequate care.

2. *Diagnosis*. In some circles there is a certain resistance to diagnostic work for multiply handicapped children, since doctors appear to put children through a

series of tests that seem to help them very little. Though there is some basis for this resistance, it partly arises out of people's confusion about the meaning of medical diagnosis and assessment. Diagnosis aims to reveal the cause(s) of a particular condition, to identify the nature and the body site of the particular pathological process, to determine the temporal cause of that pathological process and its probable outcome, that is, whether or not the individual will survive.

Diagnosis is not intended to say anthing directly about the functioning of the individual; that is what assessment docs. Diagnosis is useful because it may lead to curative or preventative steps. Parents or caretakers gain some understanding of the nature and cause of the child's condition; however, diagnosis in itself provides little by the way of management. Diagnosis should be done thoroughly and completely as soon as the handicap is identified so that, if there are specific treatments, they can be applied, and, if possible, preventative measures can be employed.

Diagnosis should not be done in bits and pieces over the years, nor should it be done repeatedly. Neither should diagnosis be allowed to influence assessment as much as it has often done. For example, many trained people continue to believe that "all Down's Syndrome children are severely subnormal," which they are not. There is no straightforward relationship between Down's Syndrome and mental retardation, although there is a low correlation which tends to put them in a below-normal population.

3. *Assessment*. Assessment is concerned with the individual's functioning, and should lead to "action." The child is assessed in such categories as gross motor function, fine motor function, vision, hearing, speech and language, perceptual and intellectual development, and social and emotional development. The results of that assessment will lead to a plan of action which is different for each child, since individual children are unique, and which will vary according to available services. It will vary also as to whether the child lives in a rural area, an urban area, in North or South America.

As for normal children, assessment must be repeated at regular intervals because children's development is not predictable. Although low to moderate correlations exist from earlier to later ages, it is important to remember, when we note the stability of human characteristics, that there is always a proportion of children who do not show expected relationships. For example, a child who was initially assessed as below average in intelligence may later turn out to be very bright. Such instances of low predictability characterize handicapped children more than normal children. If to that variability in development over time one adds the differences among families—because after all we are helping a *family* with each handicapped child—one can see that generalized statements about what should or should not be done with particular children can be dangerously misleading.

4. *Management*. I am not going to discuss the ways in which the different handicaps of multiply handicapped children can be "managed." Obviously, the child with many handicaps needs the assistance of a team of specialists. I shall, however, make for the practitioner some general points based on my own experience.

1. Make quite clear to the family the distinction between treatment which might be curative and that which is only ameliorative. We cannot cure many handicaps, e.g., the motor disorder of cerebral palsy, but we can help the child make the best use of his abilities. It is very common to find parents thinking that physiotherapy will in time "cure" their child.

2. See that the handicapped child does not get a "worse deal" than the normal child. When a handicapped child is admitted to a hospital or residential centre, this is likely to happen. Is the multiply handicapped child getting all the care and attention which parents lavish on their children, including their handicapped children? Are the child's common problems being treated? Handicapped children have feeding problems, sleeping disorders, coughs and colds as frequently, if not more so, than other children and these demand not less but more attention than they do in other children because the consequences for the family can be serious.

3. At first consultation, parents evidence many anxieties. The most common one is their need "to do something" for their child. Whenever possible, therefore, make practical suggestions about what they can start doing tomorrow that will help them involve themselves in their child's difficulties. In working with multiply handicapped children, one inevitably sees a child who has problems that are outside the range of one's own experience. Nevertheless, by using one's knowledge of normal development, one can often suggest an activity which, while not of any great long term significance, will be something that the child can enjoy and will give the parents good and early feedback.

4. Always have a plan involving specific goals for the child. The parents want short and long term counselling; they want immediate understanding of their child's condition, what the diagnosis is, and an immediate detailed programme of day-to-day management of the child which you will work out together with them. They also want a more flexible, long term programme and it is necessary to think about alerting them to some of the problems ahead, while at the same time not over-burdening them with anxieties.

WHO HELPS THE HANDICAPPED CHILD?

A common theme in family reactions to services received is the need for continuity. They prefer having one person with appropriate experience to advise them throughout their child's development. One has to remember that the multiply handicapped child is going to become a handicapped adolescent and later, a handicapped adult. Not only do professionals change jobs but those of us who have expertise with an individual's problems at one age level may be less effective with their problems at another age level. I have worked for many years with a person who was internationally known for her work with handicapped children; yet her attitude towards handicapped adolescents was outmoded. She found it extremely difficult, for example, to cope with their sexuality and favoured segregation by sex. It is important that we acknowledge our own failings in this respect. We should see that families get advice from a professional who works effectively with the age level the handicapped person has reached and who has the knowledge and experience needed to give the appropriate advice.

With respect to the question of who helps the child, I should like to draw on the work of Dr. Albert Kushlick and his colleagues, who run units for handicapped people in the Wessex region of the United Kingdom. He and his colleagues have defined the types of people who come into contact with handicapped "clients." The first group are the whole-timers—people like parents, nurses and houseparents who are with the client for most of the day. Parents of course are there 24 hours a day; as for houseparents in an institution, even though they do have time off, they are often on duty for 12 hours of the day. They are involved in everything that the client does—dressing, talking, reading, and in every other aspect of the client's education. Everything in the child's life is mediated through them. Of course they may be unaware of their comprehensive influence; for instance, nurses in longstay hospitals may think only of their responsibility for the physical care for the patient and not be aware that their own speech and body language are inevitably part of the environment in which the client finds himself.

The next group of people are part-timers who have very specific tasks. They may teach or give physiotherapy or occupational therapy. They do this task for perhaps two or three hours a day, but usually less, with a client, and then they go away. Their role is usually rather precisely defined and they know what it is. They often become uneasy if they are asked to move outside that role. Thus, a teacher will say "I am here to teach him to read, not to handle his temper tantrums."

The third group of people has been defined as the "hit and run merchants." They are the experts and I suppose I must count myself as one of these. We turn up, or rather we have the client brought to us; we carry out diagnostic and assessment procedures. If the client is very favoured, we may see him once a week, but perhaps we will see him once a month or once every six months. What the expert does is quite varied. He can decide how he should use his own time and what his role should be, because he has an expert knowledge of how to do everything! Within the field of psychiatry alone we can see an enormous range of therapeutic and diagnostic techniques being used.

There are two other groups of people involved who deserve at least a bare mention. First are the monitors and supervisors. These are the people who administer out lives; they may come into some contact with the client. Then there are the providers and the planners. We may all play some part in this, but in the end these are the people who have the power to organize our society; these are the people we call politicians.

The problem with this type of structuring of help for the multiply handicapped person is that the person who has the most training, although not necessarily the most appropriate training, is the least available of the helpers. He is the expert; he will have had six to nine years of training to reach his position and theoretically may have an enormous amount of knowledge about the needs of multiply handicapped children. The whole-timers—the parents and houseparents—have had very little training; yet they are expected to handle the very complex needs that some of these children have. It is analogous to the situation in a World War I battlefield, when the generals in the command posts often knew very little about what was happening to the infantry in the trenches. If effective care is to be brought to handicapped children, we have to think of some way of closing the gap between knowledge and action by providing more knowledge for the whole-timers and restructuring the expert's lives so that they see more of the "problems in the trenches."

PROBLEMS AND DIFFICULTIES

I now want to mention some difficulties which seem very important when we think about the problems of handicapped children.

1. *How to measure our effectiveness in what we are doing.* The traditional role of the physician, when he sees a multiply handicapped child, is to suggest some form of intervention—a drug treatment or a therapy programme or an educational programme. We need to know later whether the programme or treatment has been effective. It is very difficult to measure treatment effectiveness. We tend to say things like, "We are going to increase the child's potential, change his attitudes, develop his awareness; we are going to provide intensive care, improve hospital morale, provide a supporting community environment and coordinate services." All of these aims are very laudable but very difficult to measure.

One has to decide what one can measure and one has to then try to determine the extent to which one can identify possible factors that lead to any changes. One can observe and record what an individual is doing at a particular time. It is possible, for example, to sample the child's behaviour between 10:15 and 10:20 AM; it is possible to measure the way the child moves, it is possible to record how he feeds and how he dresses himself, and it is then possible, later, to look at some of these behaviours and see how things have changed. It is possible to record the number of outbreaks of disruptive behaviour occurring over a period and to see whether they have increased or decreased in succeeding weeks. It is possible to set specific goals, e.g., "the child learns to manage a spoon," and to see if this goal has been achieved within a short period of time. When we find that we are not getting positive results, we must think of a different strategy to try or we must recognize that specific goal as not achievable.

2. *Communication.* Let us assume the client's perspective and raise a rather provocative issue. The parents of a young multiply handicapped child want to get some good advice. First of all, they have to find an expert, or several experts; secondly, they need to know whether an expert really has the expertise they need. Most of us are aware, for example, that many kinds of therapy are available for a multiple handicap, such as cerebral palsy, and that some of these therapies are a complete waste of time or may actually be harmful. But in various parts of North America and Europe an expert might advise the family that this type of therapy was what the child needed. In time, the family might come to doubt their expert. We can not, therefore, avoid the question: "How do people judge the quality of experts?" This is a task faced, not only by families with handicapped children, but by people in many areas of life. There is no simple answer to this question, but we can at least explain how we look at these issues, namely, by the scientific method.

One feature of the scientific method is that it does not provide you with cut-and-dried answers. It provides you rather with a way of critically assessing what you do. It also provides you with a way of doubting. One has to try and put it across to families that you are not certain that a recommended method is best but that you believe it to be the best *at the moment*. We can indicate to the parents that we are constantly trying to appraise different systems of therapy and that we do have methods for thinking about them critically. Many of the books and papers we use are written in such a way that people without specialization in the biological sciences cannot understand them. I see no simple answer to this question of communication.

3. *Motives for working with the handicapped.* Some years ago, when I was concerned with the selection of teachers to work in special schools, it was considered rather suspect for anyone to say that they "felt the call" or the "need" to work with handicapped children. The appropriate answer to a query from the interviewer about motivation was to say "I think it will be an interesting job and better paid than the one I now have." I was perplexed by this attitude, because it seemed to me that, if one were going to work for the handicapped, one should feel concerned and moved about their fate. At the same time I knew how this attitude had originated, especially from my experience with the over-zealous, mud-

dled enthusiast who often hinders rather than helps some multiply handicapped children. On the other hand, one has found individuals who seemed to have remarkable skills and attitudes which allowed them to be unusually effective in looking after handicapped people. It is time that we recognized these differences and took some steps to identify what skills and what personality traits make the person effective to this work. If one is at all concerned with the care of the handicapped, motivation must be recognized as a very important factor of that care.

References

Oswin, M. (1978) *Children Living in Longstay Hospitals* Spastics International Medical Publications Research Monograph No 5., Heinemann Medical Books, Lippincott.

Rutter, M., Graham, P. & Yule, W. (1970) *A Neuropsychiatry Study in Childhood* Clinics in Developmental Medicine 35, 36 London: Spastics International Medical Publications, Heinemann Medical Books: Philadelphia, Lippincott.

Kushlick, A. Palmer, J. Felce, D. & Smith, J. (1977) *Summary of Current Research in Mental Handicap 1977* Research Report no 126.

17

Management of Children with Special Handicaps

STELLA CHESS, M.D.

Abstract

A longitudinal view of children whose development was affected by the rubella virus following the epidemic of 1964 shows that these children had visual, hearing, neuro-motor and cardiac defects. Many had these problems in combination. In addition to physical problems, behaviour problems began to emerge after two years. Mental retardation and autism were the most prominent, but other learning difficulties were also evident. Developmental milestones were often delayed.

There is reason to believe that in the case of multiply handicapped children, developmental milestones compiled for normal children are not a good indication of what the prognosis is. The fact is that it is the minority of handicapped children who do not improve and that it is important not to give up too early.

L'auteur présente une perspective longitudinale des enfants dont le développement a été affecté par le virus de la rubéole à la suite de l'épidémie de 1964. Ces enfants ont été atteints de défectuosités visuelles, auditives, neuromotrices et cardiaques. Plusieurs avaient ces problèmes tous ensemble. En plus des perturbations, des troubles du comportement se mirent à apparaître après deux années. L'arriération mentale et l'autisme étaient les plus évidents, mais d'autres difficultés d'apprentissage se manifestèrent également. Souvent les étapes du développement se trouvaient reculées.

L'auteur est d'avis que, dans le cas des enfants à handicaps multiples, les étapes ou normes de développement proposées pour les enfants normaux ne sont pas de bons indices de pronostic. Elle fait remarquer que seule une minorité d'enfants handicapés ne donnent pas de signes d'amélioration et que, par conséquent, il est important de ne pas abandonner les efforts prématurément.

Though I am by training a child psychiatrist, I became involved with multiply handicapped children in the New York area as the result of the Rubella epidemic of 1964. At that time there were an estimated twenty to thirty thousand affected children born across the United States who survived the pre-natal period. The head of pediatrics at the New York University Bellevue Medical Centre was asked by the Department of Health to undertake a study of the children of the larger New York area—initially a purely physical study. The area hospitals were asked to report any birth of a child who was defective and the

Department of Health also supplied a list of women whose obstetricians had reported them as having had rubella during pregnancy. But in the course of the study, as the children approached the age of two, the pediatricians began to discover problems other than physical defects. It was at this point that I was asked to help.

Of the 243 children identified, 80 (33 per cent) had visual defects (usually cataracts—some glaucoma) and 177 (73 per cent) had hearing defects. The neurological findings indicated that 107 children had focal neurological problems and 59 had "soft" neurological problems and in addition, 85 of the children had evidence of cardiac problems. For 50 children, there were no physical findings. These were largely children whose mothers were reported to have had rubella during the third trimester or in the very end of the second trimester of their pregnancies. At age 14, only 34 of these 50 children had no physical findings because the other 16 had other defects which had manifested themselves since early childhood. Seventy-two of the 243 children identified had one defect area; 47 had two defect areas, 47 had three defect areas, and 27 had 4 defect areas. These four categories, visual, auditory, neuro-motor, and cardiac are clearly noticeable but they lead to oversimplification because there are other kinds of problems in this sample.

As the children were studied behaviourally, other categories had to be added, of which mental retardation was the most prominent. A history and some testing showed one-third of the sample to be in the sub-average group. Also, the intellectual levels of the children in the normal range had, in general, risen.

One-half of these mentally retarded children were in the severe and profound group. Most of the others were in the moderate group, and only a few were classified as mild. We also found an unexpectedly high proportion of autistic children. Evidently, rubella can frequently result in autism. Ten of the children were fully autistic, and another eight, who gave fleeting evidence of awareness, I classified as under partial syndrome.

These children are not representative of a total population, but of the selective effects of this particular virus. The children have been studied three times, first in the pre-primary period or early childhood, next at 8 to 9 years of age, and finally as 13 to 14 year olds.

The services to parents in this longitudinal study included (1) an informing interview to parents following the studies, (2) further discussions with any of our personnel on special issues, and (3) helping to search out appropriate treatment facilities. Some parents have mentioned that this was the one time when they were able to get a total view of their child, because the previous reports had been unrelated. For instance, the cardiologist reported on the cardiac problem; if the child had any hearing defect, an isolated report was given on this aspect; if the child had a visual defect, a statement was made as to whether, for example, the cataract should be extracted or not. A total discussion had never been held. Consequently, we not only discussed the child's behavioural integrity and the absence or presence of retardation, but also encouraged the parents to ask us any question they wished. After reporting on the findings and on the child's physical status, one learns to say to the parents, "Everyone has questions. Frequently parents feel that they just should not be asking professionals lay questions, but really, what else do you want to talk about?" Once parents or caretakers realize that they need not frame a professionalized question, practical everyday concerns tend to come out.

The data indicated that the vast majority of the rubella children were deaf. Often deafness was combined with other handicaps.

CHILDREN WHO WERE "DEAF ONLY OR DEAF PLUS CARDIAC"

The cardiac problem for the children who survived was largely *pulmonic stenosis* and *patent ductus arteriosis*. Fortunately, the cardiac defect for these children did not represent great functional defects. They were mostly in cardiac classifications 1A and 1B, and only one or two children had been told to guard against fatigue. Therefore, the "deaf only or deaf plus cardiac" children could be categorized largely as deaf only. Most of these children were of average or above-average intelligence. Some of the children were of quite superior intellectual level; these children tended to be at day schools, either in day schools for the deaf or main-streamed with resource teachers.

CHILDREN WHO WERE "DEAF AND VISUALLY IMPAIRED"

By contrast, the "deaf and visually impaired" (with or without cardiac difficulty) were most frequently multiply handicapped children, a large proportion also having neuromotor difficulty and mental retardation. A small group of "deaf and visually impaired" were average or above average in intelligence.

CHILDREN WHO WERE "DEAF AND BLIND"

Those who are classified as deaf-blind are frequently in residential schools Monday through Friday or in full residential care. They are frequently referred to as low-functioning—a term that usually means retarded.

We found that our children grouped themselves very quickly into those of average or above average intelligence with deafness of some degree, a very small proportion of whom also had visual impairment or neuromotor difficulty, as opposed to retarded youngsters with multiple handicaps. They needed to be at day schools if they were of average or above average learning ability and in developmental centres if they were below average.

LEARNING PROBLEMS

Many terms associated with learning difficulties are used in vastly different ways by different people. A great deal of confusion exists concerning appropriate terminology with respect to rubella children. For example, teachers would say, "Oh, yes, this is a typical rubella child; he has a mind like a sieve," or "this is not a typical rubella child; he does not have a mind like a seive." Somewhere the idea had originated that the rubella virus almost universally causes long and short term memory problems and it had led to prejudgements which not infrequently became self-fulfilling prophecies. Other teachers, of course, found the expected memory problems a challenge and made a special effort to provide a great deal of repetition. Those who had the most severely damaged children assumed that the problems they faced were representative of all children with congenital rubella. When teachers and caretaking personnel met at conferences this idea was reinforced and the expectation of memory deficits affected their perception of children who, in fact, did not have such problems. The retention problems are reflections of mental retardation and also, in some cases the perserveration, hyper-irritability and high distractability characteristic of neurologically damaged children with impulse disordered which have influences on learning beyond those of the cognitive defect itself. These behavioural symptoms reflect the degree and kind of damage to the central nervous system that had occurred in certain children but not in others. It is frequently a great surprise to the institutional personnel serving low-functioning children to learn that there could be children with deafness, blindness, and/or neuro-motor problems who are of average or above average intelligence and might have been spared behavioural or cognitive problems.

Another term that was inaccurately used in many different ways, often tying the hands of the personnel who were trying their best to handle the children, was "autism" and variations thereof. Since an unexpectedly high proportion of autistic children was found in this sample, we were quite sensitive to the misuse of the term *autistic*. Again and again, we heard; "This child is autistic." "There are autistic features," "Pseudo-autism is present," or "At times the child shows autistic behaviours." Since the word, *autism*, has been too widely and carelessly applied, it might be worthwhile to explain its true meaning. The diagnosis autism is shorthand here for *childhood autism*, which is also often called Kanner's syndrome because it was first described in 1943 by Dr. Leo Kanner as a distinct clinical entity. Dr. Kanner borrowed the word autism from adult psychiatry, where it refers to preoccupation with inner thoughts, while actual reality is excluded or distorted. Initially, childhood autism too was so defined, but most of these children gave no real indication of what their inner thoughts might be. The most prominent symptom is in fact the absence of affective relatedness to people. Autism has, thus, a somewhat different meaning when applied to children than to adults. The essential basis for diagnosis is the reduced awareness of affective relatedness to other people. One must be careful to make sure that the unresponsiveness is well beyond the degree that would be fully accounted for by the retardation present. Autistic children exhibit many mannerisms and rituals, which constitute a very prominent aspect of their functioning. Flapping hands, whirling, and odd finger movements are some of the most prominent of these behaviours. These rituals are also characteristic of some blind, deaf, and retarded children who exhibit many stereotyped behaviours. Some application of the terms "autistic" and "autistic-like" have been based on the assumption that ritualistic and stereotyped behaviour are synonomous with "autistic behaviour." The distinction is often not made that many of the sensorially deprived or retarded children who exhibit such stereotyped behaviours are quite happy to put them aside when an opportunity is provided to interact personally with others. This is quite different from the autistic child who frequently responds to the attempt to initiate an interpersonal relationship with pitched squealing and other evidences of distress— wanting only to get back to the rituals. The presence of ritualistic behaviour patterns should not automatically lead to a diagnosis of autism per se. One has to look further.

AFFECT AND ITS VARIATIONS

Children have often been described as "without effect," as evidencing a "flat affect" or "inappropriate affect." The term *affect*, also initially used in adult psychiatry, has been adapted to child psychiatry. It is often used interchangeably with *emotion*, although attempts have been recently made to differentiate these two concepts. The word *mood* is also used interchangeably with affect. As used in adult psychiatry, affect refers to the person's emotional tone. The word affect is used with the same lack of precision in describing children as the word autism. Thus, an *affectless* child is one who indicates no mood or expression whatsoever. *Flat affect* refers to an emotional expression which has a narrow range, although it may be appropriate to the stimulus events. *Inappropriate affect* describes an emotional expression unrelated to the concomitant event. The child may laugh when hurt, put up a struggle when something ordinarily pleasurable to a child is occurring, or whine when no clear reason can be found. Both flatness of affect and inapporpoirate affect may occur in autistic children. Yet their presence does not signal "autism," since both can occur in children with other disorders. Sometimes an outward manifestation of affect does not occur, as in the case of a blind child who does not smile but is nevertheless experiencing pleasure.

MENTAL RETARDATION

A child should not be considered "mentally retarded" unless his total adaptation is sub-average. Using an IQ as the sole criterion for determining retardation is inappropriate. There are many situations in which the results of various intelligence tests will be at odds with a child's actual ability to understand his world and to learn adaptive techniques. Children who have spent long periods in institutions or who have been closely restricted to home will be unfamiliar with many situations from which test items have been drawn. Hence these children will give answers that are incorrect according to the test key. The investigator's interpretation of wrong answers as inability to comprehend is based on the assumption that all examinees have been exposed to similar problem situations, which is not accurate for these children. Physically handicapped children may lack experience, or may have limited experience with some of the items or situations used on the test, although these items are appropriate for more mobile children. Children with physical handicaps are at times administered tests which do not take into account their handicaps. For example, a partially deaf child may have limited familiarity with words, not because of lack of intelligence but because of inability to discuss, argue, play word games, learn rules and their exceptions, or otherwise build up an age-appropriate familiarity with the words used within the test. Certainly the use of a verbal scale for a severely or profoundly deaf child in computing an intelligence quotient is a highly questionable practice. Similarly, with blind or partially sighted children, certain portions of the test can either not be given, or if given would be inaccurate as a representation of the child's actual adaptive capacities, especially in timed tests using visual skills in which the score depends partially on speed. Youngsters with neuromotor difficulties will not be able to manipulate materials easily or they may lack familiarity with test stimuli to the same degree as that of non-handicapped children of the same age. Where tests exist which do not require use of the defective route for demonstration of comprehension, the IQ score will have greater validity. However, unless these tests have also been standardized with a non-handicapped population, it is not possible to make comparative judgements regarding learning ability.

Traditionally, in the preschool period, the passing of developmental milestones can be used to determine the presence of normal intelligence or the degree of retardation. Clearly, for physically handicapped children or those with specific language lags, such evidence of developmental retardation will be accurate in the absolute sense. However, one major purpose for using developmental rates as measures of adaptation is to predict the rate of future development in order to make appropriate demands and provide appropriate stimulation for the child. Youngsters with physical disabilities must use alternate routes, different intersensory complementary and supplementary connections, for they can comprehend the world only through the means available to them. It has been shown that milestones at earlier ages, still arrive at norm or above when they grow older. One must therefore emphasize that (1) the IQ and adaptive level are not always the same and that (2) the adaptive level in physically handicapped children, even when interpreted in light of their personal experiences, cannot be taken as providing the final word. Although they afford a better basis for predicting future development than the use of tests standardized for non-handicapped groups, early measures of adaptive behaviours do not always predict accurately what the future will bring.

As the child utilizes his undamaged faculties to understand the world and its sequences, and as he combines motor, tactile and sensory experiences at the higher cognitive levels that he reaches, the child may achieve a comprehension that finally equals in quality that of the non-handicapped child, or comes closer to it than early testing would have led us to believe. This does not diminish the importance of testing or of gathering data on the child's adaptive level. It means that such data should be used differently, that is, we must interpret results from later testing to see how the older child *compares with himself* at an earlier age, and then make our predictions and plans on the basis of such a comparison.

Traditionally, developmental milestones can be used in the preschool period to determine the presence of retardation. We have found in our group, and in all of the detailed longitudinal studies reviewed, that the developmental milestone data compiled for normal children are not a good basis for prognosis for the physically handicapped. Our longitudinal study of rubella children has emphasized this. It is only a small minority of the severely handicapped and the profoundly and severely retarded children that do not tend to improve. But the adaptive skills of those not in these categories do improve, given stimulating environments. Since there is a trend for the rubella child to improve his relative status as he grows older, we must counter the tendency to give up on a child too early just because it is assumed that prognostically such treatment programmes are not worth the money nor the effort.

18

Problems Experienced by Line Staff in Management of Children with Multiple Handicaps

DANA BRYNELSEN

Abstract

Using letters and the case study method, we may understand the problems experienced by line staff in getting adequate services to plan long-term care for multiply handicapped children. Delay in acquiring a comprehensive diagnosis and assessment, and fragmented services are major problems. This produces prolonged, unsuccessful caretaking experiences for parents where the optional care for the child would be available, and puts them at greater risk for withdrawing from the child's primary care.

The involvement of both parents, early access to informed medical information and counselling, as well as follow-up referral to a community resource team would help the management process significantly. The management of these children by involved professionals, and the direction of the programme by one professional who would assume the role of "educational synthesizer," would produce a better outcome for multiply handicapped children.

The problems experienced by line staff in management of children with multiple handicaps are many. Parents, whether natural or foster, are even more "on the line" than paid staff. The problems they both face have similar roots and this presentation will focus on the problems common to both the primary caregiver and the staff.

I have attempted to select examples of problems we have in B.C., cases that have been reported in the literature or documented at international conferences. Some of these issues have been discussed for over 100 years. Nineteenth century concepts relating to the provision of services to children with handicaps include assessment, early intervention, in-home support and group homes. As twentieth century phenomena these expanding services have been criticized, it would seem, in direct proportion to their growth, as being fragmented, overspecialized, uncoordinated, inefficient and ineffective.

In 1925, Smith deplored the fact that different specialists dealt with the handicapped child at different stages of growth and development, as follows: in infancy—the physician; schoolage—the educator; adulthood—the social worker.

The result was that the handicapped person was not seen as a human being but rather as a plastic mass to be moulded to fit the situation at hand. Smith felt that the goal should be normal family life in which "supervised and intelligent training among understanding parents or foster parents is dominant and where accessible, the assistance of specially trained workers . . .".

In 1948, Yepson said, "it was well recognized yet appalling that although it was ¾ of a century since organized services for the handicapped were first initiated that not a single American state or Canadian province had a well integrated or well coordinated program for the handicapped." He added, "new objectives were not needed, nor was there a need to re-examine present objectives. What was needed was a positive dynamic program of action."

To illustrate the impact that inadequate and inconsistent services can have on a family, I would like to quote portions of two letters here. Both letters were written by the same parent. The first was written three years ago when her son, who has multiple handicaps, was four years of age. It was addressed to Eileen Scott, the former National Consultant, Children's Services, C.N.I.B.

> Dear Miss Scott:
> Thanks for your letter—I was impressed by the fact that you remembered Tim personally after nearly two years.
> Tim is indeed severely handicapped, as you know, by brain damage as well as functional blindness. He is small for a four year old, has a good disposition, and certainly isn't an unbearable burden at this point; most of my worrying over him concerns his future.
> In this regard, I'd like to ask you for some information. . . .
> First, I would really like to know just exactly what makes Tim blind—what's wrong? I have found doctors we've seen decidedly hard to communicate with on this subject, but I would really appreciate a detailed, medical explanation, and I'm quite willing to do whatever research is needed in order to understand it . . . . I would like to explore any possibility there may be for improving his vision; if there is no possibility, I'd like to know that, too.
> I'm interested in any information you have on stimulating blind children to learn—I realize much may have to be adapted or disregarded in light of the fact that Tim can't walk, crawl, etc. to explore his environment. . . . I feel that in attempting to get his interest, to teach him anything, I'm working by trial and error, and I could really use some help.
> I feel that unless Tim's condition improves drastically, there is going to come a time, whether in five years or ten, when I will be physically unable to care for him alone. . . . But I feel that in any of the existing institutions Tim would be just maintained as a live blob, fed, changed, and rotated to avoid bedsores, and whatever potential he may have for learning would die

of neglect. . . . 'Institutional care must undergo a radical transformation before I'll be able to submit Tim's fragile psyche to its tender mercies.

Looking farther into the future I wish I could see Tim living in a small, local group home, or something of the sort, where I could spend lots of time with him, keep an eye on his care, and continue to give him the love which I will always have for him, on a daily basis. . . . I would be greatly interested in knowing how to contact any individuals or groups who perceive these needs for support, and are pursuing such goals.

Last, I would like to know if any financial support, pension, etc., is available to assist families in meeting the special needs, travelling expenses, equipment, etc., for children like Tim.

Thanks a lot for your concern and consideration. I'm not too proud to admit that I need all the help I can get in caring and planning for Tim, and your kind letter brought me hope.

The problems this parent was experiencing or anticipating when her son was four include the following points:
- inadequate access to information relating either to her son's handicapping conditions or remediation activities
- concern for the future in terms of Tim's education and long term care

Three years later, a second letter was written by the same parent to a senior government official. There is a great deal of anger in this letter but I do not feel that it overdramatizes the problems this family was experiencing.

Dear Mrs. Smith:

I have recently heard with great (morbid) interest your statement that group homes, as well as large institutions, for the mentally and physically handicapped should be phased out, with parents and foster parents assuming care of their present and potential residents. As the mother of a blind, spastic quadruplegic and profoundly retarded six year old boy who lives with me, and is known to you as a number on the Extended Care waiting list, I suggest that you, Mrs. Smith, pioneer this progressive program by fostering my son Tim.

Of course this will change your life dramatically. Since Tim's care will demand a great deal of your emotional and physical energy, you may find yourself forced to give up a career. . . . In the meantime, any weight problems you may have will disappear, as feeding and diapering Tim, and worrying about him will effectively discourage your appetite, as well as burning many calories. . . . If you love doing laundry, he'll be glad to keep your hands full of it. . . . Your constant backache is normal; take two aspirins and call me in the morning.

Despite all this and more, you may learn to love Tim, as I do, for his responsiveness, affection and nice nature. You may come to see him as I do, as a *person*, with a personality, a human spirit trapped behind a useless pair of eyes, a useless body, a damaged brain. . . . You may see his overwhelming needs for affection, physical care, mental stimulation, his increased spasticity and withdrawal when left "just sitting" for too long. You may come to see him, as I do, as a child worthy of the *best* care and training that money can buy.

When you no longer deny the fact that Tim is making no progress, receiving little attention, and withdrawing into apathy, you can appeal to your school board for a program of education for him. If you have done your homework well, they will praise your articulateness and courage, and regretfully inform you that the one-to-one, intensive program he needs is, sadly, financially out of reach.

Should you find yourself considering seriously the possibility that Tim's needs might be better met in a group setting in a house chosen for accessibility to wheelchairs, with staff who have chosen this work because it interests them, you may want to discuss your ideas with social workers who are well trained to tell you how much they admire you, and how they would really like to help, if only someone else would foot the bill. Bask in their appreciation of your devotion and self sacrifice. Put your hat back on your head. Pray to the lord for strength as you kneel beside the bathtub. Your government is behind you all the way!

What will your rewards be? For fostering Tim, you receive a family allowance cheque (I hear it's being decreased), and up to $500.00 per month in salary, which is of course, $500.00 more than I have been receiving for doing this work. This should cover the depreciation of your body, intellect and spirit. In addition, you will receive the satisfaction of doing an extremely difficult job, quite possibly singlehandedly, and when you finally lay your burden down, you'll certainly get your crown in Heaven.

Sounds super, eh? When can you start?

P.S. Mrs. Smith, I hope you understand that I mean no disrespect for you or Tim. The facts here are of the utmost seriousness to me; it's my life, and the lives of many other parents, being discussed somewhat flippantly here; a choice between trying to laugh and crying the blues. We don't need sympathy; we sure could use your understanding and concrete assistance with the dilemma of caring for these children and surviving ourselves.

I have included these two letters, by way of introduction, to give us a glimpse of the long-lasting, cumulative effects of inadequate and inconsistent service. Too often, we who serve these families, are isolated by physical space, funding source, disability group or ideologies. There is little, as isolated individuals, that we can do to make whole, systems that are chronic fragments. . . . However, as individuals, regardless of profession or role, who are working with these families and their children, we can bring about significant improvements in parent-child relationships. We can provide expertise that will encourage developmental progress with children with multiple handicaps. We can continue to foster, with parents and colleagues, working relationships that facilitate both processes, and this is what the present paper hopes to illustrate.

CASE STUDIES OF INFANTS IN INFANT DEVELOPMENT PROGRAMMES:

As part of that illustration I will present two case studies of infants with multiple handicaps who are at present receiving service from Infant Development Programmes in B.C. These infants were selected to represent how individual case management practices can hinder or facilitate the parent-child relationship and the development of the infant. These infants were selected for presentation out of a group of 50 infants with multiple handicaps and do not represent the worst or best examples of case management, although the first represents inadequate management and the second, at this time, adequate management.

Tammy:

Tammy was seven weeks premature and weighed 4½ pounds at birth. After a three week stay in hospital she was discharged and her mother was told that she was doing well. Over the next two months, the mother became increasingly concerned over Tammy's development, specifically over her low level of alertness and responsiveness, her irritability and general developmental delay. The mother also suspected seizures. These concerns were brought to the attention of the physician when Tammy was three months of age. The mother had older children and felt she had a basis for comparison. Tammy was referred for assessment at eight months of age and hospitalized for neurological examination at ten months. The mother visited daily. After one month of hospitalization, and extensive assessments, Tammy was discharged with a diagnosis of seizure disorder, suspected mental retardation, cortical blindness, hearing impairment and cerebral palsy. She was referred to the Infant Development Programme at discharge; the reason for the referral being the above diagnosis as well as support to the mother and family. No further developmental information beyond the diagnosis was made available to the Infant Development Programme staff although the social history was well presented.

During the initial home visit the mother expressed anger at the delay in securing what she felt to be appropriate medical attention for her daughter and said she felt she had not been given enough information about Tammy's present condition or future potential. She wanted information on institutionalization and felt that although she loved Tammy very much, the care Tammy demanded and the lack of positive feedback she received from Tammy were disrupting her family life and her ability to care for the rest of the family was deteriorating. The Infant Development Programme worker discussed foster care as an alternative to an institution . . . but the mother rejected foster care as she felt she could not cope with the idea of another person doing what she should be able to do. Tammy spent the next month in the hospital. The Infant Development Programme staff, the mother and a social worker visited a small institution 40 miles from the parents' home. The mother was impressed by the physical facility and physical care given to the children. Her continued involvement with Tammy was initially encouraged by the Supervisor of the institution and by the Infant Development Programme staff and social worker. Tammy was taken from the hospital and placed in the institution. Mom visited Tammy bi-weekly. Staff at the institution began to express concern over her involvement. They requested the Infant Development Programme staff to discourage the mother from visiting as she disrupted the schedule. The mother was not allowed to feed Tammy, and subsequently asked not to visit the nursery and requested to visit for only twenty minutes in a room separate from the nursery. Attempts to have physio consultation for Tammy in this facility were not successful. Staff considered physiotherapy to be cruel and unnecessary. With increasing restrictions on visiting and no therapy, the mother began to consider foster placement as an alternative, and when Tammy was observed by visitors as attempting to pull to stand and smiling to gain attention, arrangements were made for a full assessment.

Tammy, then eighteen months of age, was assessed and two months later was placed in a rehabilitation hospital for two months, a foster home for one month, and now has been with the present foster parents for eight months. The foster parent, at placement and up to this time has only Tammy's name and birthdate. As Tammy has had continued involvement with certain individuals in the community, there is some information of her developmental history available for programme planning purposes.

The foster parent, Infant Staff and physiotherapist (who visits bi-weekly) have been encouraged by Tammy's developmental progress over the past eight months. The foster parent, shortly after Tammy arrived, questioned the diagnosis of blindness, as Tammy appeared to peer in her direction without auditory cues when "misbehaving" (e.g.: reaching for a coffee cup on a low table.) She has subsequently been seen by an opthamologist and eye surgery is planned for the near future. Her year of hospital and institutional placement without intensive therapy have contributed to increased spasticity and corrective orthopedic surgery is scheduled. Psysiotherapy will continue. Tammy at age 30 months is imitating sounds, has a five word vocabulary, is gaining skills in the fine motor area, and will be attending a pre-school for exceptional children this fall. The foster parent has applied to be permanent caregiver for this child.

The major issues that this case study presented are, briefly:

- the delay experienced in initial assessment.
- the mother's feeling that she has not received enough information regarding her daughter's problems
- the decision to place Tammy in an institution rather than foster care, primarily on the basis of the parents feeling that it would be difficult for them (the parent) to cope with the idea of foster care.
- a government funded facility that does not permit developmental programming or parent involvement
- the decision to move Tammy from the institution to the community based on circumstance and personalities involved rather than scheduled semi-annual assessments to ensure appropriate placement
- restricted access of the present primary caregiver to developmental information that relates to appropriate individual programme planning which is further compounded by six placements in eighteen months

Over forty professionals have been directly involved with Tammy since she was assessed as multiple handicapped, eighteen months ago. These professionals represent medicine, nursing, physiotherapy, occupational therapy, social work, and education and many sub-categories within each profession. Some have provided 24 hour care, others on-going intervention and still others consultation. These professionals also represent the most highly skilled manpower available to young children in our province, and many have worked with great diligence to provide the best services possible for this young child.

This case study represents several problem areas which impedes families and line staff in successful management of children with multiple handicaps. Some of these problem areas have solutions even within our fragmented human delivery service system.

The first major problem this case represents is the eight month delay the parent experiences in acquiring a comprehensive assessment. Some parents have described the period between suspicion of delay and confirmation of their concern as being the most difficult period to cope with emotionally. Our experience is, it would seem that the longer this period continues the more difficult it is to intervene in effecting change in parental attitudes and in helping the parent to set realistic goals for their child's development. One key to this, of course, relates to how the parent perceives him or herself in relation to their child's development. Studies elsewhere as well as one study of 59 developmentally delayed infants in Infant Development Programmes in this province, which included many infants with more than one handicap, demonstrate that generally, parents providing the most optimal home environment were those who believed in their ability to influence their child's development and felt a personal sense of responsibility towards that development. The parent with prolonged, unsuccessful caretaking experiences is at risk for withdrawing more and more from parenting practices. These pre-diagnostic experiences can be significant factors in postdiagnostic decisions regarding out of home care.

Successful attempts to bridge the gaps between suspicion and confirmation include those hospitals with well-established follow-up clinics which monitor the development of high risk babies and ensure comprehensive developmental assessments at regular intervals. Referral to, and close consultation with community resources when delay is evidenced should constitute their reason for existence. As Meier has said, under the sub title of Paralysis of Analysis, "when a satisfactory comprehensive developmental screening system has been selected from available tests and procedures, . . . it is useful only if it feeds into practical intervention programmes."

However, with or without this follow-up, community professionals should be aware that research demonstrates that parental observations regarding deviant development are generally well founded. However, 1979 research conducted by Robinson/Sheps of Population Paediatrics involving 287 developmentally delayed infants registered in intervention programmes in B.C. revealed a certain "nonchalance" on the part of the physicians with regard to parental concerns when they were first approached for help. Parents should also be well informed of available avenues for assessments so that one unsatisfactory or discouraging encounter does not deter a continued pursuit of appropriate help.

A second major problem area was that the mother felt she had not received enough information regarding her daughter's problems. There are two points here. One is that both parents must be included in all major discussions relating to assessment, diagnosis and intervention. It is an unfortunate cultural condition that mother as primary caretaker is also deemed primary recipient and transmitter to her family of assessment, diagnostic and intervention information. Needless to say, much is lost in the translation, not just in terms of accuracy, but also in terms of potential meaningful involvement of the father in decisions and management issues. The effectiveness of intervention strategies is in part predicated on parents in partnership with each other as well as in partnership with staff.

The second point is that parents must have access over time to informed and empathetic counselling regarding their child's diagnosis. Simple practices such as requesting the parents to write down questions or concerns for discussion at the next visit have proved very helpful. This simple practice allows the professional to see how effective he/she is in sharing information with a family.

Billy:

Billy was five weeks premature and weighed four pounds, thirteen ounces at birth. After a three week stay in the intensive care nursery he was discharged home. Billy was the first born for this family and they suspected delay by six months of age. The paediatrician involved the parents in ongoing assessments and requested the parents to chart Billy's progress. At 8½ months Billy was hospitalized when seizures appeared and underwent extensive neurological assessments. The consulting neuropaediatrician and both parents had the opportunity to meet frequently during the month Billy was hospitalized. Both parents were kept well informed on a daily basis as to the attempts to control the seizures, the neurological assessments and the initial diagnosis which included infantile spasms, developmental delay, cerebral palsy and visual impairment. The parents were counselled as to the implications of each handicap and the compounding effect of these handicaps on developmental progress. The parents were given realistic expectations with regards to Billy but were encouraged to assist him to acquire new developmental skills.

The neurology team referred the family to the Infant Development Programme. Both parents met with the Infant Programme staff to discuss the programme and a schedule of weekly home visits was set up.

In brief, Billy at nine months was able to lift his head in prone momentarily and with arms positioned over a roll could maintain it for 20 seconds. Billy was starting to mouth objects and occasionally put his hands on a bottle when being fed but preferred to put his hand on his mother's hand.

A programme of activities was worked out by the parents and staff to encourage Billy's development. Physiotherapy was prescribed and the consulting therapy incorporated appropriate gross motor exercises into the daily home programme by visiting the home with the infant worker. The C.N.I.B. were involved and are available for further consultation as Billy's visual abilities change.

Billy's development at 16 months was encouraging. He is now able to sit unsupported for up to five minutes. He has well established object permanency, and he responds to his name and can say two words.

In addition to the home programme Billy is assessed every six months by a team for visually impaired children. Both parents, the infant worker, neuropaediatrician, therapist and team public health nurse participate in this assessment and copies of the reports are sent to the family as well as the other involved professionals.

The family are consistent in their work with Billy. They do not expect miracles but are encouraged by his progress.

The issues that this case study present that seem to be relevant to a more successful management approach are briefly:

- the involvement of both parents by the paediatrician in developmental on-going assessments and charting from the point of suspicion of delay.
- the access for both parents to informed medical information and counselling on an on-going basis during hospitalization.
- direction, at discharge from the hospital to a community resource and

follow-up by a team with the parents and community resource on a regular basis.
- involvement of both parents in programme design and implementation
- involved professionals with one assuming primary involvement

SUMMARY

As a summary, I would like to go into this last point in greater detail. Primary involvement of one professional is considered by some experts to be critical to the successful maintenance of children with multiple handicaps in their own community. One model, developed by Dianne Bricker, describes this professional as an "educational synthesizer or one who can gather information from a variety of specialists and incorporate it into effective daily intervention strategies." Obviously, throughout the course of childhood, this person would change. The difference between this approach and one bemoaned by Smith in the introduction, where the physician, teacher and social worker have age related influence, is that, although the person changes the role does not. Therefore, one may assign the role to the most relevant person involved with the child as his/her needs and services change. For some children, this person may be the parent, and certainly the parent in most instances is the only constant adult in a child's life. Regardless of who assumes the role, this must be shared with the parent to whatever degree possible.

Primary involvement of one professional requires many modifications to present professional practices. The person assuming this role must have the following skills: the ability to relate to children, their families and other professionals; the ability to assess the needs of the child in terms of ongoing programme development and the family in terms of support services and information; knowledge of professions's other than one's own and the potential contributions other professional's can make to programme development and family needs; and the ability to decipher specialist input and incorporate it into daily practical use that will effect measurable change.

Consultant specialists to this primary professional as well must have certain skills. These are: the ability to relinquish traditional powers in order to foster a climate that encourages open interaction; the ability to reduce professional jargon to minimum; and the ability to explain why certain procedures are relevant to a child's development or family needs and to describe these procedures within the context of functional interaction.

In closing, I would like to reiterate Yepson's statement. "New objectives are not needed, nor is there a need to re-examine present objectives. What is needed is a positive dynamic programme of action."

References

Baker, B.L. "Support Systems for the Parent as Therapist." In *Research to Practice in Mental Retardation, Vol. I Care and Intervention*. Mittler, P.M., Ed. Baltimore: University Park Press, 1977.

Bricker, D. "Educational Synthesizer." In *Hey, Don't Forget About Me*. CEC, 1976.

Dunn, *H.G. et al. Canadian Paediatric Society Ross Conference on the Unmet Needs of Canadian Children*. Montebello, Quebec, 1973.

Heifetz, L.J. "Professional Preciousness and the Evolution of Parent-Training Strategies." In *Research to Practice in Mental Retardation, Vol. I, Care and Intervention*. Mittler, P.M., Ed. Baltimore: University Park Press, 1977.

Meier, John "Screening, Assessment and Intervention for Young Children at Developmental Risk." In *Issues in the Classification of Young Children*, Vol. I, 2 Vols., Hobbs, Nicholas, Ed. San Francisco: Jossey-Bass, 1974.

Robinson, G. and S. Sheps *Children With Developmental Handicaps: Is There A Gap Between Suspicion and Referral?* Department of Paediatrics, UBC, 1979.

Sloan, W. and H. Stevens *A Century of Concern: A History of the American Association on Mental Deficiency*, A.A.M.D. Inc., 1976.

Tolleson, L. *Parents' Beliefs, Attitudes and Values and Their Relationship to Home Environment Provided for Developmentally Delayed Infants Involved in a Home-Based Intervention Programme*. Unpublished M.A. Thesis, UBC, 1978.

"Problèmes rencontrés par le personnel de base dans leur travail avec les enfants à handicaps multiples".

DANA BRYNELSEN

Sommaire

S'appuyant sur des documents épistolaires et sur la méthode d'étude de cas, l'auteur décrit les problèmes rencontrés par le personnel de base dans leurs efforts pour obtenir des services qui permettraient la planification à long terme des soins à donner aux enfants à handicaps multiples. Le retard dans l'obtention d'un diagnostic et d'une évaluation compréhensive et la fragmentation des services représentent des problèmes majeurs. Ceux-ci entraînent pour les parents l'expérience de soins prolongés et inefficaces, là où il serait possible de donner à l'enfant des soins optimaux, et un plus grand risque de voir ces parents se désintéresser des soins primaires à fournir à l'enfant.

L'auteur laisse entendre que la mise à contribution des deux parents, la possibilité d'avoir accès dès le début à une information médicale et à un counseling éclairés, de même que l'orientation ultérieure vers une équipe de ressources communautaires, faciliteraient sensiblement le processus de traitement. Elle prétend que la prise en charge de ces enfants par des professionnels engagés et celle du programme par un spécialiste qui accepterait le rôle de "synthétisant pédagogique" donneraient des résultats plus favorables aux enfants à handicaps multiples.

INTRODUCTION

On m'a demandé de traiter des problèmes que rencontrent les membres du personnel de ligne (ceux qui sont sur la "ligne de front") dans leur travail auprès des enfants à handicaps multiples. Puisque les parents, naturels ou nourriciers, sont plus sur la "ligne" que les employés rémunérés, et puisque les problèmes que ces deux groupes affrontent ont des racines semblables, cette communication portera sur les problèmes qui sont le lot commun, tant des premiers responsables des soins que du personnel directement affecté à ces enfants.

J'ai essayé de choisir des exemples de problèmes que nous rencontrons ici en Colombie Britannique, problèmes rapportés dans des publications ou présentés à des conférences internationales précédentes qui ont eu lieu ailleurs. Certaines de ces questions ont fait l'objet de discussion depuis plus de cent ans. Les notions que nous a léguées le XIXe siècle en ce qui a trait aux services à donner aux enfants handicapés comprennent l'évaluation, l'intervention précoce, dans l'aide au foyer et dans les maisons de regroupement. En tant que phénomème du XXe

siècle, l'expansion de ces services a été critiquée, en proportion directe de leur prolifération, apparemment pour leur fragmentation, leur spécialisation excessive, leur manque de coordination, leur mauvaise utilisation et leur inefficacité.

En 1925, Smith déplorait le fait que des spécialistes différents s'intéressaient à l'enfant handicapé à des stades différents de sa croissance et de son développement; durant la tendre enfance—le médecin; à l'âge scolaire—l'éducateur; à l'âge adulte—le travailleur social; avec ce résultat que la personne handicapée n'était pas perçue comme un être humain, mais plutôt comme une boule de plasticine à modeler en fonction de la situation qui prévaut. Smith était d'avis que l'objectif devrait être la vie de famille normale dans laquelle "la formation supervisée et intelligente entre parents naturels ou nourriciers compréhensifs prédomine et où (on a) accès à l'assistance de travailleurs qui ont subi un entraînement spécial . . ."

En 1948, Yepson disait . . . "on admettait volontiers le fait pourtant navrant que, bien qu'il se soit passé trois quarts de siècle depuis qu'on avait institué pour la première fois des services organisés pour les handicapés, il ne se trouvait pas un seul état américain ou une seule province canadienne qui possédait un programme pour handicapé bien intrégré ou bien coordonné." Il ajoutait "nul n'était besoin de nouveaux objectifs, ni de remise en question des objectifs actuels. Ce dont on avait besoin c'était d'un programme d'action positif et dynamique."

Pour illustrer l'impact . . . que des services inadéquats et incohérents peuvent exercer sur une famille, j'aimerais vous présenter des extraits de deux lettres. Ces deux lettres sont de la même maman. La première a été écrite il y a trois ans quand son fils, qui est frappé d'handicaps multiples, avait quatre ans. Elle est adressée à Eileen Scott, qui était alors Conseiller national des Services aux Enfants C.N.I.B.

Chère Miss Scott,

Merci de votre lettre—j'ai été touchée de constater que vous gardiez un souvenir personel de Tim presque deux ans plus tard.

Tim est, en effet, grandement handicapé, comme vous le savez tant par atteinte cérébrale que par une cécité fonctionnelle. Il est petit pour un enfant de quatre ans; il est d'un bon naturel et il ne représente sûrement pas actuellement un fardeau insupportable; la plupart de mes soucis à son égard se rapportent à son avenir.

A ce propos, j'aimerais vous demander certains renseignements. . . .

D'abord, je désirerais vraiment savoir très exactement ce qui rend Tim aveugle—qu'est-ce qui ne vas pas? J'ai trouvé les médecins que nous avons consultés peu disposés à parler de ce sujet, mais j'apprécierais réellement (qu'on me donne) une explication médicale détaillée et je suis tout à fait disposée à faire toutes les recherches nécessaires pour la comprendre

. . . j'aimerais explorer toute possibilité qui puisse exister d'améliorer sa vue; s'il n'y a pas de possibilités, j'aimerais le savoir également.

Je m'intéresse à toute information que vous puissiez posséder sur les moyens d'amener les enfants aveugles à apprendre—je comprends qu'il peut y avoir beaucoup (de points) à adapter ou à laisser de côté étant donné que Tim est incapable de marcher, de se traîner, et ainsi de suite, pour explorer son entourage . . . . J'ai l'impression que dans mes efforts pour susciter son intérêt, pour lui apprendre quelque chose, je procède par essai et erreur et que j'ai réellement besoin d'aide.

Je sens que, à moins que l'état de Tim ne s'améliore de façon inattendue, il viendra un moment, dans cinq ou dix ans peu importe, où je serai physiquement incapable de prendre soin de lui toute seule. . . . Par contre, je crois que dans n'importe laquelle des institutions existantes Tim ne serait qu'entretenu comme une nullité vivante, alimenté, changé et retourné dans son lit pour éviter les plaies et que tout potentiel d'apprentissage qui pourrait être le sien s'évanouirait dans l'oubli. . . . Les soins ''institutionnels'' devront subir des transformations radicales avant que je me sente disposée à confier le psychisme fragile de Tim à leurs bons soins.

En regardant plus loin dans l'avenir, je souhaiterais voir Tim placé dans une petite résidence commune locale, ou quelque chose de semblable, où il me serait possible de passer beaucoup de temps avec lui, de surveiller ses soins et de continuer à lui apporter l'amour que je ressentirai toujours pour lui, sur une base quotidienne. . . . Je suis fortement intéressée à apprendre comment entrer en communication avec tout individu ou groupe qui serait sensible à ses besoins d'aide et qui poursuivrait de tels objectifs.

Enfin, je désirerais savoir s'il existe quelque appui financier, pension, etc., de disponible pour aider les familles à pourvoir aux besoins spéciaux, frais de déplacement, équipement, etc., pour des enfants comme Tim.

Merci beaucoup de votre intérêt et de votre considération. Je ne suis pas fière au point de ne pas admettre que j'ai besoin de toute l'aide que je puisse obtenir pour prendre soin de Tim et planifier (son avenir) et votre lettre bienveillante m'a apporté de l'espoir.

Les problèmes que cette maman rencontrait ou qu'elle prévoyait alors que son fils avait quatre ans comprenaient l'insuffisance de l'accès à l'information se rapportant soit au handicap affectant son enfant, soit aux activités susceptibles de le corriger . . . et une inquiétude de l'avenir en termes de l'éducation de Tim et des soins de longue durée.

Trois années plus tard, la même maman écrivait une seconde lettre à l'intention d'un officier supérieur du gouvernement. Cette lettre exprime beaucoup de colère, mais je ne crois pas qu'elle dramatise abusivement les problèmes que rencontrent présentement cette famille . . .

Chère Madame Smith:

J'ai récemment écouté avec un grand intérêt (morbide) votre déclaration à l'effet qu'on devrait éliminer progressivement les résidences en groupes, de même que les grandes institutions pour handicapés mentaux et physiques, en laissant les parents naturels et nourriciers se charger du soin des résidents actuels et éventuels (de ces maisons). En ma qualité de mère d'un garçon de six ans, aveugle, tétraplégique spasmodique et profondément arriéré, qui vit avec moi et qui vous est connu en tant que numéro sur la liste d'attente des soins de longue durée, je propose, Madame Smith, que vous lanciez vous-même ce programme progressiste en prenant en charge mon fils Tim.

Cela changera votre vie de façon dramatique, bien sûr. Puisque la garde de Tim va accaparer une grande partie de vos énergies physiques et émotionnelles, il se peut que vous vous voyiez forcée d'abandonner une carrière. . . . Entre temps, tout problème d'embonpoint que vous puissiez avoir s'évanouira, car (les efforts employés à) nourrir Tim et changer ses couches et à vous inquiéter à son sujet vous couperont effectivement l'appétit, de même qu'ils brûleront bien des calories. . . . Si vous aimez faire la lessive, il se fera un plaisir de vous en mettre plein les bras. . . . Vos maux de reins constants sont normaux; prenez deux cachets d'aspirine et téléphonez-moi le lendemain.

Malgré tout ceci et plus encore, il se peut que vous appreniez à aimer Tim, comme je l'aime, pour sa sensibilité, son affection et son bon caractère. Il est possible que vous en arriviez à le percevoir comme je le fais, comme une *personne*, avec sa personnalité, une âme humaine emprisonnée derrière une paire d'yeux inutiles, un corps inutile, un cerveau abîmé. . . . Peut-être sentirez-vous ses besoins irrésistibles d'affection, de soins physiques, de stimulation mentale, l'accroissement de sa spasticité et de son repli sur lui-même quand on le laisse "tout simplement, à lui-même" pendant trop longtemps. Vous en viendrez peut-être, comme moi, à le percevoir comme un enfant digne des *meilleurs* soins et de la *meilleure* éducation que l'argent puisse procurer.

Quand vous en serez arrivée à ne plus nier le fait que Tim ne fait pas de progrès, qu'il reçoit peu d'attention et qu'il se renferme dans son apathie, vous pourrez faire appel à votre commission scolaire pour (qu'elle vous offre) un programme d'éducation à son intention. Si vous avez bien fait vos devoirs, on vous félicitera de votre façon de vous exprimer et de votre courage et on vous apprendra, avec regrets, que le programme individuel et intensif dont il a besoin est, malheureusement, hors de prix.

Se présenterait-il que vous envisagassiez sérieusement la possibilité que les besoins de Tim soient mieux servis dans le cadre d'un groupe, (logé) dans une maison où l'on peut avoir accès en fauteuil roulant et dont le personnel a choisi ce travail à cause de son intérêt, vous pourrez vouloir discuter de vos idées avec des travailleurs sociaux qui sont bien préparés pour vous dire jusqu'à quel point ils vous admirent et combien ils aimeraient vraiment (vous) aider, si seulement quelqu'un d'autre était disposé à payer la note. Plongez-vous dans le bain réconfortant de leur appréciation de votre dévouement et de votre abnégation. Remettez votre chapeau sur votre tête. Agenouillée près de la baignoire, priez le Seigneur qu'il vous donne de la force. Votre gouvernement vous appuie jusqu'au bout!

Quelle sera votre récompense? Pour la charge de Tim, vous recevrez un chèque d'allocations familiales (j'ai entendu dire qu'on réduisait le montant attribué) et jusqu'à 500 $ par mois de salaire, ce qui représente évidemment 500 $ de plus que ce que j'ai reçu jusqu'à présent pour ce travail. Cette somme devrait compenser la dépréciation de votre corps, de votre intellect et de votre moral. Vous aurez, en sus, la satisfaction de remplir une tâche extrêmement difficile, fort probablement toute seule, et quand finalement vous déposerez votre fardeau, vous recevrez assurément votre couronne dans le Ciel.

Formidable, n'est-ce-pas? Quand pouvez-vous commencer? P.S. Madame Smith, vous comprendrez, j'espère, que je n'ai pas voulu manquer de respect, ni à vous, ni à Tim. Les faits (en cause) ici sont pour moi des plus graves; c'est de ma vie et de la vie de beaucoup d'autres parents dont je discute ainsi de façon plutôt cavalière; (c'est) un choix entre tenter de rire et se laisser aller au cafard. Nous n'avons pas besoin de sympathie; mais il est bien certain que nous pourrions tirer profit de votre compréhension et de votre assistance concrète face à ce dilemme de prendre soin de ces enfants et de survivre nous-mêmes.

Comme je l'ai dit plus haut, je présente ces deux lettres en guise d'introduction pour laisser apercevoir les effets cumulatifs et de longue durée de services inadéquats et incohérents. Trop souvent, nous qui pourvoyons à ces familles, nous sommes isolés les uns des autres par l'espace physique, les ressources financières, les regroupements en fonction du handicap ou les idéologies. Il y a peu de choses que nous puissions faire, en tant qu'individus isolés, pour donner de l'unité à des systèmes qui sont chroniques et fragmentés. . . . Toutefois, peu importe notre rôle ou notre profession, nous pouvons à titre d'individus qui travaillons auprès de ces familles et de leurs enfants, susciter des améliorations sensibles dans les rapports parents-enfants. Nous pouvons donner des conseils d'expert pour favoriser l'épanouissement de ces enfants à handicaps multiples. Il nous est loisible d'encourager chez les parents et les collègues l'institution de relations de travail qui facilitent ces deux processus.

Etudes de cas de nouveaux-nés participant à des programmes de développement.

Je vais maintenant présenter deux études de cas de nouveaux-nés souffrant de handicaps multiples qui reçoivent actuellement des services de la part des *Programmes de Développement des Nouveaux-nés de la Colombie Britannique*. Ces bébés ont été choisis dans le but d'illustrer comment les façons de pourvoir aux cas individuels peuvent entraver ou faciliter la relation parent-enfant et l'évolution du nouveau-né. Ces deux cas ont été sélectionnés pour fins de présentation parmi un groupe de cinquante nouveaux-nés souffrant de handicaps multiples et ne représentant ni les pires, ni les meilleurs exemples de traitement de cas, bien que le premier illustre un traitement inadéquat et le second, un traitement adéquat, dans les circonstances présentes.

Tammy:

Tammy est née sept semaines avant terme et pesait à peine plus de deux kilos. Après un séjour de trois semaines à l'hôpital elle fut confiée à sa maman à qui l'on déclara que l'enfant allait bien. Au cours des deux mois suivants, sa mère devint de plus en plus inquiète du développement de Tammy, plus particulièrement de son niveau d'éveil et sa sensibilité peu prononcés, de son caractère irritable et du retard dans son évolution générale. Elle se demandait également si le bébé ne faisait pas des crises d'épilepsie. Ces inquiétudes furent portées à l'attention du médecin, alors que Tammy avait trois mois. La maman avait des enfants plus âgés et considérait qu'elle disposait de points de comparaison. . . . On recommanda que Tammy subisse une évaluation à l'âge de huit mois et elle fut hospitalisée pour examen neurologique alors qu'elle avait dix mois. Sa mère la visitait à tous les jours. Après un séjour d'un mois à l'hôpital et de nombreuses évaluations, elle fut renvoyée chez elle avec un diagnostic d'épilepsie, d'arriération mentale probable, de cécité corticale, de surdité partielle et de parésie cérébrale. Au moment de quitter l'hôpital, Tammy fut recommandée aux soins du Programme de Développement des Nouveaux-nés. . . . Cette recommandation s'explique à la fois par le diagnostic que nous venons de mentionner et par le besoin d'aide de la mère et de sa famille. A part du diagnostic, aucune information additionnelle portant sur le développement n'a été transmise au personnel du Programme de Développement, mais l'histoire sociale a été bien présentée.

Au cours de la première visite au foyer, la maman a exprimé son indignation face au retard à obtenir ce qu'elle considérait comme une attention médicale adéquate pour sa fille et dit qu'elle ne croyait pas avoir reçu assez de renseignements sur l'état actuel de Tammy et sur son potentiel éventuel. Elle voulait qu'on l'informe des possibilités de mise en institution et elle avait le sentiment que, même si elle aimait Tammy de tout son coeur, les soins que cette dernière exigeait et l'absence de réaction positive de sa part étaient en train de perturber sa vie familiale et que sa capacité de vaquer aux besoins du reste de sa famille allait en se détériorant. La visiteuse du Programme de Développement parla des soins en foyer nourricier comme solution autre que le placement en institution . . . mais la maman rejeta le foyer nourricier, car elle se sentait incapable d'admettre l'idée qu'une autre personne fasse ce qu'elle-même elle ne pouvait faire. Tammy passa le mois suivant à l'hôpital. Le personnel du Programme de Développement, la mère et une travailleuse sociale visitèrent une petite institution située à environ 65 kilomètres de la maison des parents. La mère fut impressionnée par l'équipement et les soins physiques donnés aux enfants. Le directeur de l'institution, le personnel du Programme de Développement et la travailleuse sociale encouragèrent la mère au début à continuer de s'employer auprès de Tammy. Cette dernière passa de l'hôpital à l'institution. Maman la visitait deux fois la semaine. Les membres du personnel de l'institution commencèrent alors à s'inquiéter de la présence de la mère. Ils demandèrent à ceux du Programme de Développement de convaincre cette dernière d'abandonner ses visites parce qu'elle perturbait l'horaire. On ne permettait pas à maman de nourrir Tammy et par la suite on lui demanda de ne pas se présenter à la pouponnière et on exigea qu'elle limite ses visites à vingt minutes, dans une salle distincte de la pouponnière. Les efforts pour procurer à Tammy des consultations en physiothérapie dans ce milieu échouèrent. Le personnel était d'avis que la physiothérapie était cruelle et non indiquée. Avec l'accroissement des restrictions appliquées aux visites et à la thérapie, la maman commença à penser au placement en foyer nourricier comme solution de rechange et, quand des visiteurs eurent remarqué que Tammy s'efforcait de tirer, de se tenir debout et de sourire pour attirer l'attention, des dispositions furent prises pour que l'on procède à une évaluation complète.

Tammy, qui avait alors dix-huit mois, fut examinée et deux mois plus tard on la plaçait dans un hôpital de réhabilitation pendant deux mois, dans un foyer nourricier durant un mois et elle vit maintenant avec sa mère nourricière actuelle depuis huit mois. Au moment où le placement s'est fait et jusqu'à maintenant ce parent nourricier n'a connu de Tammy que son nom et sa date de naissance. . . . Etant donné que Tammy a été l'objet de rapports continus avec certains individus dans le milieu communautaire on dispose de certains renseignements sur son évolution, renseignements qui peuvent servir à des fins de planification de programme.

La mère nourricière, le personnel du Programme de Développement et la physiothérapeute (qui lui rend visite deux fois par semaine) sont encouragés par le progrès dans l'évolution de Tammy au cours des derniers huit mois. . . . Peu de temps après l'arrivée de Tammy, la mère nourricière remettait en question le diagnostic de cécité, car Tammy semblait regarder d'un air inquiet dans sa direction, et ceci sans indices sonores, quand elle "faisait un mauvais coup" (par exemple, chercher à atteindre une tasse de café sur une petite table.) On a consulté par la suite un ophthalmologiste et on se prépare à pratiquer une intervention chirurgicale aux yeux dans un avenir rapproché. Son année à l'hôpital et en placement institutionnel, sans thérapie intensive, a contribué à accroître la spasticité et on a prévu une chirurgie orthopédique corrective. La physiothérapie va continuer. Tammy, maintenant rendue à 30 mois, imite les sons, elle a un vocabulaire de cinq mots, elle acquiert de la dextérité dans le domaine de la motricité fine et, cet automne, elle fréquente une école préparatoire pour enfants exceptionnels. . . . La mère nourricière a fait application pour obtenir la garde de cette enfant en permanence.

Commentaires

Cette étude de cas révèle plusieurs domaines où des problèmes viennent nuire au succès des familles et du personnel de ligne dans leur action auprès des enfants à handicaps multiples. Dans certains de ces domaines, les problèmes trouvent des solutions, même dans les limites de notre système fragmentaire de distribution de services aux êtres humains. . . .

Le premier problème majeur que ce cas présente est le délai de huit mois que les parents doivent essuyer avant d'obtenir une évaluation compréhensive. Certains parents ont décrit cette période entre le soupçon d'un retard et la confirmation de leur inquiétude comme la période la plus difficile à affronter émotionnellement. D'après notre expérience, il semble bien que plus cette période se prolonge, plus il est difficile d'intervenir pour effectuer des changements dans l'attitude des parents et pour aider ces derniers à fixer des objectifs réalistes au développement de leur enfant. Une clef de la solution se trouve, évidemment, dans la façon dont le parent se perçoit, lui ou elle-même, par rapport au développement de l'enfant. Les études faites ailleurs, de même qu'une étude de 59 enfants dont le développement était retardé et qui étaient inscrits aux Programmes de Développement de Nouveaux-nés de cette province, groupe au sein duquel se trouvaient plusieurs enfants souffrant de plus d'un handicap, ont démontré que les parents qui procuraient l'environnement familial le plus favorable étaient, en général, ceux qui avaient foi dans leur capacité d'influencer le développement de leur enfant et qui avaient un sens personnel de responsabilité à l'égard de cet épanouissement. Le parent qui a connu des échecs nombreux et prolongés dans les soins à donner à son enfant court le risque d'abandonner de plus en plus son action éducatrice. Ces expériences prédiagnostiques peuvent devenir des facteurs significatifs dans la prise de décision postdiagnostique par rapport aux soins à l'extérieur du foyer. . . .

Les professionnels qui travaillent dans les centres communautaires devraient savoir que la recherche démontre que les observations des parents sur le développement anormal sont généralement bien fondées. Pourtant une recherche de 1979, faite par Robinson et Sheps de la Section de Pédiatrie de la Population auprès de 287 nouveaux-nés retardés sur le plan du développement et inscrits aux programmes d'intervention de Colombie Britannique, révèle une certaine ''nonchalance'' de la part des médecins face aux inquiétudes manifestées par les parents la première fois que ceux-ci s'adressent à eux pour obtenir de l'aide. Les parents devraient aussi être bien au courant des divers moyens dont ils disposent pour faire faire une évaluation, afin qu'un refus de secours adéquat ne les amène pas à abandonner leurs efforts.

Une seconde source importante de problèmes venait du fait que la maman avait l'impression de ne pas avoir reçu suffisamment de renseignements sur les difficultés de sa fille. Deux points à noter ici. D'abord il est nécessaire que les parents participent tous les deux aux principales discussions se rapportant à l'évaluation, au diagnostic et à l'intervention. C'est un usage culturel déplorable qui veut que la mère, en tant que première préposée aux soins, soit considérée par rapport à la famille comme le récipient et le véhicule primaire de l'information concernant l'évaluation, le diagnostic et l'intervention. Inutile de dire qu'il y a beaucoup de perte dans la communication, non seulement en termes d'exactitude, mais aussi en termes de participation significative du père dans les décisions et les questions de soins. L'efficacité des stratégies d'intervention est en partie dévolue aux parents conjointement de même qu'en partage avec le personnel.

Le second point c'est que les parents doivent avoir constamment accès à du counseling bien informé et sympathique à propos du diagnostic de leur enfant. . . . Des trucs simples, comme le fait de demander aux parents de présenter par écrit les questions ou les inquiétudes à débattre à l'occasion de la prochaine visite, se sont avérés d'un grand secours. Cette pratique toute simple permet au professionnel en cause de constater jusqu'à quel point il réussit à faire profiter la famille des renseignements dont il dispose.

Billy:

Billy était prématuré de cinq semaines et pesait un peu plus de deux kilos à la naissance. Après un séjour de trois semaines dans la section des soins intensifs de la pouponnière il a été confié à ses parents. Billy était le premier né de cette famille et ses parents soupçonnèrent du retard à l'age de six mois. Le pédiatre engagea ses parents dans un processus d'évaluation continue et leur demanda de tracer sur un graphique les progrès de Billy. A huit mois et demi on hospitalisa Billy à la suite de crises épileptiques et il fut soumis alors à des évaluations neurologiques détaillées. Le neuropédiatre de service et les deux parents eurent l'occasion de se rencontrer fréquemment pendant ce mois d'hospitalisation. On tint les deux parents quotidiennement bien informés des tentatives faites pour contrôler les attaques, des évaluations neurologiques et du diagnostic initial qui comprenait des spasmes infantiles, un retard dans le développement, de la parésie cérébrale et des troubles visuels. . . . . Les parents furent avisés des conséquences de chaque handicap et de l'effet conjoint de tous ces handicaps sur l'évolution de l'enfant. On leur dit de façon réaliste à quoi ils pouvaient s'attendre de Billy, mais on les encouragea à l'aider à acquérir de nouvelles capacités de développement.

L'équipe neurologique dirigea la famille vers le Programme de Développement des Nouveaux-nés. . . . Les deux parents rencontrèrent le personnel du Programme de Développement pour parler de ce programme et on établit un calendrier de visites hebdomadaires à domicile.

Bref, à neuf mois, Billy était capable, couché sur le ventre, de soulever la tête momentanément et, les bras placés pour l'empêcher de tourner, de la garder levée pendant 20 secondes. . . . Il commençait à placer les objets dans sa bouche et occasionnellement il posait les mains sur le biberon quand on le nourissait, mais il préférait placer sa main sur celle de sa maman.

Les parents et le personnel composèrent un programme d'activités visant à favoriser le développement de Billy. On prescrivit de la physiothérapie et le thérapeute consultant incorpora des exercices appropriés de mouvements globaux dans le programme quotidien à domicile, en se joignant au travailleur qui venait visiter l'enfant. Le personnel du C.N.I.B. participait à l'opération et était disponible pour consultations additionnelles, au fur et à mesure que les capacités visuelles de Billy évoluaient.

A 16 mois, le progrès de Billy est encourageant. . . . il est maintenant capable de se tenir assis sans appui pendant cinq minutes . . . il maîtrise parfaitement la notion de permanence des objets . . . il réagit à l'appel de son nom et a un vocabulaire de deux mots.

En plus du programme à domicile, Billy est évalué à tous les six mois par une équipe pour enfants partiellement voyants. Les deux parents, le travailleur préposé à l'enfant, le neuropédiatre, le thérapeute et l'infirmière de l'équipe de santé publique participent tous à cette évaluation et des copies du rapport sont envoyées à la famille, de même qu'aux autres professionnels concernés.

Les efforts de la famille sont constants. Ils ne s'attendent pas à des miracles, mais ils sont encouragés par le progrès accompli.

Commentaires

Voici, en bref, les points présentés dans cette histoire de cas qui semblent pertinents pour indiquer une façon plus efficace de pourvoir aux besoins de l'enfant:

- l'effort fait par le pédiatre pour intéresser les deux parents aux évaluations continues du développement et les amener à faire le tracé de l'évolution de l'enfant à partir du moment où ils se sont douté du retard. . .

- la possibilité pour les deux parents d'avoir accès à une information médicale éclairée et à des consultations de façon continue durant l'hospitalisation. . .
- la direction de l'enfant, au moment de quitter l'hôpital, vers des ressources communautaires et le contrôle ultérieur sur une base régulière par une équipe comprenant les parents et les ressources communautaires. . .
- la participation des deux parents à l'élaboration et à l'application du programme. . .
- la participation de professionnels dont l'un assume une responsabilité primaire.

SOMMAIRE

En guise de résumé, j'aimerais examiner ce dernier point en plus de détails. L'acceptation par un professionnel de la responsabilité première est considérée par certains experts comme essentielle au succès des efforts pour garder les enfants à handicaps multiples au sein de leur propre milieu communautaire. Un modèle, proposé par Dianne Bricker, représente ce professionnel comme un "synthétiseur éducationnel ou une personne capable de réunir l'information fournie par une variété de spécialistes et de l'intégrer dans des stratégies d'interventions quotidiennes efficaces". De toute évidence, cette personne est appelée à changer, durant cette longue période de croissance. La différence entre cette façon de voir et celle déplorée par Smith dans son introduction, c'est-à-dire celle où c'est l'âge de l'enfant qui détermine qui, du médecin, du professeur ou du travailleur social, a une influence à exercer, c'est que même si la personne change le rôle lui ne change pas. Par conséquent, on peut confier ce rôle à la personne la mieux indiquée parmi celles qui travaillent avec l'enfant, selon l'évolution des besoins de ce dernier et des services qu'il reçoit. Pour certains enfants, cette personne sera la mère et assurément c'est dans la plupart des cas la maman qui est le seul adulte permanent dans la vie de l'enfant. Mais peu importe qui assume ce rôle, celui-ci devre être partagé par les parents dans la mesure du possible.

L'acceptation de la responsabilité primordiale par un professionnel exige plusieurs modifications aux pratiques professionelles courantes. La personne qui assume ce rôle doit avoir les qualifications suivantes: l'art de créer des liens avec les enfants, les familles et les autres professionnels; la capacité d'évaluer les besoins de l'enfant en fonction du programme de développement en cours et ceux de la famille en termes de services et de renseignements d'appoint; la connaissance des autres professions que la sienne et des contributions éventuelles que les autres professionnels pourraient apporter au développement du programme et aux besoins de la famille; et, finalement, le talent voulu pour déchiffrer les rapports des spécialistes et les incorporer dans des pratiques quotidiennes capables d'apporter des changements tangibles.

Les spécialistes que consulte ce professionnel en charge doivent aussi avoir des aptitudes spécifiques. Ce sont: la capacité de sacrifier leurs pouvoirs traditionnels dans le but de créer un climat qui favorise l'interaction libre; le don de savoir réduire au minimum le jargon professionnel; et l'art d'expliquer pourquoi certaines mesures sont propices à l'épanouissement d'un enfant ou aux besoin de la famille et de décrire ces procédés dans le cadre d'une interaction productive. . .

En terminant, j'aimerais répéter cette affirmation de Yepson: ''Nul n'est besoin de nouveaux objectifs, ni de remise en question des objectifs actuels. Ce dont on a besoin, c'est d'un programme d'action positif et dynamique.''

VI.   L'ENFANT MALTRAITÉ

editor: Jean-Marie Honorez

19

Battered Adolescents

DR. MAURICE BARKER, PH.D.

Abstract

In the case of adolescents there are four kinds of child abuse. It can be collective, against a particular group, such as that of Francophones outside Quebec; or institutional, stemming from interaction with the schools or the courts; it can be against the individual either through active abuse, or neglect; or it can be preventive in an attempt to prevent the adolescent from becoming abusive.

The connective situation today is an absurd one in which the child may be further abused by the system instead of being offered rehabilitative therapy. The objective of treatment should, therefore, include freedom from incipient psychopathology, the encouragement to live an autonomous adequate life, and normal emotional and intellectual development.

I work as a psychologist as a member of a multidisciplinary team at Ste. Justine's Hospital in Montreal with adolescents and children who have been victims of abuse. These patients usually have a long case history which includes problems with their parents, social workers, foster homes, and even rehabilitation centres. Many are now adolescents.

Pediatricians, social workers, nurses, and psychologists, that is, all the professional staff, work with and follow the development of the adolescent boys and girls up to the time their problem is resolved or to the time of maturity or legal majority. Our clients are 12 to 18 years of age.

I believe that violence or aggression must be given a wide enough definition if we are to be in the least realistic. In a practical sense it refers to the *recourse to force*, a force which is *justified* if it is aimed at the recuperation of a right, such as security, which is jeopardized when an adolescent boy or girl makes a brutal attack on one of his or her parents or on the siblings; or it may be *unjustified*. This force may be *physical* or it may be *psychological*, ranging from the chronic deflation of one's self-esteem to "psychocide." This recourse to force, justified or unjustified, physical or psychological, may materialize itself in terms of feelings, such as long term rejection. It also finds its expression in verbal forms, such as affective blackmail. This recourse to force may also take the form of *behaviour* which may or may not leave physical scars. The object of this use of force is to inflict harm or damage to the *self* or to the *child*, who may be the instigator of self-punishment or deserve it on account of provocation (Blumbert, 1976; Barker, 1975).

As a parallel to this personal definition of violence, I wish to specify that adolescent and child abuse occurs at four different levels. First, it can be *collective* in the sense that it takes the form, for instance, of linguistic and cultural discrimination against Francophones outside Quebec and against Anglophones inside the province. Adolescent abuse is also *institutional* when schools and courts of law, such as the Youth Tribunal, impose a penalty on the normal development of moral judgment (Barker, 1976 b). The use of force also occurs at the *individual* level when parents and/or guardians neglect or abuse a teen-ager (Alvy, 1975). In my mind the fourth type of abuse originates in the attempt to prevent the adolescent from acting out. It is absurd to try to prevent abuse at the expense of rehabilitation and care which should be provided to battered adolescents. Judge for yourself. Consider the following protocol. A teen-age girl has been the victim of sexual abuse and the parents are offered marriage therapy. If one of the parents is involved, sex therapy is offered. If the culprit is a known rapist, desensitization treatment of a "clockwork orange" type is used. No personal treatment is offered to the patient, unless a medical doctor chooses on his own to make such a recommendation.

I must repeat at this point that I believe in active care in the case of adolescents who have been subjected to sexual assault. They must have access to honest and frank professional help, which often should be intermittent on a long term basis, if they are to overcome the trauma they have experienced. I am also skeptical about the overemphasis on prevention. It will be easier to accept when it becomes possible to detect the aggressors adequately *after* the fact and, when *predictive* efforts begin to be effective (Barker, 1976 b; Lester, 1976).

All parents are tempted, at one time or another, to use their coercive power; fortunately, only a small minority (Blumenthal, 1978) believe that violence is *necessary* to bring changes.

The reality of the situation is also that during adolescence, violence is bidirectional: the teenagers are just as violent as their parents! Delinquency, drug use and suicidal attempts constitute some current adolescent manifestations of aggression. The bombardment of violence from T.V. and the newspapers maintains a high level of emotional arousal and a sensitivity to violence (Green, 1975), both in the parents and the adolescents themselves. Adolescents are not the simple victims of family violence (Paulson, 1976). They sometimes come from environments in which aggression is a means of social adaptation. This occurs more often in the under-privileged sectors (Dembo, 1975; Berkowitz, 1972). They are the victims, and often the aggressors as well, towards their fathers who try to recover their masculine self-esteem through manifestations of strength and power (Woods, 1972) and they are, most of all, as much negatively affected as their parents by the fact that they have not learned to find relief in verbal insult (Richmond, 1976), or to control their impulses through empathy, humour or mild counter-conditioning seduction (Baron, 1976). One must recognize the great number who are psychologically immature (Symonds, 1975), who "benumb" themselves with drug and alcohol, in order to forget everything (Calogeras and Camp, 1975). The novels of Vonnegut, the films of Fellini and of Bergman, the words of Dylan, Heller's *Catch 22* and Cleaver's *Soul on Ice* convey very well the reactive alienation of the adolescents confronted with violence directed towards them (Berger and Rosembert, 1976).

In sexual assault and violence, the factors of age, time of day and place (Page and Moss, 1976; Depp, 1976) seldom have any influence. These individuals are rarely incapable of abstract thinking, like the other violent criminals (Lester, 1976; Kunce *et al.*, 1976), nor are they candidates for neurosurgery (Spurgeon, 1970). They are not antisocial without any ambition (Young, 1976). Their individual characteristics seem to matter little. They are *ordinary people*, more often than not, well known to their victims.

It should be noted that the number of murder trials in Quebec was 17 in 1955, 53 in 1965 and 185 in 1975. We live violently, in a violent world, and we are all sometimes violent.

This brings me to three conclusions about battered adolescents:

1. There is no realistic definition of an adequate or inadequate environment for an adolescent: therefore, there is no special criterion for ideal parents.

2. There is no clinically positive choice between an abusing parental home and three social workers for every two years, responsible for adolescents living in foster homes, which are sometimes also abusive.

3. The motive for separation from the parents is the impossible one of changing the surroundings of the adolescent and the parents.

Here is an example of what I mean. A 14 year old girl was a witness to the murder of her mother by her father using a kitchen knife. The mourning related to the mother's death has been complicated by the equally traumatic effects of the father's incarceration (Sack *et al.*, 1976). A hemophilic condition had caused the girl to run away from a foster home where she was being battered; she also ran away from a second home where an attempt was made to rape her. As a result, she is today deprived of her freedom, kept under surveillance with lack of privacy in an artificial environment composed of cement bed, unbreakable window panes, insurmountable wall, locked doors and plastic utensils, all because she has fled from foster homes.

Even if she is intelligent, since she has a poor scholastic backgound, she has less than a 50% chance of socially rehabilitating herself (Egloff, 1975). To top it all, in spite of the fact that her therapeutic relationships have been good for the last two years, the social worker appointed by the office of youth protection would not allow this patient to consult with her psychologist at the hospital, for fear that she might run away.

I shall conclude with the following recommendations:

1. The object of therapy for battered adolescents is to deliver them from all forms of incipient psychopathology.
2. The perspective of an autonomous and adequate life must be encouraged as a long term objective.
3. Continuous and repetitive attention should be given to the normal development of a self-image which includes intellect, affect, body image, aptitudes, strength, socialization and sexuality.

The goal is not a question of reconstructing a life, nor of making up for affective deficiencies, but rather of completing and developing the potentialities related to the actualization of the adolescent.

References

1. Alvy, K.T.: Preventing child abuse. *American Psychologist*, 1975, 30, 921–928.
2. Baron, R.A.: The reduction of human aggression. *Journal of Applied and Social Psychology*, 1976, 6, 360–274.
3. Barker, M.: *Le suicide adolescent*. Présentation clinique à l'hôpital Sainte-Justine le 29 avril, 1975.
4. Barker, M.: *Le climat de violence des centres de detention pour adolescents*. Présentation clinique au Centre hospitalier Universitaire de Sherbrooke en janvier 1976 b.
5. Barker, M.: Le développement normal à l'adolescence. *Union Médicale du Canada*, 1976.
6. Bergen, B.J. and Rosembert, S.D.: Culture as Violence, *Humanitas*, 1976, 12, 195–205.
7. Berkowitz, L.: Frustrations, comparisons and other sounds of emotion aroused as contributors to social unrest. *Journal of Social Issues*, 1972, 28, 77–91.
8. Blumenthal, M.D.: Thinking about violence. An overview. *Humanitas*, 1976, 12, 207–220.

9. Blumbert, M.L.: Treatment of the abused child and the child abuser. *American Journal of Psychotherapy*, 1976, *30*, 204−214.
10. Calogeras, R.C. and Camp, N.M.: Drug use and aggression. *Bulletin of the Menninger Clinic*, 1975, *30*, 329−344.
11. Dembo, R.: Critical factors on understanding adolescent aggression. *Social Psychiatry*, 1973, *8*, 212−219.
12. Depp, F.C.: Violent behavior pattern of psychiatric wards. *Aggressive Behavior*, 1976, 295−306.
13. Egloff, M.: Results of neglect in adolescents. *Acta Paedopsychiatrica*, 1975, *42*, 151−166.
14. Geen, R.G.: The meanings of observed violence. *Journal of Research in personality*, 1975, 270−281.
15. Kunce, J.T., Ryan, J.J., and Eckelman, C.G.: Violent behavior and differential wais characteristics, *Journal of Consulting and Clinical Psychology*, 1976, *44*, 45−45.
16. Lester, D.: Homicidal and suicidal impulses in the Nazi Leaders. *Perceptual and Motor Skills*, 1976, *43*, 1316.
17. Page, R.A. and Moss, M.K.: Environmental influence on aggression: The effects of darkness and proximity on victim. *Journal of Applied Social Psychology*, 1976, *6*, 126−133.
18. Paulson, M.J.: Child trauma intervention: a community response to family violence. *Journal of Clinical Child Psychology*, 1975, *4*, 26−29.
19. Richmond, J.: The art of the insult, *The Montreal Star*, Saturday, January 24, 1976.
20. Sack, W.H., Seidler, J. and Thomas, S.: The children of imprisoned parents; a psycho-social exploration. *American Journal of Ortho-psychiatry*, 1976, *46*, 618−628.
21. Spurgeon, D.: The search for a way to stop human violence, *The Globe and Mail*, 1970, Dec. 7.
22. Symonds, M.: The psychological patterns of response of victims to rape. *Seminar on rape, John Jay College of Criminal Justice*, April, 1975.
23. Woods, S.M.: Violence: psychotherapy of pseudo-homosexual panic. *Archives of General Psychiatry*, 1972, *27*, 255−258.
24. Young, I.L.: Personality characteristics of high and low aggressive adolescents in residential treatment. *Journal of Clinical Psychology*, 1976, *32*, 814−818.

"Adolescents Maltraités"

MAURICE BARKER, PH.D.

Sommaire

L'auteur témoigne de son expérience de psychologue à une section pour adolescents dans un centre hospitalier. Pour avoir une définition large de la violence, il faut distinguer entre celle qui est légitime ou illégitime dont la force est non seulement physique mais aussi psychologique. Elle se traduit dans les sentiments, le langage et les comportements.

La violence aux adolescents se produit à quatre niveaux: le collectif, l'institutionnel, l'individuel ainsi qu'au niveau de la suremphase sociale privilégiant la prévention de l'abus au détriment de la réhabilitation. La violence à l'adolescence est bidirectionnelle: les adolescents et leurs parents peuvent être agresseur ou victime.

Il est suggéré, qu'au lieu de refaire des vies d'adolescents par la séparation parentale, il serait préférable de parfaire le potentiel des adolescents maltraités en centrant l'intervention sur l'adolescent.

Ma pratique est constituée d'adolescents dont plusieurs sont maltraités et j'en parlerai plus loin, mais aussi et peut être surtout par des enfants maltraités de façon longitudinale, d'abord par leurs parents puis par leur tuteur, puis les travailleurs sociaux, ensuite par leurs foyers nourriciers et enfin par les centres d'accueil. Ils sont adolescents et donc normaux (Barker 1976) et il ne faut pas oublier que les adolescents sont numériquement majoritaires au Canada et chez nous où ils constituent 57% de la population, la majorité silencieuse.

Je suis psychologue et je pratique à la section aux adolescents de l'hôpital Sainte-Justine depuis plus de six ans. Nous avons formé à cette époque et nous demeurons une équipe multidisciplinaire, avec un fonctionnement horizontal plutôt que pyramidal pour diagnostiquer et traiter les adolescents. Pédiatres, travailleuses sociales, infirmières et psychologues, tous les professionnels voient et suivent les adolescents et les adolescentes jusqu'à la cure, jusqu'à maturation ou jusqu'à maturité civile.

De 12 à 18 ans, nous diagnostiquons et traitons les adolescents dont on a abusé. Et c'est de cette perspective de "thérapeute" d'adolescents maltraités, non pas j'espère *à*, mais *de*, l'hôpital Sainte-Justine que je m'adresse à vous.

Je crois qu'il faut d'abord définir la violence ou l'agression d'une façon suffisamment large pour être le moindrement réaliste. En pratique il s'agit de l'*usage de force;* légitime si elle vise à corriger la privation d'un droit tel que la sécurité lorsqu'un adolescent ou adolescente attaque brutalement sa mère, sa fratrie ou son père, ou *illégitime* lorsqu'il s'agit de la privation d'un privilège tel que la tolérance parentale à l'égard du fait que l'enfant est un adolescent en évolution normale; cette force peut-être *physique* pour offrir des sévices corporels—et je m'inscris contre cette seule définition étroite d'adolescents maltraités—ou bien elle peut-être *psychologique* allant de la déflation chronique de l'estime de soi jusqu'au psychocide; cet usage de force, légitime ou illégitime, physique ou psychologique peut s'exprimer en termes de *sentiments* (par exemple le rejet explicite ou pire encore implicite caché insidieux et à long terme comme dans la génèse de certains divorces), la force s'exprime en termes aussi de langage (surtout ici les fameux chantages affectifs schizophrénogènes), et cet usage de force s'exprime aussi évidemment en termes de *comportements* qui laissent mais le plus souvent ne laissent pas de sévices corporels. Cet usage de force vise la blessure ou des dommages à *soi* (le parent qui parle fort pour s'autopunir) et/ou à l'*enfant* (qui peut provoquer l'autopunition ou la mériter par provocation) (Blumberg 1976; Barker, 1975).

En parallèle avec cette définition personnelle de la violence, je veux préciser que l'abus des adolescents et des enfants se produit à quatre niveaux différents: d'abord il est *collectif* au sens où par exemple la discrimination linguistique et culturelle favorise socialement les anglophones hors Québec et les francophones dans ce qui est maintenant depuis le 22 mai, le royaume libéral, j'accepte évidemment que cet effet collectif s'exerce également à l'intérieur du Québec. L'abus des adolescents est également *institutionnel* lorsque les écoles, les centres d'accueil (what a misnomer in some instances) et les cours telles le tribunal de la Jeunesse pénalisent le développement normal du jugement moral (Barker, 1976 b.) et l'abus de force est également du niveau *individuel* lorsque les parents et/ou tuteurs pêchent par omission, négligence ou abus (Alvy, 1975). Le quatrième volet d'abus, je le situe dans la suremphase sociale de la prévention de l'abus des adolescents au détriment de leur réhabilitation. Il est absolument aberrant que l'on tente de prévenir l'abus au détriment des soins aux adolescents abusés. Je vous cite l'horreur de mon système. Les adolescentes victimes d'abus sexuel à Montréal se voient offrir des mesures de traitement matrimonial pour les parents si l'abuseur est un parent, traitement sexologique si l'abuseur est un agresseur connu et traitement de désensibilisation genre "clock work orange" pour un abuseur inconnu. Aucun traitement personnel pour la patiente, à moins d'une référence médicale optionnelle.

Je dois ici répéter que je me place du côté des soins actifs aux adolescents victimes d'assaut sexuel et donc maltraités. Ils ont besoin de la disponibilité d'aide honnête et franche, professionnelle et souvent intermittente à long terme pour surmonter leur (s) traumatisme (s) sinon leurs carences vitales. Et pour en finir avec la suremphase préventive, je l'accepterai mieux lorsqu'on pourra bien *post*-dire adéquatement les abuseurs et encore plus évidemment lorsque les tentatives de *pré*-diction commenceront à porter fruit (Barker, 1976 b.; Lester, 1976).

Après cette définition du domaine, je présente quelques réalités avant de diagnostiquer. La réalité veut que tous les parents ont la tentation à un moment ou à plusieurs moments de se servir de leur force coercitive mais que, seule une minorité (Blumenthal, 1976) croit que la violence est *nécessaire* au changement, en dépit des modèles de plus en plus nombreux à la télévision.

La réalité veut aussi que durant l'adolescence, la violence soit bidirectionnelle: les adolescents sont aussi violents que leurs parents! La délinquance, l'usage de drogue et les tentatives de suicide sont des manifestations adolescentes courantes d'agressivité. Le bombardement de violence observé à la TV et dans les journaux maintient un éveil émotif et une sensibilité à la violence (Green, 1975) autant chez les parents que chez les adolescents eux-mêmes. Les adolescents ne se réduisent pas à l'équation simpliste de la victime de la violence familiale (Paulson, 1976); ils proviennent parfois de milieux où l'agression est un mécanisme d'ajustement social surtout dans les zones défavorisées (Dembo, 1975; Berkowitz, 1972), ils sont les victimes et souvent les agresseurs aussi de pères qui tentent de restaurer leur estime de soi masculine par des démonstrations de puissance et de force (Woods, 1972) et ils sont surtout autant victimes que leurs parents de ne pas avoir appris à se soulager par l'insulte verbale (Richmond, 1976) ou à contrôler par empathie, humour ou légère séduction contre-conditionnante (Baron, 1976). Enfin, il faut aussi admettre un grand nombre qui continuent à présenter la réaction traumatique d'infantilisme psychologique—le "frozen and fright response"—(Symonds, 1975), ceux qui très souvent se "gèlent" avec drogue et alcool pour régresser et tout oublier (Calogeras et Camp, 1975). Les romans de Vonnegut, les films de Fellini et de Bergman, les paroles de Dylan, "Catch 22" de Heller et "Soul on Ice" de Cleaver expriment bien l'aliénation réactive des adolescents face à la violence à leur égard (Berger et Rosenberg, 1976).

Quant aux agresseurs des victimes d'assauts sexuels et de sévices corporels, les facteurs d'âge, de temps, du jour et de l'endroit (Page et Moss, 1976; Depp, 1976) sont rarement des facteurs déterminants. Ils sont rarement des incapables de pensée abstraite comme les criminels violents (Lester, 1976, Kunce *et al,* 1976) candidats à la neurochirurgie (Spurgeon, 1970) et ils sont encore moins des antisociaux non-arrivistes socialement (Young, 1976). Les caractéristiques individuelles semblent peu compter puisqu'*ils sont du monde ordinaire*, plus souvent qu'autrement bien connus des victimes. Je ne peux pas oublier que les causes de meurtre entendues au Québec étaient de 17 en 1955, 53 en 1965 et de 185 en 1975. Nous vivons d'une façon violente, dans un monde violent et nous sommes tous violents, à tous les moments et partout. (Ne le suis-je pas à ce moment-ci?).

J'arrive maintenant à mes trois conclusions diagnostiques sur le phénomène des adolescents maltraités:

1. Il n'y a pas de définition réaliste (même pas idéale) d'un milieu adéquat ou inadéquat pour un adolescent: il n'y a donc pas de critère de parentectomie.

2. Il n'y a pas de choix positif cliniquement entre un foyer parental abuseur et une moyenne de trois travailleurs sociaux par deux ans responsables d'adolescents placés dans des foyers nourriciers parfois abuseurs à leur tour ou dans des centres d'accueil sécuritaires.

3. Les indications pour la séparation parentale demeurent l'impossibilité de changer l'abord, l'adolescent puis les parents, condition qui survient rarement.

Je vous offre maintenant un exemple de la violation de ces principes. Il s'agit du cas d'une adolescente de 14 ans dont le crime est d'avoir été témoin du meurtre de sa mère par son père au moyen d'un couteau dans la cuisine. Le deuil du traumatisme de la mort de la mère a été compressé par les effets également traumatiques de l'incarcération du père (Sack *et al.* 1976) et d'autant plus qu'une condition d'hémophilie l'a fait fuguer d'un foyer nourricier où elle était battue et d'un second où l'on a tenté de la violer. Le résultat l'amène aujourd'hui à être privée de liberté dans un milieux artificiel avec surveillance et absence d'intimité, lit de béton, vitres incassables, murs infranchissables, portes verrouillées et ustensiles en matière plastique parce qu'elle a fuguée des foyers nourriciers. Ainsi, même si elle est intelligente, parce qu'elle est mal scolarisée, il est bien connu qu'elle garde moins de 50% de chance de se réhabiliter socialement (Egloff, 1975). Et le bouquet: même si sa relation de thérapie est bonne et profitable depuis deux ans, le travailleur social délégué à la protection de la jeunesse défendait à la patiente de consulter son psychologue à l'hôpital, à cause du risque de fugue.

En terminant, je passe maintenant à mes recommandations consécutives à mes volets diagnostiques:

1. La thérapie avec les adolescents maltraités vise à les débarasser de toute forme de psychopathologie en herbe.

2. De favoriser à long terme une perspective de vie autonome et adéquate.

3. De veiller continuellement, répétitivement à une estime normale de l'image de soi qui comprend l'intelligence, l'affect, la volition, l'image corporelle, les aptitudes, la force, la socialisation et la sexualité. *Il ne s'agit pas* de refaire des vies ni de combler des carences affectives mais bien de parfaire et de potentialiser l'actualisation des adolescents.

References

1. Alvy, K.T.: Preventing child abuse *American Psychologist*, 1975, 30, 921–928.

2. Baron, R.A.: The reduction of human agression. *Journal of applied social psychology*, 1976, 6, 360−274.
3. Barker, M.: *Le suicide adolescent*. Présentation clinique à l'hôpital Sainte-Justine le 29 avril, 1975.
4. Barker, M.: *Le climat de violence des centres de détention pour adolescents*. Présentation clinique au centre hospitalier Universitaire de Sherbrooke en janvier, 1976 b.
5. Barker, M.: Le développement normal à l'adolescence. *Union Médicale du Canada*, 1976.
6. Bergen, B.J., Rosenberg, S.D.: Culture as Violence. *Humanitas*, 1976, *12*, 195−205.
7. Berkowitz, L: Frustrations, comparisons and other sounds of emotion aroused as contributors to social unrest: *Journal of Social issues*, 1972, *28*, 77−91.
8. Blumenthal, M.D.: Thinking about violence. An overview *Humanitas*, 1976, 12, 207−220.
9. Blumberg, M.L.: Treatment of the abused child and the child abuser, *American Journal of Psychotherapy*, 1976, *30*, 204−215.
10. Calogeras, R.C., Camp, N.M.: Drug use and aggression *Bulletin of the Menninger Clinic*, 1975, *39*, 329−344.
11. Dembo, R.: Critical factors in understanding adolescent agression. *Social Psychiatry*, 1973, *8*, 212−219.
12. Depp, F.C.: Violent behavior pattern on psychiatric wards. *Aggressive Behavior*, 1976, 295−306.
13. Egloff, M.: Results of neglect in adolescents *Acta Paedopsychiatrica*, 1975, *42*, 151−166.
14. Geen, R.G.: The meanings of observed violence. *Journal of research in personality*, 1975, 270−281.
15. Kunce, J.T., Ryan, J.J., Eckelman, C.C.: Violent Behavior and differential wais characteristics, *Journal of Consulting and Clinical psychology*, 1976, *44*, 42−45.
17. Lester, D.: Homicidal and Suicidal impulses in the Nazi Leaders, *Perceptual and Motor Skills*, 1976, *43*, 1316.
18. Page, R.A. Moss, M.K.: Environmental influence on aggression; The effects of darkness and proximity on victim. *Journal of applied social Psychology*, 1976, *6*, 126−133.
19. Paulson, M.J.: Child Trauma intervention: a community response to family violence. *Journal of Clinical child psychology*, 1975, *4*, 26−29.
20. Richmond, J.: The art of the insult, *The Montreal Star*, Saturday, January 24, 1976.
21. Sack, W.H., Seidler, J., Thomas, S.: The children of emprisoned parents: a psycho-social exploration. *American Journal of Ortho-psychiatry*, 1976, *46*,618−628.

22. Spurgeon, D.: The search for a way to stop human violence. *The Globe and Mail*, 1970, dec, 7.

23. Symonds, M.: The psychological patterns of response of victims to rape. *Seminar on rape, John Jay College of Criminal Justice*, april, 1975.

24. Woods, S.M.: Violence: psychotherapy of pseudohomosexual panic. *Archives of general psychiatry*, 1972, 27, 255−258.

25. Young, I.L.: Personality characteristics of high and low agressive adolescents in residential treatment. *Journal of Clinical Psychology*, 1976, 32, 814−818.

20

Le Devenir D'Enfants Maltraités

JEAN-MARIE HONOREZ, D.PS. L.CR.

Abstract

Une recherche sur le devenir des enfants maltraités a été entreprise dans une clinique hospitalière procédant au dépistage et à l'orientation thérapeutique de tels sujets. Des données préliminaires sont rapportées quant au groupe expérimental (N=54) composé d'enfants maltraités, identifiés en moyenne trois ans et demi auparavant, non affectés de troubles neurologiques.

Au dépistage, les sujets présentaient surtout des retards psychosociaux et de langage. Le milieu familial était défavorisé socio-économiquement et affectivement.

A l'expérimentation, on observe des retards développementaux, intellectuels et scolaires. Depuis leur prise en charge, les enfants ont été déplacés du milieu naturel et ont connu de fréquents changements de milieu. Les données recueillies orienteraient l'action clinique vers la prévention.

INTRODUCTION

L'enfance maltraité a été, ces dernières années, l'objet de nombreuses théorisations et expérimentations (Kalish, 1978) dont certaines tendent à mieux cerner l'évolution, les effets ultérieurs chez les sujets exposés à de telles situations.

Grâce à un fonds du Ministère de la Santé et du Bien-Etre Social du Canada, la Clinique de Protection de l'Enfance de l'Hôpital Sainte-Justine pour les Enfants de Montréal (Jéliu, 1977) et l'Université de Montréal (Honorez, 1976) ont entrepris une étude comparative sur le devenir des enfants maltraités. Cette recherche ayant comme cadre la dite clinique, il sera intéressant de développer tout d'abord l'organisation de ses services. Dans un second temps, on exposera les premiers résultats de l'étude.

SERVICES CLINIQUES

Depuis 1971, la Clinique de Protection à l'Enfance procède au dépistage, à l'évaluation et à l'élaboration du plan de traitement des enfants identifiés comme maltraités dans les divers départements et services de l'hôpital: jusqu'en 1977, elle en a examiné 546. Sous la direction d'un pédiatre, l'investigation multidisciplinaire implique deux travailleurs sociaux, un psychiatre. Au besoin, la clinique recourt à l'expertise des diverses spécialités de l'institution.

Parallèlement à ce service d'expertise, la clinique offre depuis quelques années, une consultation hebdomadaire pour enfants requérant une surveillance pédiatrique, notamment quant à la croissance. Ces sujets, en plus de l'évaluation médico-sociale du dépistage, bénéficient donc d'examens de contrôle.

Ces examens ont fait ressortir que, dans nombre de cas, la récupération par l'enfant n'était pas aussi positive qu'escompté: dans certains cas, elle était nulle, voire négative. Ceci a donc tout naturellement amené à s'interroger sur le devenir des enfants maltraités par la mise au point d'un modèle de recherche.

SERVICE DE RECHERCHE

Une revue de littérature (Honorez, 1977), a tout d'abord souligné que le taux de mortalité chez les enfants maltraités représentait environ 10% et qu'en plus, 30% conservaient des séquelles physiques irrécupérables. La question posée dans la présente recherche est de savoir ce que deviennent le 60% restant.

Pour ce faire, 54 sujets maltraités ont été examinés: ils étaient âgés de cinq à huit ans et avaient été dépistés au moins deux ans avant l'expérimentation. Furent exclus, les enfants victimes d'atteinte cérébrale, de séquestration ou d'abus sexuel. Un groupe contrôle est actuellement vu en tenant compte des variables suivantes: absence de mauvais traitement, âge à l'expérimentation, sexe, ethnie, niveau socio-économique.

Le matériel est constitué par l'anamnèse somatique ainsi que sociale, informatisée et issue des dossiers hospitaliers. A l'expérimentation, on procède à un examen médical incluant la croissance, à un questionnaire scolaire, à un examen psychométrique (Griffiths, WISC, Bender, Goodenough-Harris, Hand-Test).

LES ANTÉCEDENTS

Au dépistage, les sujets présentaient 85% de retard socio-affectif, 83% de retard de langage, 54% de lésions cutanées, 41% de retard de croissance, 41% d'hygiène déficiente, 38% de retard moteur et 24% de fractures ou brûlures. Le tableau initial semble donc dominer par les retards de développement.

Dans les $^2/_3$ des cas, les enfants vivaient avec leurs parents naturels; dans un cas sur six, avec un seul parent. La moitié des pères avait un métier non-qualifié; 83% des mères étaient ménagères, 66% des familles recevaient des allocations de chômage ou de Bien-Etre Social. Enfin, 68% des mères et 51% des pères avaient connu la négligence, la carence ou des placements.

L'ensemble de cette esquisse suggère évidemment la pauvreté sociale, affective et économique.

L'ÉVOLUTION:

La croissance physique a été étudiée en terme de retards pondéral, statural ou pondéro-statural. Selon les courbes anthropométriques de Stuart, 41% des sujets avaient de tels retards au dépistage; 22% à l'expérimentation.

L'échelle de Griffiths donne un quotient développemental global sous le premier écart-type (QDG: 86). Les retards des sujets se situent essentiellement sous le premier écart-type au niveau écouter-parler (QD: 81), coordination oculo-manuelle (QD: 81), raisonnement pratique (QD: 76).

L'échelle d'intelligence WISC, donne un Q.I. global de 82.4. Celui-ci est particulièrement affecté par le Q.I. verbal: 78.7, alors que le Q.I. nonverbal est de 89.6.

Au plan scolaire, 49% des sujets fréquentent une classe régulière correspondant à leur âge chronologique. Le restant, 51% sont en classe non régulière: la moitié d'entre eux fréquentent une classe spéciale et l'autre a un an de retard tout en fréquentant une classe de type régulier.

Entre le dépistage et l'expérimentation, l'intervalle de temps moyen était de trois ans et demi. Au départ de cette période, 89% des sujets demeuraient dans leur milieu naturel, et 39% à la fin de la période. Les 61% restant vivaient lors de l'expérimentation en milieu substitut. De plus, au cours de l'intervalle, chaque sujet vécut en moyenne cinq changements de milieu: un à chaque neuf mois.

CONCLUSIONS

Les conclusions de cet exposé seront partielles et temporaires puisque les données rapportées ne concernent que le seul groupe expérimental, l'examen du groupe contrôle étant en voie d'achèvement.

On constate néanmoins que les sujets maltraités de l'étude sont issus de milieux défavorisés où la pauvreté familiale n'est pas qu'économique mais aussi sociale et affective. Ceci renvoie au débat concernant l'étiologie du problème. Faut-il aborder la question de l'enfant maltraité, abusé et/ou négligé par le biais d'un symptôme, la violence, ou d'un point de vue plus global et sociologique (Gil, 1971)?

Les enfants issus de ces milieux présentent tant au dépistage qu'à l'expérimentation un tableau de retards développementaux. Les instruments de recherche permettent de préciser qu'il s'agit aussi de retards intellectuels et scolaires. Ces données ont déjà été rapportées (Martin, 1972; Elmer, 1977). Cependant, les données de la présente étude sont originales dans le fait que les enfants maltraités étudiés ont été épurés des sujets atteints de séquelles neurologiques: les mauvais traitements pourraient laisser des séquelles psychosociales. Ceci soulignerait que les "mauvais traitements" réfèrent à autre chose que la seule violence.

Enfin, le plan de traitement initié au dépistage s'est avéré drastique et chaotique: enfant déplacé de son milieu naturel et instabilité géographique élevée dans les milieux substituts.

Au point actuel de la recherche, il est malaisé de pousser plus avant les conclusions. Il semble néanmoins que le dépistage fut peut-être trop tardif. Pouvait-il en être autrement?

Il apparaît aussi que le dépistage ne suffit pas. En plus de la stratégie thérapeutique élaborée dans l'intérêt de l'enfant, il conviendrait de s'assurer que les moyens de la concrétiser existent réellement et ce, toujours, dans l'intérêt de l'enfant.

Ce dépouillement préliminaire des données orienterait l'action clinique vers la prévention. Les centres hospitaliers et sociaux pourraient diriger leurs efforts vers les nouveaux-nés grâce à des services pour l'enfant ou la famille à risque (Ayoub et al., 1977). Cette optique n'est cependant pas sans poser des problèmes éthiques et opérationnels. Qu'est-ce qu'un enfant ou une famille vulnérable? Quelle aide offrir? La population cible doit-elle collaborer de son plein gré ou, pour employer un euphémisme, doit-on solliciter sa collaboration? Enfin, cette stratégie ne conduit-elle pas à une stigmatisation précoce sous le couvert d'une prévention précoce?

Loin de résoudre le problème de l'enfant maltraité, il semble que les recherches entreprises dans ce domaine amènent cliniciens et chercheurs à poser de nouvelles questions de plus en plus précises mais aussi plus nombreuses.

References

Ayoub C. et al. (1977). An approach to primary prevention: the "at risk" program. *Children Today 46* (no. 3), 14−17.

Elmer, E. (1977). *Fragile families, troubled children. The aftermath of infant trauma*. Pittsburg: University of Pittsburg Press.

Gil, D.G. (1971). A sociocultural perspective on physical child abuse. Child Welfare, 50, 389−395.

Honorez, J.M. (1976). Etude sur le devenir psychologique d'enfants abusés physiquement. Projet de thèse inédit, Université de Montreal.

Honorez, J.M. (1977). Le devenir des enfants maltraités. Revue critique de la littérature. Montréal: *Carnet de pédo-psychiatrie de l'Hôpital Sainte-Justine.*

Jéliu, G. (1977). Le devenir des enfants maltraités: étude comparative entre un groupe d'enfants abusés physiquement et un groupe d'enfants négligés par rapport à un groupe contrôle. Projet de recherche inédit, Santé et Bien-Etre Social Canada.

Kalish, B.J. (1978). *Child abuse and neglect, an annoted bibliography*, 535 p. Westport (Conn.): Greenwood Press.

Martin, H.P. (1972). The child and his development, in: C.H. Kempe, R.E. Helfer (Ed.): *Helping the battered child and his family* (pp. 93–114). Philadelphie: J.B. Lippincot.

Stuart, H.C. et al.: Anthropometric chart. Boston: *Children's Medical Centre*.

The Fate of Battered Children

DR. JEAN-MARIE HONOREZ, D.PS, L.CR.

Abstract

The Clinique de protection de l'enfance of Ste. Justine Hospital in Montreal and the University of Montreal have been, for some time now, constructing a study of the evolution of battered children. Since 10 per cent of these children die and 30 percent suffer from irreversible physical damage, these were excluded when the investigation was started. The data on the remaining 60 per cent suggest that they continue to experience serious developmental problems. Data from medical screening procedures indicate that a very significant percentage of these battered children continue to suffer from socio-affective, language, growth, and motor retardation and other developmental delays. Three and a half years after the initial assessment, intellectual and academic achievement were found to be well below average.

Social environment continues to be unstable, with an average of one move every nine months. These children came from impoverished homes where parents are poorly educated and often unemployed.

It also appears that the treatment programme has been drastic and chaotic and instead of benefitting the child it seems to have aggravated the original problem. It would, therefore, be useful to steer clinical treatment towards prevention and to begin with "high risk" newborns.

Such a strategy, however, raises ethnical and operational questions. The research is, thus, valuable not so much in solving the battered child's problems as in raising new questions.

INTRODUCTION

In the course of the last few years, the situation of battered children has given rise to numerous theoretical and experimental studies (Kalish, 1978), some of which tend to bring into sharper focus the evolution of the situation and the later effects of exposure to such conditions.

With the financial assistance of the Department of Health and Social Welfare of Canada, the Clinique de Protection de l'Enfance of Ste-Justine Hospital in Montreal (Jéliu, 1977) and the University of Montreal (Honorez, 1976) have undertaken a comparative study of the evolution of battered children. Since this research is carried out in the Clinic mentioned above, it should be of interest to speak first of the organization of the services provided. In a second part, we will report the preliminary results of this study.

CLINICAL SERVICES

Since 1971, the Clinic has dealt with the screening, the evaluation and the development of treatment programmes for the children identified, in the various departments and services of the hospital, as having been the victims of abuse and cruelty. In 1977, 546 cases were processed. Under the direction of a pediatrician, this multidisciplinary investigation involved two social workers and a psychiatrist. When needed, the Clinic could call on the expert advice of the various specialists working in the institution. A medical-social screening procedure was used.

Examinations revealed that, in a number of cases, the child's recuperative progress was not as positive as expected. In some cases it was non-existent or indeed negative. This observation has thus naturally given rise to questions about the fate of battered children and to the design of a research project.

RESEARCH FUNCTION

A review of the relevant literature (Honorez, 1977) has shown that the mortality rate of the battered children population is about 10 per cent, and that 30 per cent of these victims have irreversible physical damage. The present research concerns the fate of the remaining 60 per cent.

In an attempt to discover why these negative results occurred, 54 battered children were examined. Their age ranged from five to eight and they were all identified as battered children at least two years before the experiment took place. Victims of cerebral damage or sexual abuse were excluded. A control group was selected on the basis of the following variables: no experience of ill-treatment, age at the time of experimentation, sex, ethnic origin, and socio-economic status.

The material consists of a computerized physical and social case history drawn from the hospital files. Data included a medical examination and was based on growth information, a scholastic achievement questionnaire and a psychometric exam (Griffith, WISC, Bender, Goodenough-Harris, Hand-Test).

THE SUBJECTS' PAST HISTORY

At the moment of screening, 85 per cent of the subjects gave signs of socio-affective retardation, 83 per cent of language retardation, 54 per cent of cutaneous lesions, 41 per cent of growth retardation, 41 per cent of inadequate hygienic conditions, 38 per cent of motor retardation and 24 per cent of fractures or burns. Thus, the first examination shows the group as being dominated by developmental lags.

Two thirds of the children were living with their natural parents and one out of six had only one parent. Fifty per cent of the fathers were unskilled laborers; 83 per cent of the mothers were housekeepers; and 66 per cent of the families were receiving unemployment or welfare compensation. Finally, 68 per cent of the mothers and 51 per cent of the fathers had had experiences of neglect, deficiency or foster homes themselves.

Clearly, this sketch as a whole is suggestive of social, affective and economic poverty.

DEVELOPMENTAL HISTORY

Physical growth was assessed in terms of weight, height or weight-height lags. On the basis of Stuart's anthropometric curves, 41 per cent of the subjects showed such lags at the moment of screening and 22 per cent when the research data was collected.

The Griffiths Scales gives a global development quotient lower than the first standard deviation (GDQ: 86). The retardation scale places the subjects essentially below the first standard deviation for listening-speaking (DQ: 81), visuo-manual coordination (DQ: 81), practical reasoning (DQ: 76).

The WISC intelligence scale gives a global IQ of 82.4. This general score is greatly affected by the verbal sub-score, which is 78.7, while the non-verbal score is 89.6.

The academic situation is as follows. Forty nine per cent of the subjects attend a regular class corresponding to their chronological age. The remainder, 51 per cent, do not follow the normal pattern. Half of these children attend special classes and the other half regular classes, but with a year lag.

The mean period of time separating the screening and experimental phase was three and a half years. At the moment of screening, 89 per cent of the subjects were living in their natural setting, while at the time of experimentation, 61 per cent were living in a substitute environment. Moreover, during the interval between these two phases, each subject had experienced an average of five changes of milieu, that is, one every nine months.

CONCLUSION

The conclusions of this report will necessarily be incomplete and of a preliminary nature since the data available deals only with the experimental subjects. The examination of the control group is currently taking place.

We may note, nevertheless, that the battered children of this study come from underprivileged environments where the family's poverty is not only of an economic, but also of a social and affective nature. This reopens the debate on the etiology of this problem. Must one tackle the question of the battered, abused and/or neglected child from the angle of a symptom, violence, or from a more global and sociological point of view? (Gil, 1971)

The picture presented by the children coming from these backgrounds is, both at the time of screening and of data collection, that of a series of developmental lags. The research instruments used here show that the retardation is also of an intellectual and a scholastic nature. Similar data has already been reported by previous investigators (Martin, 1972; Elmer, 1977). The particular and original characteristic of the results of the present study is that the battered children used as subjects were screened in order to exclude those suffering from neurological sequelae; abuse may entail psychosocial after-effects. This would indicate that the term "abuse" would refer to something more inclusive than just violence.

Finally, the treatment plan operating at the moment of screening proved to be drastic and chaotic: the children were taken out of their natural setting and there was a high geographical instability in the substitute environments.

At the point where the research is now, it is difficult to push the conclusions any further. It would seem, nevertheless, that the screening may have come too late. Was it possible, however, to do otherwise? It seems also that the screening is insufficient. In addition to the elaboration of a therapeutic program in the best interests of the child, it would seem desirable to make sure in advance that the means for the implementation of this plan really exist.

This preliminary analysis of the data would appear to steer the clinical activity towards prevention. Hospital and social centres could direct their efforts towards the newborn by means of their services to the child and to the "high risk" family (Ayoub *et al.*, 1977). This position does, however, raise operational and ethical problems. What is the definition of a vulnerable child or family? What help should be offered? Must the target population be absolutely free to cooperate or not, or should their cooperation be solicited? Finally, is it not possible that such a strategy would lead to a precocious denunciation under the trappings of early prevention?

Far from solving the battered child problem, the research being carried out in this field would seem to stimulate clinicians and investigators in raising many new questions.

References

Ayoub, C. et al. (1977). An approach to primary prevention: the "at risk" program. *Children Today* 46 (no. 3), 14–17.

Elmer, E. (1977). *Fragile families, troubled children. The aftermath of infant trauma*. Pittsburgh: University of Pittsburgh Press.

Gil, D.G. (1971). A sociocultural perspective on physical child abuse. *Child Welfare*, 50, 389–395.

Honorez, J.M. (1976). Etude sur le devenir psychologique d'enfants abusés physiquement. Directeur: M.C. Kelly; Projet de thèse inédit, Université de Montréal.

Honorez, J.M. (1977). Le devenir des enfants maltraités. Revue critique de la littérature. *Montréal: Cahiers de pédo-psychiatrie de l'Hôpital Sainte-Justine*.

Jéliu, G. (1977). Le devenir des enfants maltraités: étude comparative entre un groupe d'enfants abusés physiquement et un groupe d'enfants négligés par rapport à un groupe contrôle. Projet de recherche inédit, Santé et Bien-Etre Social Canada.

Kalish, B.J. (1978). *Child abuse and neglect, an annotated bibliography*, 535 p. Westport (Conn.): Greenwood Press.

Martin, H.P. (1972). The child and his development, in: C.H. Kempe, R.E. Helfer (Ed.): *Helping the battered child and his family* (pp. 93–114). Philadelphia: J.B. Lippincot.

Stuart, H.C. et al.: Anthropometric chart. Boston: *Children's Medical Center*.

VII. PLENARY SESSION: THE DEVELOPMENT OF POLICIES FOR THE DELIVERY OF SERVICES TO EXCEPTIONAL CHILDREN

editor: Pat Woodward

21

Opening Statement at Plenary Session

GRAHAM CLARKSON, M.D.

The plenary session was directed at discussing the development of policies for the delivery of services to exceptional children. After the concentrated discussions of the previous sessions covering many of the multi-faceted aspects of research and services to exceptional children and the development of programmes for these services, the plenary session attempted to take a comprehensive view of the development of policies for the delivery of services to exceptional children.

The development of policies depends upon subscribing to a philosophy or an ideology. This requires dissent and discussion, not just by professionals or administrators, but by society at large; and certainly it has been my experience that this is the only way unless you wish to build policies and programmes on quicksand. The child and the family have rights; the child cannot be regarded simply as property. The rights of the exceptional child, who is particularly vulnerable, require special safeguards. It seems to me that the measure of the maturity and concern of a society is reflected in the goals that it adopts and attains for the disadvantaged groups within that society.

22

Planning and Integrating a Model of Health and Medical Care Services

GEORGE SILVER, M.D.

Abstract

As judged by child mortality figures, health care in North America lags behind comparable programmes in European countries, particularly those in Northern Europe.
Health care for children involves three basic elements that should be lookd at sepa-
rately; (1) social policy to protect children, (2) prevention services and (3) medical
care.

There is need for a separate health care policy for children. When there is a clearly
identifiable programme for all children, exceptional children would receive the special
care that they need.

The models and successful examples from the European experience could provide
the basis for what is needed in North America. Since these materials are available it
would be a pity not to put them to use.

Si on se base sur les taux de mortalité infantile, les soins médicaux offerts en
Amérique du Nord sont en retard par comparaison avec les programmes comparables
des pays européens, tout particulièrement ceux de l'Europe du Nord. L'auteur considère que les soins de santé qui s'adressent aux enfants comportent trois éléments fondamentaux qu'on devrait envisager séparément: 1) les politiques sociales de protection
de l'enfance, 2) les services de prévention, et 3) les soins médicaux.

Il fait ressortir la nécessité d'avoir une politique spécifique de soins de santé pour
les enfants et prétend que, lorsqu'on disposera d'un programme clairement identifiable qui s'adressera à tous les enfants, les enfants exceptionnels seront également bien
pourvus.

Les modèles schématiques et les exemples de réussite de l'expérience européenne
pourraient servir de base pour évaluer les besoins de l'Amérique du Nord. L'auteur
conclut en disant qu'il serait bien dommage de ne pas en profiter.

The growing concern for the health of children reflects the changing aspects of
social and cultural pressures. Private philanthropists contributed generously to
early efforts to ameliorate the shockingly high infant mortality, to provide
models, and to generate the public pressures that resulted in the inauguration and
extension of governmental action for the improvement of public health and particularly children's health. Later, agitation against the economic exploitation of

children resulted in legislation against child labour (in 1912 in the United States), led to the establishment of the Children's Bureau and the development of the Decennial White House Conferences on Children and Youth.

These conferences gave national visibility to the expression of child health needs and stimulated programmes for the improvement of children's health, but the gap remains. Ironically, many of the same problems have been discussed and many of the same kinds of programmes have been proposed at successive Decennial Conferences. The Children's Charter of 1930 seems to fit the situation in 1980 as well.

Strong statements of dissatisfaction about the *status quo* have begun to emerge from both professional and children's interest groups. It appears that, despite increasing legislative action, more money dispersed from the public purse, and an increasingly specialized and complex medical care system, the indicators of statistics on child health have not markedly improved. Certainly they have not caught up with or surpassed, as they should have, the standards of child health in countries less well-endowed with material and medical resources.

The same pattern seems to have set in in Canada. In a document called "Poor Kids" published by the National Council of Welfare in 1975, a dramatic attack was made on the failures of Canadian social services to meet children's needs— this despite the fact that Canada has broader social services for children than does the U.S. In its introductory statement that report said, "to be born poor is to face greater likelihood of ill health in infancy and childhood and throughout your adult life"; and later the report adds, "the advent of Medicare in Canada during the 1960's was supposed to end inequality of access to medical care among income groups in this country, but the evidence is that it has not."

It is not too difficult to recognize that the United States does not measure up to the accomplishments of countries of comparable technological advancement; for example, we are 12th or 16th, depending on who is counting, in infant mortality. This socio-medical indicator which is commonly used, although perhaps its importance is exaggerated, reflects many elements of the measures that symbolize health: nutrition, the status of women, medical care services (both in its availability and quality).

Other standards are deficient as well: a lower percentage of children immunized against infectious disease, a higher mortality rate in children under five, fewer handicapped children found and treated.

In recent years, we have seen a number of new and sombre additions to the list of illnesses that characterize childhood: no longer epidemic infectious diseases, but socially derived and maintained; problems such as drug and other substance abuse, venereal disease, pregnancy in younger unwed teenagers. These illnesses too seem to be out of control despite our abundant technology and medical care, swarms of specialists and very expensive medical services.

During a four year period, a multi-disciplinary group sought to define some of the factors in the U.S. governmental health apparatus that might be reasons for our failure to provide effective medical care and health services for America's children. It became apparent that the term ''Medical Care'' includes several interrelated programme aspects. This clarification helped not only to define the causative factors, but also after some study of European child health policies and programmes, to define possible solutions as well. Medical care for children, much more so than for adults, comprises three elements.

First, there is a social policy with regard to the protection of children. This includes the protection of the fetus during pregnancy and at birth, nutrition, welfare services, financial support to the family, legal protection, educational opportunities and programmes, all comprising, ''society's consideration for the child.''

Second, there is prevention. Under this heading can be included: health supervision in institutional settings (such as, day care centres and schools), examinations for discovery and treatment of handicapping conditions, immunization against infectious diseases, and the psychological and social guidance to parents, children and family units.

The third element is what is commonly called ''medical care,'' namely, the diagnosis and treatment of illness.

In both Canada and the United States, where all these aspects are grouped under medical care, the characteristics of these different elements become confused; and such confusion militates against the possibility of carrying out any one of them properly. Some essential factors are ignored; others are delegated to untrained or unconcerned agencies which fail to accept and fulfill responsibilities. In an important area where children could be uniformly protected, custom opposes; the legal rights of children are bound up with traditional attitudes towards family responsibility so that the mothers and fathers are dealt with, treated, punished or rewarded in the expectation that this will be reflected in the care of the children. Children, themselves, receive insufficient concern and frequently short shrift in social decisions abour their care. Specific prevention services are also insufficient in the United States; well-baby clinics and preschool centres have been replaced by physicians' office care (in which low-income families tend to restrict necessary visits to a minimum) or to hospital clinics where indignity, hustle and irregular physician attendance offer little promise of solicitous preventive care. School health services seem to have become a farce in many school districts in the United States, with little if anything being done to see to it that illness, psychological disturbance or handicapping conditions discovered in the school are treated, even in those districts where school health examinations have been carried out. The United States Congress, for example, legislated a requirement in 1967 that every child who is eligible for Medicaid, should be examined for possible handicapping conditions and treated if necessary in an ''Early Periodic Screening Diagnosis and Treatment Program.'' During the first five years, less than 8 percent of the eligible children have been so examined and there is no record of how many of that 8 percent were actually treated for whatever conditions were found. The situation is better now, but still uneven; few states look after the majority of eligible children.

Given these facts, the lack of a social policy for the protection of children, lack of preventive services for children, and lack of a universally available medical care system, it is clear that much of the undistinguished public health record of the United States children is easily explainable. For reasons of low income, geographic inaccessibility, racial or cultural differences, many children do not receive needed preventive health services or medical care. A great many studies bear testimony to the fact that the poor minority children, in the United States especially, do not have the same access to medical services as does the rest of the population.

We all realize that institutional deficiencies reflect essentially social decisions and are expressions of social values. We should be seeking a three-dimensional attack on these inadequacies: (1) to create a powerful advocacy group for children to direct the battle for change; (2) to re-organize the health and medical care structure; and finally, (3) to provide simultaneously, a social support system for children,

Europe has had longer experience with social welfare systems, including medical care services, and it's useful to look at what is being done there and how successful the various systems have been. While all European governments do have some type of social support system and some type of comprehensive medical care system, not all are equally effective. One has to look at the public health data to see how variously the different countries have been affected. In European countries, almost universally, there is social recognition of the fact that higher costs for support of the larger family unit could be detrimental to the child's health in limiting food, clothing or shelter. Therefore, not only allowances to children and families, but in some countries, rent subsidies are provided to help assure that children do not suffer the consequences of the high cost of renting large houses. Children's allowances may be modest, as in the United Kingdom, or quite substantial, as in France, where fully 25 percent of a large family's income could come from this source. Rent subsidies could be substantial too, as in Denmark, where a low-income family of five might draw their entire rental cost from the government. In the United Kingdom, the children's allowance is taxed along with other income, with the result that upper-income families benefit very little. In other European countries, the children's allowance is untaxed and all families benefit regardless of income. Maternity leave may range from a few weeks, as in the United Kingdom, to six months paid leave and up to 90 percent of the earnings of a working woman, or even to a full year's leave, as in Sweden.

In European countries then, despite the fact that the parents are recognized as the agents responsible for children, the law also takes into account the fact that the child is a person who deserves protection under the law, even sometimes against his parents. All European countries have in place a system of official or informal agencies for children and youths to hear complaints regarding child abuse and to assess and assign needed legal or social sanctions. The Dutch have a very elaborate system including medical referees, like ombudsmen for children, to intervene on demand and spread protective wings over an abused or potentially abused child. In Sweden, rather than take an abused child out of the home, creating another set of difficult circumstances to which the child must adjust, a social worker may be assigned to live with the family as a form of protection for the child. Finally, all European countries have either a health insurance system or health service in place which provides all or nearly all citizens with needed medical care; the financing mechanism eliminates any means test for obtaining medical services for children as needed; what this means is that children receive such care regardless of the parents' income.

The question that arises is, then, whether universal entitlement to medical services is a sufficient guarantee that children will receive needed preventive services. If the social conditions are met, does the comprehensive medical care system fulfill all the child's health and medical care needs?

As it turns out, if one takes seven northern European countries and ranks them, for example, by infant mortality and percentage of children immunized, an interesting grouping is observed. Nations with a specific child health service rank higher. So it is plain that a distinctive preventive service for children is quite helpful in raising or maintaining a high level of child health. Judging from data on infant mortality and percentage of children immunized, those countries stand at the head of the list which have positive social policies favoring children and clearly distinguishable preventive service, plus a strong nursing input into that service. Some of the things we concentrate on in the United States turn out to be relatively unimportant, e.g. obstetricians in place of mid-wives or hospitals rather than homes for child-birth. The issue of public or private control of health service also seems less significant when there is a strong advocacy programme for children.

Some arbitrary administrative actions can make a difference as well. The professional decision in Scotland, for example, to eliminate the health visitor from the public health programme and to place the public health nurse in the physician's office, has not been beneficial for well-child or school health services. Although it is theoretically sensible to have doctor and nurse work together out of the same office and let the doctor combine preventive and curative roles in child care, it does not work that way in actuality. The doctor is still impatient with well-child care, relates principally to illness, and assigns the nurse to more and more service responsibility for older people, reducing the time and opportunity available for child care. In addition, and again for sound professional reasons, an upheaval has taken place in Scotland administratively, with the responsibilities for administration in public health reduced to a single community management specialist. This is still not dealing effectively with both roles; the child health services suffer accordingly. These changes may be the source of declining immunization rates, the persistence of a relatively high infant mortality rate, and evidence of reduced case findings of handicapping conditions in school children.

On the other hand, administrative decisions in Scandinavia and Holland have had a powerful and *positive* impact on the legal rights of the child in those countries. Private as well as public bodies have been authorized to look into children's rights, supervise child care, seek out neglect and legally discipline families where the children are being abused or neglected. Different countries approach these matters differently, perhaps because of their different histories, or because of differing professional and social experience.

One can, therefore, review the experiences and benefits of the European programmes for child care with a mixture of emotions. Only the naive will expect that spreading the word of what happens in one country will result in legislative action to provide similar or identical programmes in another. We cannot expect this, nor should we. The European experiences, as emphasized, vary from country to country. There is no European system of child health care: there is a Dutch, a French, a Swedish, a Finnish system; and there ought to be an American and a Canadian system.

A skeleton outline of what is needed can surely be derived from the study of various European experiences. Certain basic elements must obviously be included. Creating a child health system that incorporates the best of the European experiences should not be too difficult. Nor should the introduction of major changes in the way in which this new child health system model would be carried out, provided that the contesting parties are given an opportunity to try out preferred solutions. So there should not be too much difficulty in designing a law that permits expression of the intent of that legislation in more than one way. Certainly we are long past the stage of believing that there is only one perfect way of carrying out a social policy.

Charles Schultz, chairman of The Council of Economic Advisors, made this point very well in the prestigious Godkin lectures delivered at Harvard University a few years ago. He described how some ten years earlier the government supported one kind of pilot programme, making it necessary for the target population to use that system exclusively, whether or not it suited them all or even the majority. He asked if it would not be possible, first, to establish what he called market analogues, whereby a number of different forms of the intended programme could be established and then, after a period of their operation, to see which one or ones achieved the greatest success.

In a sense, this approach would be giving the welfare system a market operation test. The government and the clients would all benefit. Assessing responses to alternatives may allow us to reach a consensus in law-making as well; this approach may disarm controversy and hasten effective action on behalf of child health. Such questions as, ''Is the nurse a better preventive medicine specialist than the physician?'' can be tested; so can the question as to whether supervision and accountability is better mediated at the local or the national level. The proper role of the private sector can be tested by stimulating the development of neighborhood health education and support groups on the Dutch model. Nothing that might conceivably play a beneficial role in promoting child health services need be overlooked in such testing.

In this connection, the political system in Canada may work to the advantage of those most concerned with stimulating changes in child health practice. It is well known that national politics is much less susceptible to radical change than local politics, despite the evidence that specific local communities tend to be more conservative than the national community. It is easy to see why national legislatures will be more hesitant to put large-scale social changes into operation with the accompanying destabilization and confusion. In the United States, Justice Brandeis noted fifty years ago that the states were natural laboratories for social experiments, implying that no large-scale social change ought to be undertaken on the national stage without some pre-existing experience at the state level.

Let me be more specific: the Saskatchewan experience, a bare thirty years ago, in province-wide health insurance taught us many lessons in the United States. The success of that experiment facilitated the introduction of nation-wide health insurance in Canada. The experiment may have fallen short of fulfilling the total vision of its protagonists. Nevertheless, all the critical pieces of its design were included in the final accomplishment.

If we in the United States had managed to obtain one state's participation in a comprehensive medical care insurance programme during the past 30 years, we would probably have a national programme today. Perhaps it would not be as good as Canada's, and certainly different, since each country must find its own way of carrying out common objectives; but at least we would have had a national health insurance programme. One province, politically sophisticated, accepting the responsibility for a child health programme, could set the pattern for the country. One state in the United States, doing the same, could establish a pattern for us.

Accepting the responsibility in this sense does not mean simply legislating; it means recognizing the critical factors enumerated earlier and designing a programme that deals with them. It means negotiating with the professions and the unions for the experimental task assignments and reimbursement formulas. It means advocacy education towards the development of private resources for cooperative action. It further means redirecting public health activities to ensure positive access for every child to a health system that provides at least the minimum services required by law. Canada is fortunate in having a national medical care programme already in place. Focusing on a comprehensive preventive service for children can be more easily accomplished without the competition for programme funds and hesitation that might be induced by the lack of such a programme.

Canadians have the advantage over Americans in getting such a new programme initiated. I mean this as a tribute to the parliamentary form of government which can make social decisions more rapidly than can a representative government. In the U.S., for example, every congressman must be elected on his appeal to his local constituency. He therefore cuts his political cloth to the measurement of the variety of needs of his own voters. One advocacy group has to be played off against another in this way. Every congressman has the same problem. Advocacy has to be addressed to 435 constituencies and therefore requires enormous amounts of individual effort, unless you are in steel, oil or banking and can afford a powerful lobby in the nation's capital. Parliamentary government, on the other hand, has the benefit of party discipline to control the votes within the party in power. One need only convince the policy making group within the party in order to command a policy change. I realize it is not quite that simple in practice, that many individuals and certain powerful representatives need to be influenced; but basically the argument does hold. It is easier to engineer policy changes within a parliamentary democracy than within a representative one.

There are, basically, three components of health and medical care needs for children: (1) a social area compromising such economic factors as cash assistance to families and housing subsidies, legal protection and social services; (2) a preventive service based on the physical examination, parental guidance, immunization, and school health supervision; and (3) medical care for sick and disabled children.

In conclusion, I would say that the general pattern of an effective child health service must provide for (1) a separate and clearly identifiable programme for children; (2) emphasis on the preventive aspects, supervised and directed by specially trained nurses; (3) services to the schools, day care centres and other institutions where children congregate; and (4) a strong liaison with legal and social services for more general protection of children. The necessary advocacy to maintain proper oversight and to prevent backsliding could be in the hands of three agencies: (1) a parents' group organized around some tasks of the delivery of services; (2) an official ombudsman to protect the children's interests and to represent the child in court and in society; (3) an Inspector-General Service within the government to make sure that the entire system works as it should. Specifically, so far as exceptional children are concerned, they would benefit from the comprehensiveness and universality of the system suggested. However, the research potential would aid this minority perhaps even more than the majority because their special problems would then become part of the problem testing process which is the essence of a dynamic social system.

23

Components of Health Services for Children

ROBERT HAGGERTY, M.D.

Abstract

The philosophy of waiting until the consumers come to get health care services is more expensive in the long run and does not serve the interests of the children. There is need for "out reach" to find the children who need help as early as possible. Once problems are diagnosed they should be followed up in order to prevent more significant costs to the health care system later on.

Stressful events in a family's life increase their call on the health care system. Because these stresses are economic, social, behavioural and educational, an integrated, multi-faceted service must be available, with parents and non-medical professionals participating. This would be the least expensive and most beneficial approach in times of tight funding policy.

L'attitude qui consiste à attendre que les clients viennent réclamer des services de santé est à la longue plus coûteuse et ne répond pas aux intérêts des enfants. L'auteur démontre la nécessité de faire des efforts spéciaux pour aller repérer le plus tôt possible les enfants qui ont besoin d'aide; une fois que les problèmes auront été identifiés, on devrait les garder sous surveillance afin de prévenir l'imposition dans l'avenir de coûts ultérieurs plus considérables au système de santé.

L'auteur démontre comment les circonstances difficiles dans la vie des familles accroissent la fréquence de leur recours au système de soins de santé. Comme ces stress sont de nature économique, sociale, comportementale et éducationnelle, il considère qu'un service intégré à facettes multiples, comportant la participation des parents et des professionnels qui ne sont pas médecins, représenterait la stratégie la moins coûteuse et la plus bénéfique dans cette époque où les politiques de financement sont très restrictives.

As a generalist, rather than an expert in exceptional children, I propose here to address the needs of exceptional children from a general point of view.

Dr. Silver has made a very good case for a distinct and separate child health service and I agree with that emphasis. He has pointed out that there are three action centres: the social action centre, the preventive action centre and the curative medical action centre. I would first like to move on from this viewpoint to discuss what I think are some of the components of the services that need to be delivered within those centres, with a special emphasis upon the family and the meeting of family stress needs. Then I would like to suggest how we can put these components together into some sort of package. I fear that the separation into three separate services (or in our country, I think, we now have four—education, health, legal and medical) creates the problems of coordinating those services to serve an individual child. It also poses the problem of how to get professionals from different disciplines and different training backgrounds to agree on how best to do this.

Now, what are some of those components? First, we have heard about the early identification of problems. This requires not only a lowering of barriers—financial, geographical, and cultural barriers—but it also involves a matter of philosophy. There are people, families, who find it difficult, for a variety of reasons, to accept services. The helping services, therefore, need to have an outreach programme to find such people, to identify early the children in need, and to do a variety of things to help the families accept needed services. To many that sounds like an intrusion into family life and that is where the moral conflict arises on this issue. There are many people in the United States who now argue that an outreach programme is morally indefensible, that we should not reach out to families who do not want services, that we should provide all the services needed for those who come of their own free will, but not intrude into families who, for a variety of reasons, do not want services. I wish to make my point very clear: I do not think children are well served by that attitude.

The development of a programme for early identification and outreach will run into that philosophical barrier in addition to all of the other barriers. Reaching out to find families in need who are not now using services and bringing these families into the service assumes (1) that the service can do some good for the child and (2) that finding such a family earlier is better than finding them later. These are two points which have not always been well documented, and which I believe, are points for research and demonstration. But problems abound, from the social to the medical, in which early identification, and provision of services known to be beneficial exist. In some instances provision of services may require finding families in need, and doing a variety of things to ease their way into the system. I remain convinced that outreach is basic to any effective child health service, and especially so for exceptional children.

Secondly, the system has to have a follow-up component. One of the largest gaps in preventive or early identification programmes in the United States has been the lack of follow-up. Dr. Silver has mentioned our poor success rate with the Early Periodic Screening Diagnosis and Treatment Program. This programme not only failed to find children and bring them into the system, but it failed even more miserably to follow up after the initial screening. Many children whose difficulties were identified received no follow-up; hence, the number of children who finally got a planned management programme carried through has been very small. Follow-up also runs into the same philosophical barriers as the outreach on identification. Many people say that if you once got the family and child into care, then, if the care did not meet their needs or did not satisfy them and they did not come back, it would not be the responsibility of the health care or any other system to go out after them. Some of us who have advocated the more active role have been labelled by the pejorative term, in favor of 'patient pursuit.' However, both early identification and follow-up are clearly very important. This may require an active role by providers.

Another basic fact to remember is that all children need primary general health services, the exceptional child as well as the non-handicapped child. Several studies have documented the lack of primary care services for children with handicaps. Most recently, Dr. Palfrey in The Children's Hospital Medical Center, Boston, has looked at children attending regularly the specialty clinics for the handicapped; she found that 50 percent of them had not been immunized, had not had a hearing test, had not had a vision screening test, had not had ordinary preventive services and did not get care when they had an acute febrile infection.

The organization of primary care services for the handicapped raises a special problem in our country. Parents of children who get into a very specialized institution like a children's hospital expect that the institution will give the children all the services that they need. But the specialized service, on its part, will provide care for a heart condition, or cerebral palsy, or learning disorder, but will not assume responsibility for any other services. I think that primary care is a concern which needs to be addressed in any plan to organize health services. One of the difficulties in setting up clinics with high specialization is that specialists do not want to deliver primary health care and show little concern about organizing a service that will provide it.

Yet another vital issue is that of what I might call "boundary areas" that extend across the boundary of services for children into the family. We have evidence that families with handicapped children have special needs that one cannot meet if one serves only the handicapped child. When these needs move across boundaries into welfare, education, or law, we do not have a good mechanism for integrating those various services to serve the family and the children.

For sometime now, we have been studying services for children in several communities where a notable effort has been made to integrate these services. We were particularly intrigued by the Mott Child Health Centre in Flint, Michigan, because under one roof they have four components of service: an educational service, a behavioural or psychiatric service, a medical service and a dental service. This is well funded and finances have not been a problem. We undertook to look at what happens to children who flow through this particular system. Unfortunately in practically no case was the child receiving services from more than one of those component parts in spite of the fact that our assessments often indicated need for two or more such services. The children entered a system which was set up to provide comprehensive care under one roof but, because of the way the professions were organized and the departmental services structured within that centre, the children did not get behavioural services when they had a medical problem, or they did not get medical services when they had an educational problem and vice versa. So I am well aware of the complexities of trying to solve this problem of integration by merely putting the component services under one roof. Clearly, more than just physical aggregation of services has to be ensured.

Now, why should we do this sort of thing anyway? What makes one believe in the need to integrate services across disciplines? Well, for several years, I have been interested in studying the effects of family stress in health and illness. Presenting some of our data should emphasize that the boundaries between health and behavioural and educational services are very blurred. I find it very difficult to think of setting up separate services by different disciplines for these different needs.

The model that we have been working with over the years has shown that in families stress (that is, environmental stress affecting children, such as, family stress, separation and divorce, father losing his job, family moves, being evicted from the house, siblings being arrested) has two effects: (1) it lowers resistance to disease; and (2) once you have a disease, it tends to determine when and how you use health services. The fact that not all families react this way raises the interesting question of what are the protective features. We believe most social support systems in time of stress are one of the major protective factors.

Twenty years ago, we studied streptococcal infections in families, culturing the family, and culturing the child. On the basis of diaries kept by sixteen families, we were able to show that in the two-week period preceding the onset of streptococcal illness, there had been a three to four-fold increase in the number of these stressful life events. This relationship of these preceding stressful events to the precipitation of common physical illnesses is something that more and more people are recognizing. Yet how often do we think that providing families with income maintenance to avoid the family stress resulting from a father's losing his job might, in fact, reduce the incidence of streptococcal illness? That is an example of the kind of interaction that I would like to see our services address.

As another illustration of this point, our data show that the level of chronic stress as rated by the social worker was positively correlated with the frequency of acquiring streptococcal illness. Even the immunologic response (an antibody response) to a streptococcal infection will increase as the level of chronic family stress increases. We know, for instance, that families under social stress are the ones who are more likely to have rheumatic fever. It may well be that that kind of stress induces a different kind of immunologic response once you have this common infection due to streptococcus.

There are a large number of studies that would, I believe, convince most people that these kinds of social stresses, (which can only be ameliorated by a social policy that addresses such factors as income and jobs) have a major effect on the incidence of illness. So that is the first effect of stress.

The second effect concerns the question: "If a patient is sick, when does he use health services?" Our data come from a study we did in Rochester where we measured the chances on any given day of a person's using the health services (e.g.—calling the doctor, going to his office, going to an outpatient clinic, going to the emergency department or going to another clinic). On days when there is no illness and no stress, there is obviously no need of health services. With increased illness but no stress, people go to the doctor; but when you add to illness the presence of one of these stressful events in the family, the chances of the doctor being telephoned are doubled. The number of office visits does not change, because office visits have to be scheduled, and schedules lack flexibility; but the frequency of outpatient visits doubles, so do the chances of using the emergency room, and the chances of using any health service for the child almost double when there is a stressful event. The relationships are complex. On the first day of a stressful event, the chances of using health services diminish slightly, for both mother and child; but for illnesses that last a little longer, the chances of the *mother* using health services when under stress decrease from 10 percent to 8 percent but the chances of the *child* being taken to the doctor on that day almost double. All these comparisons involve the same kind of illness but vary in the presence or absence of some other stressful event. Health service personnel need to understand this, because the doctor, faced with a child brought in with a relatively minor illness feels irritated until he realizes that the reason for a visit on that particular day may be the fact that the father has just lost his job. This relationship is, in my view, one argument for the integration of services.

To proceed to the third question: Why do most people not get sick when faced with these daily stressful events? What protects them? Consider a study showing the incidence of *angina-pectoris* in adult males. This study determined whether or not the men were under heavy work stress and whether or not they had a wife who supported them in that particular situation. With low work stress, the rate of *angina-pectoris* does not vary with the degree of wife support. However, under heavy stress at work, the incidence of *angina-pectoris* is significantly less if there is a good deal of support from a wife. In fact, the incidence is almost half of what we find in the case of men who did not have the support of a wife at those times of stress. Other studies show the ameliorating effect on both children and adults of being in a social support system. This is the basis for another of my arguments for putting social and medical services together.

One of the social support systems that we as health workers could put into place, but rarely have, is the family counsellor system. I propose this because it probably has the greatest relevance to people dealing with exceptional children. Consider a study done by a Canadian who worked with me in Rochester for ten years and is now back in Montreal. He studied children who had severe physical handicaps (cerebral palsy, cystic fibrosis, etc), randomly dividing them into two groups. Into the study group, as a family counsellor, he put a mother who was sympathetic. She met the family with the handicapped child; she gave a certain amount of support at that time, educated the family as to the kind of problems coming up, and made herself available as a support service in times of crisis. He studied the children's functioning in school and their general mental health before and after the family counsellor was provided. The data show that after a year in the study group with this supportive person added to the system, the child's psychological status rose in nearly two-thirds of the cases; this result was significantly higher than that for the control group. Apparently, there are some practical applications of this principle to everyday services, applications that have proved to be relatively inexpensive. This investigation found that mothers were, extraordinarily interested, willing and able to provide this kind of service to a family with an exceptional child. Professionals have at times been afraid to bring parents in because they are viewed as too emotionally involved. I believe that parents have a major role to play in this kind of supportive service. So my point about boundary areas is that these services are very difficult to label as health or education or social welfare and that we, in fact, are going to have to learn to work across these boundaries.

We may now turn to a few other components of child care and then come to at least a potential solution. Funding is clearly a problem. Traditional curative services have commanded the greatest share of the health care dollar, with the social, educational and preventive services having a much smaller share. In Greek mythology, Panacea, the god of cure, was always seated higher than Hygeia, the god of prevention. In citing this point Dr. Dubos reminds us that that is the way life has been for a long time and we are going to have to live with the fact that curative services have an emotional appeal that commands resources greater than fall to the educational and preventive ones. I think that this is a good argument for Dr. Silver's point that we should identify separate budget items for the preventive, social, and educational areas. If they are all lumped together, there is a real danger that funds will get diverted into the curative programme exclusively. The financial constraints that we are all facing require especially careful threading through this funding maze. As we try to put these services together we should be careful not to lump all the funds together. At the same time we need to be careful not to separate services.

Clearly, the manpower issue is important. In my opinion, we need to utilize non-medical people for many kinds of services. I have mentioned the role of mothers and the role of nurse practitioners as particularly important.

Another component, also mentioned by Dr. Silver, is consumer advocacy. We clearly need an articulate group of people, parents as well as non-parents who are committed to improving services for children and educated in the strategies of politics to help us command the resources and develop the organization and the policies that are essential for children. At times I find it rather difficult as a physician to advocate improved health services; it may look like feathering one's own nest. Whenever any professional group argues for policies to support its own area, such activity can be viewed as self-serving. I think it is far more effective to have a consumer advocacy group who take a more general approach to these kinds of problems.

A final component would be a data system which would help us to know what we have accomplished and what it is costing us. We know that group services have been provided but we lack information on who has been served and who is being missed in the community; we do not have adequate data on costs and outlays. Now those are some of the components that I consider are important in this service for children with handicaps, and generally for all children.

The integration of services is, to my mind, one of the greatest problems that we face, and I have no solution to recommend. Nobody has yet shown a clear-cut way to solve that problem. I agree with Dr. Silver that one has to have a variety of demonstrations in order to find out how to achieve such integration. How do we decrease the medical dominance that seems to develop if we build the programme around the medical system? And yet, how do we get medical involvement if we build the programme around the education system? We are embarked in the United States on implementing the right of the handicapped to education (Public Law 94−142). Under this law, every handicapped child will have an assessment and a plan of care worked out for him between age 3 and the time he goes to school. This responsibility has been placed in the educational department. However, educational departments experience great difficulty getting health personnel involved in those assessments.

I do not minimize the problems involved in getting these services to work together. But I hope that I have made a case for the crucial importance of putting them together. I believe that more attention and effort should be given to the concept of multi-service centres. I have mentioned the centre in Flint, Michigan as having fallen short, but I think that until you at least get the disciplines working together under one roof, talking to each other about a given child and family, we have little chance of achieving the kind of integration that is necessary.

Let me end on an optimistic note. Dr. Silver and I have emphasized the problems that we face in Canada and the United States, but we should also remember that we have made a lot of progress. In starting a new programme there is the danger of thinking that it is going to magically change things within a year; such naive expectations lead naturally to a phase of depression and consequently, the whole programme faces collapse. We should guard against unrealistic expectations, but should nonetheless try to work out new programmes. I would like to end with a quote from Dr. Rogers, the president of The Robert Wood Johnson Foundation, who in his new book, *American Medicine*, speaks as an optimist about the problems of change. He says:

> Changes take place very slowly. In America, there is a long period of increasing concern, turbulence and mounting awareness of the serious nature of a defect. This is often followed by a brief frantic period of rhetoric, legislation, funding and a much publicized commitment to correct

the problem overnight. This is then followed by a short period of intense activity but with little apparent effect. At last, there usually then follows a period of discouragement and disenchantment, a general feeling that we are on the wrong track. Public attention wanes and any additional and continued efforts are derided as another example of "do gooder" ineptitude. A period passes and then, all of a sudden, changes for the better appear to take place and we are surprised, and pleased, and often forget what went before to make this happen. We need better institutional memory, a greater willingness to stay with programs, and a longer, more realistic, perspective.

In advocating demonstration projects, I wish to warn against the danger of discarding short-term demonstration projects that do not look as if they have brought immediate change in provider or recipient behaviour in the short run. Premature cynicism is as great a danger as not doing anything at all. So I end as an optimist. There are examples out there of improved services which have developed over the years. We must not discard those. We must have some new demonstrations, and we must stay with them long enough to see how we can effectively combine these multi-disciplinary services in more effective service to the child.

Plenary Session: Concluding Discussion

"Ten years ago such a multidisciplinary conference could not have occurred . . ." Dr. Graham Clarkson, who chaired the Plenary Session concluded his opening remarks with the statement that "the measure of the maturity of the society is reflected in the goals that it adopts and works out for the disadvantaged groups within it." He noted that the exceptional child who is particularly vulnerable, requires special safeguards.

In his summing up he identified three threads running through the conference sessions.

1) The need to use the family as a resource.
2) The need for earlier and more frequent assessment.
3) The growing importance of socio-economic factors in providing services to the special needs child.

As a model example of the first theme, he identified the project in Newfoundland, described by Drs. O'Neill and Neville-Smith in which the parents of profoundly deaf children were trained to teach their children language early in life.

As a model example of the second theme, he pointed to Dr. Zaleski's programme in the remote areas of Northern Saskatchewan where early assessment was part of the team's regular operation.

Dr. Clarkson suggested that we could attract the attention of government and professional groups through the use of demonstration programmes. These could help in two ways. Firstly, by showing what could be done and secondly, by changing the attitudes of both professional and government groups.

He concluded by saying "This conference surely calls for use to reaffirm and defend the rights of the child."

Discussants in the plenary session included Dr. Frances Ricks, Head of the Evaluation and Planning Unit for the B.C. Ministry of Human Resources; Dr. Don Fernandez, Research and Planning Officer of Mental Health Programmes for the B.C. Ministry of Health, and Mr. Alan Garneau, a principal for the Vancouver School Board. Each of these people looked at the issues raised by the plenary speakers in terms of their "insider views" on their respective ministries. Dr. Ricks pointed to the need to integrate service, evaluation and research in such areas as day care, foster care, infant development, etc. Dr. Fernandez called for integration at the planning stage and Mr. Garneau pleaded the case for the participation of parents who he said are often noncoping—rather than noncaring.

Drs. Silver and Haggerty in answering questions from the audience, made some final points.

Dr. Silver:

In responding to the general question—"How would you get things started?" Dr. Silver pointed out that the problem of delivery of services is essentially a political problem and that resolution required a political decision. He said "Large organizations can't provide personal services. Enlarged bureaucracies are incapable of dealing with personal difficulties. When a job has to be done, money should be given to the lowest unit, consistent with discharge and admission. Administration of the project should be at the local level so that the family, the parents, the teachers, the providers of health care, the people who are really concerned, can participate."

He calls for the money to be provided to the mediating institutions, the neighbourhood, the churches, the family itself to offset the power of the megastructures, big labour, big industry, big government.

He suggests the answer is to create a political reality, a channel of advocacy where people believe they can have an impact. He says there are two such channels of advocacy; one is private funding sources and the other is getting the government to fund services at the local level.

Dr. Haggerty agrees that advocacy is difficult. He gives us an example of groups that have achieved a reasonable level of success in Massachusetts where there are three kinds of children's advocacy groups.

1) An *Office for Children* within the State Government set up and funded by them.

2) A privately funded *Committee on Children & Youth*, started by an active professional who rounded up money and interest from private sources to keep an eye on the Office of Children and to provide a complement to them.

3) A *Grass Roots Group of People* who felt that the Committee on Children & Youth was too establishment and too professional. They grew up as a challenge to the other groups. These three advocacy groups have been a force for the good in their area, and point to a way to get started; and finally,

CONCLUSION

Dr. Schwartz concluded the conference. Dr. Clarkson said "Ten years ago such a multidisciplinary conference could not have occurred". Indeed, today in most places, and tomorrow in many places, such a meeting could not occur. Over the last two days we have crossed the defended lines between discipline, culture and language many times. We have been our own demonstration project, we have provided the model that this can be done. The special experiences we have enjoyed and the new friendships and associations we have begun, will bear future fruit and indicate that this should be done again and again in many places and at many times. We hope what we have done here has been a beginning.

Dr. Schwartz concluded the conference. Dr. Clarkson said "Ten years ago such a multidisciplinary conference could not have occurred". Indeed, today in most places, and tomorrow in many places, such a meeting could not occur. Over the last two days we have crossed the defended lines between discipline, culture and language many times. We have been our own demonstration project, we have provided the model that this can be done. The special experiences we have enjoyed and the new friendships and associations we have begun, will bear future fruit and indicate that this should be done again and again in many places and at many times. We hope what we have done here has been a beginning.

Making progress in science is like taking a journey down an unknown road. It is a road along which we sometimes walk, sometimes run, and sometimes retreat. Progress is getting further along the road and realizing that we still have much further to go.

When we make real progress we have to find ways to share the good news. Scientific journals addressed to a particular discipline may not be the medium. Nor do newspapers or even magazines where journalists often misinterpret the language of professionals inspire much replication. Indeed, they often report the sensational and leave out the substance of the project.

Perhaps this conference has provided us with the perfect forum to spread the good news. It is the hope and dream of this volume that this book will provide the vehicle for enlarging our audience of colleagues and for continuing to spread the good news about what things have already been accomplished so that we may continue to make further progress along the road.

This has been a splendid thing to do in the International Year of the Child. It is a good legacy with which to conclude the International Year of the Disabled.

Séance plénière: Discussion

"Il y a dix ans il n'eût pas été possible de tenir une conférence pluridisciplinaire de cette nature . . . ." Le président de la séance plénière, Dr. Graham Clarkson, terminait son discours d'ouverture par la conclusion suivante: "le degré de maturité d'une société se mesure aux objectifs qu'elle se donne et qu'elle cherche à atteindre en fonction des groupes d'individus défavorisés qui se trouvent dans son sein." Il a noté la nécessité de prendre des précautions spéciales dans le cas de l'enfant exceptionnel, être tout particulièrement vulnérable.

Dans sa récapitulation sommaire de la conférence, il a pu identifier trois courants qui se sont manifestés tout au long de ces journées d'étude:
1. La nécessité de recourir à la famille comme ressource.
2. La nécessité de procéder à des évaluations plus tôt et plus fréquemment.
3. L'importance de plus en plus grande des facteurs socio-économiques dans la prestation de soins à l'enfant qui présente des besoins spéciaux.

Il a pris, comme exemple typique du premier thème, le programme mis en place à Terre-Neuve et décrit par les docteurs O'Neill et Neville-Smith, où l'on entraîne les parents d'enfants atteints de surdité profonde à leur apprendre à parler dès les premières années.

Pour illustrer le second thème, il rappelle le programme appliqué par le docteur Zaleski dans les régions éloignées du nord de la Saskatchewan, où l'équipe procède de façon régulière à une première évaluation de l'enfant qui se fait le plus tôt possible.

Le docteur Clarkson fait remarquer qu'on pourrait éveiller l'attention des gouvernements et des groupes professionnels par le truchement de programmes de démonstration. Ceux-ci pourraient avoir deux effets. D'abord, indiquer ce qui pourrait être fait et ensuite contribuer à changer les attitudes de ces deux groupes, gouvernemental et professionnel. Il conclut en disant que "cette conférence nous engage sûrement à réaffirmer et à défendre les droits de l'enfant."

Ont participé à la discussion au cours de cette séance plénière, le Dr. Frances Ricks, chef de l'Unité d'évaluation et de planification du Ministère des Ressources Humaines de la Colombie Britannique, le Dr. Don Fernandez, officier de Recherche et de planification des programmes de Santé mentale au sein du Ministère de la Santé de la Colombie Britannique et Monsieur Alan Garneau, un directeur de la Commission Scolaire de Vancouver. Chacune de ces personnes a considéré les problèmes soulevés par les conférenciers de la séance plénière dans l'optique propre à leurs ministères respectifs. Le Dr. Ricks a souligné le besoin d'intégration des services, d'évaluation et de recherche dans des domaines comme ceux des soins en clinique (day care), des soins de garde (foster care), du développement des nouveaux-nés, etc. Le docteur Fernandez a parlé de la nécessité de procéder à une intégration dès la phase de la planification et Monsieur Garneau a fait un plaidoyer en faveur de la mise à contribution des parents dont l'inaction tient bien plus souvent de l'incapacité de faire face à la situation que de l'indifférence.

En réponse à des questions de l'assistance les docteurs Silver et Haggerty ajoutèrent quelques précisions finales.

Dr. Silver:

A la question générale "Comment procéder pour mettre les choses en branle," le docteur Silver fait remarquer que le problème de la prestation des services est un problème essentiellement politique et que sa solution dépend donc d'une décision politique. "Les organismes importants ne sont pas en mesure de pourvoir à des besoins personnels. Les bureaucraties hypertrophiées sont incapables de s'occuper de difficultés personnelles. Lorsqu'il y a un travail à faire, on devrait donner de l'argent à l'unité située le plus bas sur l'échelle, unité qui a affaire à l'admission et à la mise en congé. L'administration du projet devrait se faire au niveau local de façon à ce que la famille, les parents, les enseignants, les préposés aux soins de santé, les gens qui sont réellement impliqués puissent y participer."

Il demande que l'argent soit fourni aux institutions médiatrices, à l'entourage, aux églises, à la famille elle-même afin de contrebalancer le pouvoir des mégastructures, les grandes puissances du syndicalisme, de l'industrie et des gouvernements.

Il croit que la solution se trouve dans la création d'une réalité politique, un mécanisme de soutien auprès duquel les gens pourraient espérer pouvoir exercer une influence. Il y aurait selon lui deux mécanismes de soutien d'une telle nature; l'un consiste dans les sources de financement privé et l'autre se trouve dans la possibilité d'amener le gouvernement à défrayer les services au niveau local.

Le *Dr. Haggerty* est d'accord pour reconnaître la difficulté de créer des mécanismes de soutien. Il présente cependant des exemples de groupes de ce genre qui ont obtenu un succès raisonnable au Massachusetts, où l'on trouve trois ordres de mécanismes de soutien orientés vers l'enfance.

1. Un *Bureau de l'Enfance (Office for Children)* au sein du Gouvernement de l'Etat, créé et maintenu financièrement par l'Etat.
2. Un *Comité de l'Enfance et de la Jeunesse (Committee on Children & Youth)*. Cet organisme a été créé grâce à l'initiative d'un professionnel entreprenant qui a su recueillir l'argent et susciter l'intérêt des milieux privés pour les amener à exercer une surveillance sur le Bureau de l'Enfance et à entreprendre une action complémentaire à celle de ce dernier.

3. Un *Groupe de gens du milieu* qui considéraient que le Comité de l'Enfance et de la Jeunesse était trop étroitement associé aux gens et institutions en place et aux professionnels. Ils se sont constitués et se sont développés dans une attitude de défi face aux autres groupes. Ces trois mécanismes de soutien ont été une force bénéfique dans leur domaine et ils fournissent un exemple de la façon de mettre les choses en branle.

Le docteur *Schwartz* prononce ensuite une allocution finale. Reprenant les paroles du Dr. Clarkson: "Il y a dix ans, il n'eût pas été possible de tenir une conférence pluridisciplinaire de cette nature," elle fait remarquer en effet qu'aujourd'hui même dans la plupart des endroits et demain dans bien des régions une telle réunion ne serait pas réalisable. Au cours de ces deux derniers jours, dit-elle, nous avons à plusieurs reprises traversé les frontières gardées entre les disciplines, les cultures et les langues. Nous avons constitué nous-mêmes notre propre programme de démonstration; nous avons été le modèle de ce qui peut être fait. Les expériences particulières que nous avons vécues et appréciées, de même que les nouvelles amitiés et relations que nous avons formées porteront des fruits et témoigneront de l'opportunité de répéter cette expérience en plusieurs endroits et bien des fois. Espérons que ce que nous avons réalisé ici ne sera qu'un départ.

Le progrès dans le domaine scientifique ressemble à un voyage le long d'une route inconnue. C'est une route où parfois l'on marche, parfois l'on court et parfois l'on recule. Le progrès consiste à s'aventurer toujours plus loin le long de la route pour constater qu'il y a encore beaucoup plus de chemin à parcourir.

Lorsque nous réalisons des progrès réels, nous devons trouver des moyens de communiquer la bonne nouvelle. Il est bien possible que les revues scientifiques orientées vers une discipline particulière ne soient pas le véhicule idéal. Les journaux ou les périodiques populaires dans lesquels les journalistes donnent une fausse interprétation du langage des professionnels sont encore moins un stimulant à la répétition des expériences. En effet, ils ne rapportent souvent que ce qui est sensationnel et oublient l'essentiel de la contribution scientifique.

N'est-il pas possible que cette conférence nous ait fourni la meilleure tribune pour la diffusion de la bonne nouvelle? Ce volume est présenté dans l'espoir, qui tient peut-être du rêve, de le voir devenir un moyen d'élargir l'auditoire de nos collègues et de continuer à faire connaître ce qui a déjà été accompli de façon à ce que nous puissions faire des progrès additionnels sur la même route.

Cette conférence aura été une réalisation splendide au cours de cette Année Internationale de l'Enfant. Elle constitue un héritage intéressant pour la conclusion de l'Année Internationale des Personnes Handicapées.

Contributors

Barker, Maurice, Ph.D.
Secteur des Adolescents
Hôpital Ste. Justine,
3175, Côte Ste. Catherine,
Montréal, H3T 1C5,
Québec, Canada.

Bax, Martin, M.D.
Community Paediatric Section
St. Mary's Medical School,
5A Netherhall Gardens,
London, NW3 5RN, England.

Bélanger, David, D.Ph.
5609 Westminster,
Montréal, Qué.
H4W 2J3.

Berry, John, Ph.D.
Psychology Department
Queen's University,
Kingston, Ontario,
K7N 3N6, Canada.

Brown, J.K., M.B. F.R.C.P., D.C.H.
Consultant Paediatric Neurologist
Royal Hospital for Sick Children,
Sciennes Road, Edinburgh,
EH9 1LF, Scotland.

Brynelsen, Ms. Dana
Provincial Advisor
Infant Development Programmes,
2979 West 41st Avenue,
Vancouver, B.C., V6N 3C8,
Canada.

Chess, Stella, M.D.
New York University Medical Center,
School of Medicine,
550 First Avenue,
New York, N.Y., 10016,
U.S.A.

Clarkson, Graham, M.D.
J. Graham Clarkson Consultants Ltd.,
6311−129th Street,
Edmonton, Alberta,
T6H 3X9, Canada.

Coté, James
292 William St.,
Gauanoque, Ontario,
K7G 1S6, Canada.

Crichton, John U., M.B., F.R.C.P.(E)
Children's Hospital
4480 Oak St.,
Vancouver, B.C.,
V6H 3V4, Canada.

Eaves, Mrs. Linda, Ph.D.
7286 Ridge Drive,
Burnaby, B.C.,
V5A 1B5, Canada.

Glennie, Mrs. Ruth, B.N.Sc., D.S.P.A.,
Reg. OSHA
Consultant—Speech and Language,
16 Glen Elm Avenue,
Toronto, Ontario,
M4T 1T7, Canada.

Haggerty, Robert, M.D.
William T. Grant Foundation,
919 3rd Avenue,
New York, N.Y., 10022,
U.S.A.

Hardwick, David, M.D., F.R.C.P. (C)
Professor and Head,
Department of Pathology,
Faculty of Medicine,
University of British Columbia,
2075 Westbrook Mall,
Vancouver, B.C.,
V6T 1W5, Canada.

Hardy, Janet, M.D., C.M.
Department of Paediatrics,
John Hopkins School of Medicine,
Turner Building, Rm. 17,
720 Rutland Avenue,
Baltimore, Maryland,
21205, U.S.A.

Honorez, M. Jean Marie
Clinique de Protection de l'enfance,
Département de Pédiatrie,
Hôpital Ste. Justine,
3175 Côte Ste. Catherine,
Montréal, P.Q.,
H3T 1C5, Canada.

Lambert, Wallace E.
Department of Psychology,
McGill University,
Montreal, P.Q.

McConville, Brian J., M.B., Ch.B., F.R.C.P. (C)
Professor of Psychiatry,
Queen's University,
Kingston, Ontario,
Canada.

McEachern, Mr. Donald
Douglas College,
P.O. Box 2503,
New Westminster, B.C.,
V3L 5B2

MacLeod, Patrick M., M.D., F.R.C.P. (C),
F.C.C.M.G.
Department of Medical Genetics,
University of British Columbia,
Clinical Genetics Unit,
855 West 10th Avenue,
Vancouver, B.C.,
V5Z 1L7, Canada.

O'Neill, Marie J., Ph.D.
49 Jervois Avenue,
Magill, S.A.,
Australia 5072

Robinson, Geoffrey, M.D., F.R.C.P. (C)
Faculty of Medicine,
Division of Population Paediatrics,
4480 Oak St.,
Vancouver, B.C.
V6H 3V4, Canada.

Schwartz, Geraldine, Ph.D.
250–5780 Cambie Street,
Vancouver, B.C.,
V5Z 3A7, Canada.

Silver, George, M.D.
Yale University,
School of Medicine,
Department of Epidemiology
and Public Health,
60 College Street,
New Haven, Connecticut,
06510, U.S.A.

Neville-Smith, Clare, M.B., F.R.C.P. (C)   Director, Child Health Services,
Department of Health,
Province of Newfoundland,
c/o Telemedicine Office,
Memorial University,
St. John's, Newfoundland,
A1B 3V6

Spreen, Otfried, Ph.D.   Department of Psychology,
University of Victoria,
Victoria, B.C.,
V8W 2Y2

Tischler, Bluma, M.D., F.R.C.P.   Medical Director,
Woodlands Hospital,
9 East Columbia Street,
New Westminster, B.C.,
V3L 3V5, Canada.

Triandis, Harry, Ph.D.   University of Illinois at Urbana-Champaign,
Champaign, Illinois,
61820, U.S.A.

Usher, Miss Trudy, M.S.W.   Health and Welfare Canada,
926 Brooke Claxton Building,
Tunney's Pasture,
Ottawa, Ontario, K1A 1B5,
Canada.

Wilson, Robert, Ph.D.   6230 St. George's Place,
West Vancouver, B.C.,
V7W 1Y7

Zaleski, Witold, M.D., M.R.C. (Psych.),   Professor, Department of Paediatrics,
F.R.C.P. (C)   University of Saskatchewan,
Medical Director,
Alvin Buckwold Centre,
University Hospital,
Saskatoon, Saskatchewan,
S7N 0W8, Canada.